The
Magickal
Family

About the Author

Monica Crosson is a Master Gardener who lives in the beautiful Pacific Northwest, happily digging in the dirt and tending her raspberries with her husband, three kids, three goats, two dogs, two cats, many chickens, and Rosetta the donkey. Her garden was featured on Soulemama .com's 2016 virtual garden tour. She has been a practicing Witch for twenty-five years and is a member of Blue Moon Coven. Monica is a regular contributor to Llewellyn's almanacs, calendars, and datebooks. She also enjoys writing fiction for young adults and is the author of *Summer Sage*.

The
Magickal
Family

Pagan Living in Harmony with Nature

MONICA CROSSON

Llewellyn Publications
Woodbury, Minnesota

FIRST EDITION
Third Printing, 2019

Book design: Donna Burch-Brown
Cover art: Neil Brigham
Cover design: Kevin R. Brown
Interior art: Kathleen Edwards

Llewellyn Publications is a registered trademark of Llewellyn Worldwide Ltd.

Library of Congress Cataloging-in-Publication Data
Names: Crosson, Monica, author.
Title: The magical family : pagan living in harmony with nature / Monica
    Crosson.
Description: First Edition. | Woodbury : Llewellyn Worldwide, Ltd., 2017. |
    Includes bibliographical references and index.
Identifiers: LCCN 2017025403 (print) | LCCN 2017036364 (ebook) | ISBN
    9780738753225 (ebook) | ISBN 9780738750934
Subjects: LCSH: Magic. | Families.
Classification: LCC BF1621 (ebook) | LCC BF1621 .C76 2017 (print) | DDC
    299/.94—dc23
LC record available at https://lccn.loc.gov/2017025403

Llewellyn Publications
A Division of Llewellyn Worldwide Ltd.
2143 Wooddale Drive
Woodbury, MN 55125-2989
www.llewellyn.com

Printed in the United States of America

Also by Monica Crosson

Summer Sage

Essays Featured In

Llewellyn's 2015 Herbal Almanac
Llewellyn's 2016 Herbal Almanac
Llewellyn's 2017 Herbal Almanac
Llewellyn's 2018 Herbal Almanac

Llewellyn's 2015 Magical Almanac
Llewellyn's 2016 Magical Almanac
Llewellyn's 2017 Magical Almanac
Llewellyn's 2018 Magical Almanac

Llewellyn's 2015 Witches' Companion
Llewellyn's 2016 Witches' Companion
Llewellyn's 2017 Witches' Companion

Llewellyn's 2018 Spell-A-Day Almanac

To my magickal family—Steve, Joshua, Elijah, and Chloe—
who fill my life with enchantment, beauty, and song.

Contents

. . . .
Part 1: Family Magick

. . . .
Part 2: Family Sabbat Celebrations

Activities

Disclaimer

This book is not intended to provide medical advice or to take the place of medical advice and treatment from your personal physician. Readers are advised to consult their doctors or other qualified healthcare professionals regarding the treatment of their medical problems. Neither the publisher nor the author take any responsibility for any possible consequences from any treatment, action, or application of medicine, supplement, herb, or preparation to any person reading or following the information in this book.

Introduction

The Family That Dances Under
a Full Moon Together Stays Together

It was a clear July night and the moon was as round as a Chinese lantern in the sky. My friend Jean and I were in my backyard. We sipped lemonade and chatted about the garden. We had spent the day with our combined eight children at the lake and decided to enjoy the breeze that whispered through the weeping willow for a bit before she took her family home.

Quite suddenly, we both noticed a flash of white that just barely peeked from one end of my house.

"Did you see that?" Jean asked.

"Yeah," I said.

Another flash. This time something extended quickly from the glowing form—it was very much arm-like.

"What the ..." I got up to investigate. But before I made it to the side of my house, the small ghostly figure reappeared, this time hitting me square in the abdomen. It was the milky-white body of my then-seven-year-old son, Elijah.

"Oh, honey, what are you doing?"

"Well," he managed to get out between heavy gasps. "I'm dancing naked under a full moon just like you and Daddy."

Jean smirked and I could feel the waves of embarrassment begin to flood my cheeks.

We had indeed danced naked under June's Strawberry Moon. After the coven had gone home and the children were supposedly tucked in bed, there was such a lovely breeze that carried the sweet scent of honeysuckle—bewitching us both—that we couldn't help ourselves. It was something we were compelled to do.

"Go put some clothes on," I said to Elijah, "before the mosquitoes eat you alive." I ruffled the top of his red head.

"Oh, I see how it is," Jean said, then grinned. "The real magick begins after the Witches leave."

I shook my head. It had been a month and the kid had never said one word.

Later that night after my husband, Steve, had come home, I told him what had happened.

"That goofball," he said. Then he quietly added, "I hope he didn't see what was going on in the hot tub after we danced."

"Steve," I hushed him. "I was thinking—tomorrow night how 'bout we all dance together? Just the family."

"Naked?" he questioned.

"Jeez, of course not."

"Oh, good—because I just had a visual of that, and it wasn't pretty." He chuckled.

I rolled my eyes.

The next day I went up into my craft room (basically an attic space accessed through my bedroom) and dragged down everything I could find to make musical instruments. I found bells, ribbon, colorful yarn, dried beans, cardboard tubes, paint, markers, plenty of tape, and staples.

And so, after breakfast, my three children—Josh, who was eleven; Elijah, who was seven; and Chloe, who was three—got to work. They wove ribbons and bells until they had anklets and bracelets for everyone that would jingle as we moved. They made shakers that they decorated with magickal symbols—some they knew, others they made up. It was Josh's idea to get a couple of the gnarled sticks he had found on the river that they used as staffs and tie bells on them.

So, as darkness crept upon us late that hot July night, our family stood bejeweled with tinkling bells, waiting for the Thunder Moon to majestically rise above the cragged peaks. And as our Lady Moon rose ever higher in the star-speckled sky, we cheered. Elijah, who was a fan of *Where the Wild Things Are*, declared, "Let the wild rumpus start!" We twirled and jingled, rattled and spun. We laughed and sung until we were all exhausted.

When the dancing was done, I gave my seven-year-old a big squeeze. "So, how was that, Elijah?"

"Can we do it again next month, Mama?"

I smiled. "Of course we can!"

Following the Witch's path is not something our family saves for sabbats or esbats; it's part of our daily lives. I'm not saying we all parade around in ritual wear, my children yelling out "Expecto Patronum!" and waving wands at perfect strangers (okay, on second thought, maybe they have). What I am saying is that most people, including most of our extended family, are not really aware of our practices.

What we do emphasize is the Wiccan Rede (An it harm none, do as ye will) not just in our magickal practices, but in our everyday lives as well. For us it is simple: live as holistically and simply as possible and leave the lightest possible footprint we can on our Mother Earth. To instill these lessons, we look to nature—for who but the Goddess has so many lessons to teach?

- *To be thankful for what the earth provides.* Taking children outside and letting them sink their hands deep into the soil is a great start. Let the natural mood-boosting properties of the soil take effect and watch their faces shine. I put seeds in my children's hands from a very early age—teaching them not only to grow food, but to give back to the earth by properly nourishing the soil to ensure others will also experience abundance.

- *To embrace changes in their own lives through the cycle of death and rebirth.* There are many lessons to glean from nature. Spring unfurls and brings forth life, only to be struck down by winter's icy hand. Seasonal change can be used to teach our children how to deal with life's inevitable transitions. It will help them recognize growth and embrace the wisdom gained from loss.

- *To slow down and take time to enjoy life as the Wheel of the Year turns slowly.* As we journey 'round the Wheel of the Year, like the sun, we grow and recede. In our modern, 24/7 society we have created an artificial environment that keeps us in a constant fast-paced motion. Mimicking the natural rhythms of nature will allow us to teach our children to know when to express themselves outwardly and joyously but also when to slow down so that we can recharge, renew, and reflect.

- *To appreciate beauty in all its forms.* In knowing that the earth shows many lovely faces, be it mountain, ocean, desert, or grassy plain, our children can in turn see the beauty within each individual. We all have value, regardless of race, sex, religion, or sexual orientation.

- *To be grounded.* Like the mighty tree, it is important to give our children strong roots and let them grow confident in who they are so they can hold fast through the many storms life has to offer.

- *To treat every day as a celebration.* Every day is special, and the Goddess gives us so many simple things to celebrate and be thankful for if we just take a little time to look, be it the delicately opening snowdrops signifying spring's return, the sound of rain splashing gently on your roof on a summer's eve, or a night under a warm Thunder Moon dancing with your family.

So go and make yourself a cup of tea. Turn off your cell phone and curl up in your favorite chair as we explore ways to celebrate the Goddess with our families and simplify our lives just a little bit.

Part 1

Family Magick

notes

Chapter 1

Growing Up Pagan

Keep your feet firmly planted, my child—
feel what resonates to you and stand strong...

I grew up in the Pacific Northwest on a small farm nestled in the foot-hills of the North Cascades mountain range under a weeping sky and surrounded by giant conifers. I grew under their protective mantle, a changeling with wild hair and an even wilder spirit, free to discover and explore the beauty and magick of my world.

I spent my days constructing elaborate faerie houses from the crum-bled remains of fallen cedar boughs, twigs, cones, and whatever other bounty the forest floor provided. After I finished the construction, I would lie in the grass and listen to all the sounds nature had to offer up. Just under the whispering wind, I could hear the faint tinkling of faerie bells, and I would smile because I knew they were pleased.

At other times, I sat cradled in the arms of a bigleaf maple weaving tales of a people I called the "Hidden Ones," a magickal folk that only a true daughter of nature could see. I rode horses past the boundaries set by my parents and sometimes hiked the foothills past the trails of man and into virgin forest so incredibly beautiful that I would stand and weep.

I went through the public school system (reluctantly), participated in sports (not very well), and attended Sunday school every Sunday. You see, I was raised in a fundamentalist Christian household. Our family's adage was "God said it. I believe it. That settles it." So there was no room for my beloved faeries in their world, and soon I even stopped hearing the tinkling of bells.

As I grew into my teens, I tried desperately to feel that *frenzy* of joy I witnessed other parishioners experiencing every Sunday at our small community church. But no matter how hard I prayed or how loudly I sang, I never felt a thing. I became active in our youth group and spent a lot of time at conferences that preached against rock music and impure sexual thoughts. By the time I was sixteen, I was a guilt-ridden mess.

In my late teens I found a copy of Stewart Farrar's book *What Witches Do* at a garage sale. My fingers tingled and my heart jumped a little as I held it gingerly in my hands. And though I was pretty sure I was going to hell for buying it, I did it anyway. I brought the book home and tucked it safely under my bed. I soon found solace between the pages of that book, which I didn't know at the time would one day lead me … *home.*

In my early twenties, I married my husband, Steve, a male counterpart of myself. We knew we wanted to live a simple life, lightly imprinting Mother Gaia's soil. And if we were to be blessed with children, we would raise them under the Goddess's protective green mantle. That was over twenty-five years ago, a much different world for practicing Pagans. One where more of us (especially those of us in rural areas) stayed tucked neatly in our broom closets, just behind our besoms and scrying bowls, only meeting others at the occasional festival that popped up or at metaphysical shops that, at that time, seemed few and far between.

When my oldest was born, I did the best I could to attune him to the earth's natural rhythms. My baby's first friends were the birds that sung overhead, and I dedicated my first garden to his brethren, the Fae. As the thought of preschool percolated, I questioned, were there families out there that would share in the joys and frustration of raising children to be free-spirited, nature-loving individuals? Living in a tiny logging community made me wonder. I remember having nightmares of Josh being sat on by ignorant, thick-headed children who would yell, "Come on boys—kick the Witch!" and I would wake up in a panic.

Pagan Proud

Serendipitously, through our small homeschooling program called Skagit River Schoolhouse, we met not only other Pagan families, but Hindu, Jewish, Muslim, Christian, and agnostic families as well. Through Skagit River Schoolhouse, my children learned of new types of family, including polyamorous, blended, single-parent, cross-generational, same-sex, and never married. Through our homeschooling community, our children tasted sweetly dried fruit while lighting small oil lamps for Lakshmi, the Hindu goddess of wealth, for Diwali. They tossed dreidels while taking in the scent of crispy fried potato latkes during Hanukkah. They learned traditional totem carving and listened to legends as told by a Native elder sitting in the shade of Grandmother Cedar. They learned the power of compassion and the beauty of hope as they logged hours handing out food to the less fortunate at our local food bank. Above all, they learned that every individual is unique and sacred to the Goddess. Everyone has a voice, regardless of age, gender, or position.

Who knew that in this tiny valley, hidden within the cragged peaks of the North Cascades, we would find such a treasure trove of diversity! It was exactly what I dreamed for my kids.

Though I felt lucky for finding a group of people who we could identify with (some of whom became intrinsic members of Blue Moon Coven), there were times my children did feel the heady sting of ridicule for being "different." All three of my children have been told they were going to hell. All three have been taunted. And all three have experienced the loss of a friend due to ignorance and fear. I remember each time it happened—I held them tight and wiped the tears of disillusion and abandonment that stung their eyes. I felt helpless as a parent, knowing even chocolate or fresh-baked cookies weren't going to take their pain away (though the cookies helped a little).

It's sad to think that in the twenty-first century, a time in history when Paganism is growing at an incredibly fast rate, that there are still some pretty crazy myths and misconceptions out there about Paganism.[1] In many ways, we are still a persecuted group—wafts of the smoke of heresy still cling to the backs of our cloaks. Misnomers like "hidden trap" and "growing danger" can still be heard whispered by the misinformed. And though for the most part an exposed pentacle goes unnoticed, there are a few eyes that still drop—once, twice, a nervous third time. "Don't worry," I want to say. "I promise I won't eat your baby. It's my daughter you need to watch out for."

Unfortunately, we cannot always hover over our children, ready to throw hexes at the first person who dares to challenge their beliefs. But what we can do is equip them with the knowledge and the confidence to handle situations as they come up.

- *Teach the Fundamentals:* In the Goddess tradition, there are many paths to deity, each uniquely beautiful. But whether you are a Witch, Wiccan, Heathen, Druid, Shaman, Eclectic, or practitioner of one of the many other traditions that sit squarely under the umbrella of Paganism, we share similar fundamentals. Making sure our children are confident in what is true to them will make it easier for them when questions come up. And believe me, they will.

  Are you devil worshipers? Do you cast spells? Are you going to cast a spell on me? Where do you go when you die? Do you believe in God? My kids have been asked questions like these multiple times. Sometimes the questions come from someone who is curious and truly interested in understanding Paganism—that's wonderful. But

---

1. According to the American Religious Identification Survey of 2008, the amount of people who identified as followers of Wicca and other Neopagan religions had more than doubled between 2001 and 2008—and the number continues to increase.

more often than not, it's a bully trying to bait them into an argument or someone making a grand attempt to proselytize to them. In either case, knowing your child can confidently define their beliefs will make these inevitable confrontations run a lot more smoothly.

• *Walk the Talk:* Leading by example is one way to boost children's confidence in their beliefs. Telling them about the relevance of nature is one thing. Taking them out into nature and showing them its relevance is another. Involve your kids in simple outdoor rituals. Take them on nature walks through the park or around your own backyard. Get to know your native flora and fauna. Get involved in local beach, road, or trail cleanup efforts. Sing songs to welcome the moon as she rises. Build faerie houses or create a family altar. These are all simple ways to weave earthy beliefs into everyday life.

• *Erase Stereotypes:* Yes, we are one of those families that looks a little...bohemian. Both Chloe and I tend to border Gothic at times (I really like black...I can't help it). So here's the problem: How do we erase the stereotype that most Witches are Gothic wackos or hippy-dippy New-Age nutjobs that can't be taken seriously? We integrate. Now, I didn't say *simulate.* Being creative and expressing ourselves outwardly through our dress, hair, makeup, or what have you is perfectly healthy, but being dark and mysterious around the neighbors...not so much. Getting our families involved in community events, block parties, after-school programs, and other social activities gives us a chance to let people know, "Hey, we're a family just like yours. Let's have coffee." Coming out of the broom closet to the neighbors can be a freeing experience and help dispel misconceptions that could later affect your family in a negative way.

Remember, religion or spirituality, in any form, is one of our unalienable rights, and our children shouldn't have to feel afraid of ridicule. I'm not here to judge you if choose to keep your family safely tucked in the broom closet. I get it. Really, I do—I was crammed behind a cauldron and besom for years—but, inevitably the truth does seem to seep from under cracks in closet doors, and someone's going to notice. Be ready. Be Pagan proud.

"Mama, Are We Wicked?": How I Almost Threw the Wiccan Rede out the Window

My children were all predominantly homeschooled, but there have been times in our lives when I could not afford the luxury, and the kids were reluctantly put into the public school system.

You see, I am married to a very accident-prone individual. I can no longer count the times he has fallen from ladders, tripped over curbs, dropped objects onto his feet, or tumbled off a tall roof, inevitably breaking bones. He has been in a handful of car and motorcycle accidents that have put him in various trauma centers across western Washington. (I have to say the food at Saint Joe's Hospital in Bellingham is by far the best, but the waiting rooms at Harborview in Seattle are quite comfortable.) And then there's the work-related accidents, usually involving me picking him up at the nearest emergency room and being forced to help him apply ointment to one part of his body or another. (Typically his eyes. Yuck.)

Years ago, the kids and I were at a Renaissance fair hosted by our homeschooling community to celebrate the end of our medieval studies program. I remember feeling a lightness of spirit that one can only feel when being entertained by sprightly young children learning sword-handling techniques from the talented men and women from the Society of Creative Anachronism. I basked in their excitement as they learned to cut and thrust their foam swords and laughed when they tumbled to the ground. Then I received the call.

While stopping by our house, my parents had found Steve in the dirt, unconscious, his hand and shoulder severely broken. He had been on a ladder, replacing fallen shingles at the second-story level of our home, and had fallen almost twenty feet onto a very large rock. Neat. I guess if there was an upside to this story, it would be that the doctors at the emergency room had never seen a hand broken completely in two, dropped and hanging in the skin next to the wrist. They thought it fascinating and called doctors in from other floors just to marvel at it. I thought it was gross. On the downside, Steve was looking at several surgeries and a lot of physical therapy. He wasn't going to be working for a while, and someone needed to pay the bills.

Joshua, being a very self-motivated child, could continue his home-based studies, and Chloe wasn't a problem—she was only four. It was Elijah I worried about. All of my children appreciated a very hands-on approach to learning. The aha moments came when role-playing or when art projects or games were made of the lessons. This was especially true for Elijah; it was like pulling teeth to get him to do conventional schoolwork, and I knew Steve wouldn't be able coax him. So I reluctantly enrolled him into third grade before going to work as a river guide for a Seattle-based outfitter that ran trips down the nearby Skagit River.

Elijah was a sweet kid and, being raised as he was, went into the third grade unaware of the workings of the elementary school social hierarchy. At first, he chatted happily about his new friends, Jonnie, Sam, and Charlie, who I thought were boys for weeks until Sam called our house asking for Elijah in sweet, feminine tones.

"Are Jonnie, Sam, and Charlie *all* girls?" I asked.

"Yeah," he said. "Why?"

"No reason, sweetie. I think it's great that you're friends with girls. There is nothing wrong with it." I patted his head. "Personally, I think girls are awesome."

"Well…" He scrunched his nose. "The boys at school think I'm weird. They say they are my girlfriends and tease me."

I kneeled down beside my little man. "Do you like hanging out with Jonnie, Sam, and Charlie?"

He nodded his head and said yes.

"Then don't let those boys take that away from you. They're probably just jealous because they're not cool enough to make friends with girls."

He smiled. "Yeah," he said. "I'm cool."

"Go to bed, sweetie. We both have a big day tomorrow."

After a month or so, I noticed Elijah's enthusiasm deteriorate. He no longer wanted to go to school. I had to practically drag him out of bed in the morning, and when he got off the bus in the afternoon, he would go straight to his room and shut the door. If I asked him if everything was all right at school, he would just say, "Yeah, it's fine."

Well, it wasn't.

I felt I had to get to the root of the problem. I snuggled up with him one evening on his bed. "Okay, I know something's wrong, so what is it?"

He shrugged. "Nothing."

"I'm not leaving this bedroom until I know why you have been so quiet. You know, I talked to your teacher," I added. "And she says you won't even go out at recess. You just stay in the classroom and read."

"I like books." He was twisting his favorite blue blanket, a sure sign he was hiding something.

"Yeah, I know you like books." I stroked his red hair. "But I also know how much you like to play outside."

Finally, he scrunched his forehead and looked up at me with puppy-dog eyes. "Mama?" he asked. "Are we wicked?"

"What?" I was completely taken aback. "I don't understand. Of course we're not wicked. Who would say such a thing?"

"Charlie." Elijah started crying.

"Why, sweetie?" I think I knew what was coming next. "Why did she say that?"

Between tear bursts, the story unfolded. "I was playing with Jonnie and Sam when Charlie, Brent, and Rodney came over to us and said that Charlie told them we were evil." He took a gulp of air. "I told Charlie we were Pagans, and I guess she told everybody all about it."

"Go on." I could feel anger stirring deep within my gut. I was becoming so agitated that I think I could have literally spewed acid.

"He said we must be devil worshipers, and I said, no, we loved the Goddess and nature and that we don't believe in the devil." More crying. "Then Charlie asked if we were Witches, and I said yes. She said Witches are wicked, and then nobody wanted to play with me."

I have to say it was all I could do not to pull out the flying monkeys. I wanted nothing more than to throw every baneful spell I could think of at those rotten little stinkers (that was not the word I used at the time). How dare they pick on my sweet little boy.

"It's okay," I cradled Elijah. "They're the wicked ones for making you feel bad."

When I went to bed, I cried too.

When I'm upset, it is my friend Jean whom I go to. She is always thoughtful, levelheaded, and willing to let me vent. Needless to say, she has been my rock.

"They're wicked little snots!" I cried.

She handed me a cup of tea and a cookie. "No," she said, her voice steady. "They're not wicked—they're ignorant." She sipped her tea. "There's a difference."

"They're ignorant and wicked!" Crumbs spewed from my mouth as I spoke. "I'm going to go to that school, and I'll show them what a Witch can do." I gulped my tea too quickly—then tried to hide the shock of having scalding hot water hit the roof of my mouth. "I need to go to that little Charlie's house and have a little talk with her parents."

"No, what I think you need to do is invite them over." She smiled.

"Why would I do that?" I was surprised by my friend's suggestion.

"Look, Elijah has a birthday coming up, right?"

I nodded.

"Send out invitations. Show those kids what a great family you have. Let them get to know Elijah outside of school."

I sighed. "You're right. I'll do it."

Invitations were made for every child in Elijah's third grade class. When it came to the kids who had been teasing him, I went a step further and called their homes, introduced myself to their parents, and extended the invitation. "We would love for you to come," I said.

Elijah wanted a sixties hippy variation on his yearly dinosaur birthday theme. Yeah, I know ... but I pulled it off with lots of tie-dye, a few borrowed lava lamps, and a psychedelic volcano cake with crazy painted dinosaurs. As the guests arrived, I stood proudly in a tie-dye shirt with my pentacle on the outside.

The day ran smoothly, and though Elijah had been reluctant about the idea, he was having a lot of fun. And throughout the afternoon filled with happy chaos, I waited for the opportunity to set things right.

It arrived when I went to my kitchen to refill a juice pitcher. Charlie and her mother were at my sink, rinsing Charlie's hand.

"I hope you don't mind," her mother said. "She got her hand in a little mud."

"No, of course not." I handed Charlie a dish towel and noticed her eyes drift to the pentacle dangling from around my neck. "I see you're looking at my necklace. It's a pretty star, isn't it?"

Charlie shook her head. "Elijah said you are Witches."

"That's right." I looked up to her mother, who just smiled. "He told me that it scared you, and you didn't want to play with him anymore."

"Oh, Charlie," her mother said. "I hope you weren't mean to Elijah."

"I wasn't." She looked to her toes. "Do you have a cauldron?" she asked.

"Yes." I smiled and pointed to one of my small cauldrons, which was propped in the kitchen. "But that's not the one I use for cooking children. That one's outside."

Her eyes grew large, and her mother snickered.

"I'm just kidding, honey. That was a bad joke." I gave her a little squeeze.

She giggled.

"You know, I have a faerie garden where nature spirits love to dance and play."

Charlie smiled.

"I bet if you ask Elijah, he would show it to you." I tugged at her ponytail. "You know, late at night, I have quite often spied a faerie who bears a striking resemblance to you."

Charlie looked bright-eyed to her mom. "See, Mom," she said.

Her mother laughed. "Charlie always tells us she was a faerie in another life."

And that was it. Charlie, Jonnie, Sam, and Elijah were back to being the best of friends. It was a friendship that continued for many years, even after Steve healed and Elijah was back at our beloved little schoolhouse. But as with many friendships made during those tender young years, the friendship between Elijah and the girls slowly dissolved. Both Sam and Charlie moved before middle school, and high school hierarchy created a rift between Jonnie and Elijah. But it was a friendship that Elijah still treasures.

As I look back on this story I am reminded of this saying: "Never blame anyone in your life. Good people give you happiness. Bad people give you experience. The worst people give you a lesson, and the best people give you memories." And as I tell my children, be true to yourself—if someone doesn't like you for who you are, they don't deserve the privilege of being a part of your life.

Dance to the Beat of Your Own Drum

I picked up my oldest son from Skagit Valley College, where he studied creative writing and worked at the college's radio station, writing and reading local news stories. It was autumn and the sugar maple he was sitting under was ablaze with color. He sat comfortably in an old tweed jacket (the kind with the patches on the elbows). He had an English driving cap perched on his head, and as he plucked contently on an old Underwood typewriter, he seemed oblivious to the hordes of students who bustled around him in twenty-first-century attire, most tapping at their smartphones. I smiled at the juxtaposition of the scene.

He glanced up and waved and then packed his typewriter into its case. Nobody stared, nobody gawked. He exchanged a few pleasantries with students he knew and crawled into our jeep.

"What?" he asked, noticing the silly smile I was still wearing.

I wrapped my arms around him. "I love you. That's all." I gave him another squeeze. "Never change."

He laughed. "I learned it from the best, Mom." He pointed to my shredded jeans, tied with quilting scraps.

"You're right." I chuckled. "You totally did."

This is one of the things I feel I did right as a parent. I allowed my children the freedom to express themselves. Okay, I have to say it sucked when Josh was going through his 1980s phase. All those horrible geometric sweaters lying around the house—it was all I could do not to burn them.

But, really, there is nothing more beautiful than a child who is truly comfortable in their own skin, and what better time than now to celebrate your own uniqueness? Teaching our kids to embrace what sets them apart from the others can be a real confidence booster. It shows in the way they walk and in the way they interact with their peers and with adults. It's reflected in how they take on challenges and how they greet each and every day.

This is a hard feat for today's youth. Mass media bombards our children with ridiculously unattainable body images. They are saturated with ideas of how young people should act, what they should wear, and that popularity is a standard to be attained. Eating disorders are becoming more prevalent among our youth, and antidepressants are even being prescribed to children.

Helping our children learn to love themselves and discover what is true about their shining, unique souls will help them as they grow into rounded, confident adults.

Can't Is a Four-Letter Word

I taught art and writing at workshops for children for years and the saddest word (and sadly the most common word) I ever heard was "can't." Too many parents put "I can't" into their children's heads without even realizing it. Telling a child they're good at one thing and not at something else can unintentionally plant the seeds of doubt. Before you know it, "I can't" takes root. Acknowledging a child's effort in all they do is important. Yes, some skills take a little longer to master, but it can be done.

Your child may have many budding interests; allow them to explore these pursuits freely without the stigma of "you *can't* be a quitter." When Elijah was nine, he thought he was going to die if he didn't learn piano. I found a local resident who taught piano lessons. She was inexpensive and, most importantly for me, only ten miles from my home. Elijah was a natural, but, unfortunately, his desire to continue his lessons fizzled out after two years. I did make him continue until his final recital for the year (I also believe it's important to follow through with commitments). But I wasn't going to force him to continue playing an instrument that no longer sparked his soul.

What he did find out about himself through piano lessons was that he really loved music and wanted it to be a part of his life. Ultimately, it was the guitar that ignited a fire within Elijah. He hung out with local musicians and made friends with similar interests, and within a couple of years, he became a talented guitar player and singer.

Redefine Role Models

Our children learn by example, and having strong, confident leadership in their lives will help them be the same. When my daughter expressed an interest in running marathons, it was my sister Heidi, a triathlete who competes all over the United States and won her age division in her first Ironman competition, who took Chloe under her wing. She taught my daughter how to be strong physically, through proper diet and exercise, and emotionally, with her positive attitude and an astonishing will to accomplish goals no matter what obstacles may lie before her.

Also a busy career woman, Heidi took time out of her tight schedule to properly prepare Chloe for her first half marathon. Not only did she take her on long runs on her weekends off, but she also made sure Chloe was familiar with the route by running portions of it with her days before the race and giving her tips along the way. On race day, Heidi and I cried together when we saw Chloe's beaming smile as she came up over the final hill and across the finish line. Strong, positive role models who have turned their lives into an astonishing testament to the power of the human spirit will do so much more for our children's psyches than anorexic supermodels or over-privileged socialites.

Of course, the most important role model for our children is looking straight at us when we gaze in that mirror every morning. Yes! We, as parents, are the first and most influential people in our kids' lives. If we show them that breaking boundaries and being unique in our way of thinking, dressing, or acting is a positive attribute, they will learn to do the same.

Dance, Baby, Dance!

My friend Kathleen, who works at the post office where I am a substitute mail carrier, bought me a glass necklace that has a very cool steampunk image on one side and a message on the other side that reads, "It's better to be weird than to be ordinary ... Ordinary is boring."

"This made me think of you," she said. "I hope you're not offended."

"How could I be offended?" I asked. "It's perfect! I'm glad you noticed."

Why conform to society's prescribed ideal of normal? As a parent, I know we *want* our kids to be liked and to "fit in," not necessarily out of a need to see our daughter become homecoming queen or our son captain of the football team, but because we don't want to see them hurt or made fun of. Encouraging kids to seek out and join in with kids with similar interests will allow them to feel accepted and will also let them maintain their sense of self. Having them join clubs or groups of like-minded peers that foster their uniqueness will help cultivate the confidence that will ultimately allow them to bloom as adults.

It's time we proudly celebrate what truly makes us unique. And what better way to be truly heard? Whether your child is a supernerd surrounded by science books, a music geek who has to take his instrument wherever he goes, a flower-child nature freak, a Gothic princess, or the quiet writer who considers a manual typewriter his tool of trade, remember: these are the kids who are most likely to succeed—not in spite of their differences, but because of them!

I have always told my kids, "Embrace your inner weirdo!" Why? We are all born individuals—there ain't nobody else like you on this entire planet. So when you hear your drums a-beatin', dance, baby, dance!

Express Yourself

Here are some creative expression exercises to help keep those creative souls dancing to their own beat!

Mindfulness Exercises

Mindfulness is a grounding technique that focuses one's awareness on the present moment, while simultaneously accepting bodily emotions, thoughts, and feelings. It is being used in more and more public schools, and according to a 2014 article in *Frontiers in Psychology*, schools who use mindfulness techniques on a regular basis have students who think more positively, are happier, and have increased compassion for others.

Try these mindfulness exercises with your children. I have included four, focusing on each of the elements.

EARTH

Earth is stability. We want our kids to feel rooted and confident, and connecting to the element of earth can help. Take your child outdoors with bare feet and have them stand tall. Have them feel the soil between their toes. Tell them to focus on that feeling. Next, have them raise their arms and reach toward the sky, like the branches of the mighty oak. Now have them imagine their feet as roots, reaching deep into the soil. They are taking in the ground's life-giving water. Have them close their eyes and focus on the earth. Tell them or have them repeat, "You are (I am) mighty, just like a tree."

AIR

Air is freedom. Connecting with the element of air helps free your kids' minds and stir their already curious intellect. For this mindfulness exercise have your child fetch their favorite stuffed animal or doll. Have them lie comfortably on the grass (or a yoga mat or soft blanket indoors). They will place the toy on their belly. Have them close their eyes and breathe deeply in through their nostrils and out through their

mouth. As they do this, have them focus on the moving of air throughout their body through the rise and fall of the toy on their body. Tell
them or have them repeat, "Air sets your (my) imagination free."

Fire

Fire is strength. What are your child's goals? To win the spelling bee?
Maybe to participate in a marathon or win the big game. Connecting
with fire through mindfulness exercises will light the flame of action!
Have your child stand near a sunny window or outside on a nice day.
Have them close their eyes and raise their arms to the sun. Tell them
to feel the power of the sun's power as it heats their fingers. Have them
imagine that power running down their arms, into their body's core,
and finally filling their legs and reaching their toes. Tell them or have
them repeat, "You are (I am) as powerful as the sun."

Water

Water is healing. Let water wash away the blues through mindfulness exercises. This mindfulness exercise requires getting their feet
wet. On a warm day have your kids sit near a lake, stream, creek, river,
sea, or pool. On a cooler day, you could use the bathtub or a tub of
water in the kitchen. Have them sit comfortably with their feet in the
water. Have them close their eyes and focus on the flow of water and
its cleansing power as it splashes against their toes. Have them imagine
the water washing away their problems or fears. Tell them or have them
repeat, "You are (I am) filled to the brim with peace."

Affirmation Poem

This is a great activity that can be done with children as young as two.
It's a simple way to reinforce all those beautiful aspects of our children
that really make them stand out as individuals.

At the top of the page have your child (or a parent if they're too
young to write) title the poem "What I Know at (fill in their age)."

Your child will then list ten things that they truly know about
themselves, their world, or their spirituality. Make sure they start each

sentence with "I know." If your child is too young to write it, simply prompt them: What do you know you're good at? What do you know you really love to do? What do you know about the Goddess?

After the ten affirmations (or less), have your child write their name. It really is as simple as that.

What you end up with is a one-of-a-kind poem that can be framed and hung on your child's bedroom wall as a visible reminder of the positive things they know about themselves. If they're having a bad day or feeling a little insecure, have them read the poem out loud to remind themselves how absolutely unique and wonderful they are.

What's great about this exercise is that it can be repeated year after year. Keep the poems from previous years together in a scrapbook. It's fun to go back through them and recognize your kids' growth and new-found confidences.

Here is a sample of an affirmation poem my son Joshua wrote when he was seven:

What I Know at 7
I know that I am loved.
I know that I am good at climbing trees.
I know that I love sweets and candy.
I know the Goddess is in the sky.
I know that my favorite thing is writing.
I know I am good at swords.
I know I can type.
I know how to grow a garden.
I know my daddy takes me fishing.
I know the moon is a door to the Goddess.
—*Joshua*

(In case you're wondering, yes, I did cry my eyes out as I typed Joshua's poem.)

Poetry Masks

This is a project I have done many times with students for children's writing workshops all over western Washington. An artistic expression of who we are on the inside, this craft is meant to convey the message that our inner qualities are more important than our physical appearance.

You will need:

1 white cardstock or plastic mask per child (These can be purchased at any craft store or online, or you can cut one out of white cardstock.)
1 Popsicle stick per child to glue to the bottom of the mask as a handle
Fine-tipped permanent markers (black plus any other colors for decorating)
Craft glue
Decorations: colorful feathers, sequins, plastic jewels, glitter, felt cutouts, collected leaves, bark, small cones, shells, or whatever your creative mind can come up with to decorate the masks

Before I get started, I like to really help the kids understand that this mask is a picture of their beautiful souls. A way to show the world who they really are. "Who are you?" I ask. "Tell me about yourself through your mask."

Before the fun of decorating, have the kids write down everything they want to convey in words on a separate piece of paper. Have younger kids use positive adjectives to describe themselves, words like "creative," "funny," "happy," or "awesome." Older kids can use song lyrics, lines of poetry, cool quotes—anything that they positively identify with. They will then artistically write the words, quotes, etc., on the masks.

Now for the real fun! They get to use all the great craft supplies you have gathered to decorate the masks. Maybe your child feels as free as a bird when running—cover the mask in feathers to reflect that! Maybe your child is a true nature baby and is happiest climbing trees; a classic Green Man mask comes to mind. Don't forget to attach the Popsicle stick to the bottom of the mask when you're done. Your kids can also use ribbon to tie the mask around their heads.

After the masks are dry, have everyone hold them up to their faces and try this blessing:

This mask I wear portrays the potential in me,
A symbol of the beauty I want everyone to see.
As I say these words, help me bloom and grow.
Let me be an example to others—as above, so below.
Blessed be!

Rites of Passage

Honoring life's passages through ritual is a practice that goes back to our Neolithic roots, helping to shape us as individuals, reaffirm important relationships in our lives, and strengthen our connection with the Divine. So as your family journeys 'round the spiral path, acknowledge the sacred transitions and honor your loved ones. Celebrating milestones is a wonderful way to make the mundane truly magickal!

Blessingways

Of all transitions in a woman's life, entering motherhood is probably the most significant. The term "Blessingway" comes from Navajo tradition and serves as a blessing for the mother; the definition is a hint as to how it differs from a traditional baby shower. A Blessingway celebrates the mother-to-be as she journeys through this life-altering transition. Friends and family circle her, surrounding her with love, guidance, and support. The focus is exclusively on the woman preparing for birth. She is pampered with scented oils, candlelight, gifts, and decadent food. Ritual aspects of this celebration may include the lighting of candles, raising energy, washing feet, plaiting hair, and henna tattooing the celebrant's hands and belly. You may want to add a craft; blessing flags and beads can be made at the event and gifted to the celebrant at the end of the day. Both make lovely mementos and can be taken with the mother-to-be to her birthing area for meditation and positive energy.

One craft we always include at Blessingway celebrations is a belly cast for the expectant mother. I had belly casts done for me for each of my pregnancies and had assisted with several more, so when asked if I would do one for a friend of a friend, I confidently said yes. It didn't seem that difficult to do on my own, and besides, I'm an artistic person. What could go wrong?

The celebration was lovely. We held it in the backyard of my friend's beautiful home within the protective confines of her circular herb garden, surrounded by the sage, lavender, and roses. It was perfect. After a poignant ritual that included a lot of happy tears and joyful laughter, it was time to cast her belly. The expectant mother beamed as she pulled off the lovingly embroidered maternity shirt she had made herself, and I asked, "Are you ready?"

"Yes, I can't wait," she answered.

The one thing I noticed as I wiped olive oil over her belly and breasts to protect from the harsh plaster that would soon cover her belly was that she was very ... hairy. Her entire belly was coated with a downy fuzz, and her pubic hair reached almost to her belly button. Not giving it a second thought, I continued my work. I soaked the plaster gauze strips and one by one, her friends and family lovingly helped me lay them across her belly and breasts.

As the form began to quickly dry, I noticed the mother-to-be grimace. "Is it supposed to hurt?" she asked.

"No, it shouldn't hurt," I answered. "I think what you're feeling is the heat," I quickly added. "It does heat up a bit."

"No," she said, and I could tell she was beginning to panic. "This hurts!"

A couple of her friends gathered around her, asking if she was okay.

"No, I need to get this thing off!" She was in full-on panic mode and stood, pulling at the cast.

I really didn't know her very well and thought maybe she was just a drama queen. "Relax, it's dry. It should just pop right off." I tried to sound calm as I gently took the edges of the cast and began to tug. But to my horror, the cast wasn't "popping" off. In fact, it seemed glued to her belly.

She must have noticed my fearful expression because she began to scream, "Get it off! Get it off!"

As her friends and family tried to gently work the cast off her belly, I noticed the role of unused plastic wrap lying beside my casting supplies. "Oh, dear Goddess," I mumbled. "What have I done?"

My friend, the party's hostess, came to me. "Monica," she said. "What do you think went wrong?"

I pointed to the plastic wrap.

Her eyes grew wide. "You didn't cover her pubic hair with the wrap? You are aware of the amount of hair on her belly, right?" She, too, was beginning to panic. The pubic hair had adhered to the plaster.

"Maybe you should get her in a shower." I was shaking.

The approximately fifteen minutes of her shrieking and crying in the shower as her mother broke and peeled away the casting material felt like a lifetime to me. "Maybe I should call an ambulance," I finally suggested to the ten other sets of unforgiving eyes.

"Yeah," a nervous young blonde said. "That might be a good idea."

I picked up a phone, but just before I began to dial, the shrieking ceased. I put the phone down and waited as the celebrant weakly walked from the bathroom with her mother. She revealed herself to the concerned crowd, exposing an angry red belly and missing patches of pubic hair.

After seeing that, I slipped out unnoticed and ashamed. I cried all the way home.

Later that evening, my friend called me and assured me that everything was fine and not to worry—I wouldn't be lynched. A couple of weeks later, I received a nice e-mail from the hapless victim of my artistic negligence, and she thanked me for my attempt and said it was something she would always remember. She went on to tell me she kept a piece of the plaster that had pubic hair still attached and on the curved side painted a full, round moon.

She gave birth to a beautiful baby boy who is now nine years old. I saw them just after Yule this past year while replacing a reluctant shopping cart at our local grocery store. She introduced me to her son, and we laughed a little about the incident. I have done many belly castings in the past nine years and have never again forgotten to cover exposed pubic hair with plastic wrap. Lesson learned.

A Blessingway Celebration

This rite of passage is all about the mother-to-be, so I would suggest holding it in a place where she feels most comfortable, whether her own home or backyard, a favorite park, or the home of a close friend or family member. Leave that up to her. Also, decorations should reflect the celebrant. Does she enjoy old-fashioned perennial favorites with a shabby chic flair, or is she all about a simple, clean setting with a single bouquet of her favorite lilies? Maybe she's a romantic and loves rich colors and soft draping with rose petals scattered everywhere! Really, the sky's the limit, so have fun working out the details with the mother-to-be.

A couple of rules as far as setup: Keep the seating intimate and circular. Design a menu that is full of the celebrant's most decadent, sinful delights. Perfume the air with beautifully scented candles. Play relaxing music.

You will need:

Stones

Permanent markers (color of your choice)

Sage and lavender smudge

Lovely scented massage oils

Henna kit

Beads and beading kit (In the invitation for the event, remind everyone to pick out and bring a special bead that reminds them of the celebrant.)

Red yarn or ribbon for the binding

Several scraps of paper and a pencil

A large pillar candle

A large dish of sand

A pretty bowl

Yummy food!

Have a table set up with clean stones and permanent markers outside the seating area for each guest to write a blessing for the mother-to-be on. Smudge and welcome the celebrant and each guest as they enter the circle. Seat the mother-to-be in a chair or cushion of honor. Make it special so she feels like a queen, complete with a flower crown! This is all about her, so remember to have a couple of people working in the background to help keep the activities running smoothly. She shouldn't feel like she has to do anything but relax and enjoy.

After everyone is seated comfortably, the hostess will then open the Blessingway celebration with a blessing or reading of her choice. I have hosted several and have included quarter calls and a blessing for my magickal friends as well as a poem that I felt reminded me of the celebrant's wonderful qualities for my mundane friends. You can open the floor to guests who would like to say something as well.

Time for the pampering to begin! At this point it is nice to massage the mother-to-be's feet and hands with scented massage oil or henna her belly or both. You can go ahead and do this yourself, or if it's in the budget, hire a professional masseuse or henna tattoo artist. While she is being pampered, have the guests present their beads one at a time and tell the celebrant why they chose it for her. Elect someone to string the beads as they are presented, and the mother-to-be can keep this wonderful memento with her as she labors as a reminder of the support of her friends and family.

After she has been massaged and tattooed, bring out the red yarn or ribbon. Start by wrapping the wrist of the mother-to-be and continue wrapping all guests around the circle as a way of connecting everyone. At the end of the ceremony, each guest can snip a length of ribbon or yarn to wear as a bracelet until the celebrant begins labor—a symbol of unity and support.

The hostess will then hand the mother-to-be a pencil and several scraps of paper. On the papers she will write fears or concerns she may have about the upcoming delivery or about being a new mother. As she does this, the hostess will then light the large pillar candle and put it in the sand-filled dish on a table or stand near the celebrant. The mother-to-be will then read her fears one at a time, giving everyone a chance to give her advice and words of love to help dispel the fear. As each fear is dealt with, the mother-to-be will ritually dispel each by lighting it with the pillar candle and dropping it into the sand to burn out.

Now it's time to eat some delicious food! As everyone enjoys their lavish meal, have the celebrant open her gifts. Remember, guests are to bring gifts meant to pamper the new mother, not gifts for the baby.

Before everyone leaves, end the ceremony by opening your circle or with a closing of your choice, and don't forget to give the mother-to-be the blessing stones arranged in a pretty bowl and her newly strung beads.

First Moon: Coming of Age Rites for Girls

My early teenage years found me tall, gangly, and socially awkward. If that wasn't bad enough, I was a late bloomer, constantly reminded by the group of girls I sometimes hung out with at school that because I hadn't started my period yet, I truly didn't understand *anything.*

At home, it was the opposite. The oldest of four girls, I was taunted about my changing body. My sister Angela and her friends would follow me out to my favorite pasture and wooded areas proclaiming, "Monica's developing, Monica's developing!"

My two baby sisters would look at my budding breasts wide-eyed. I was no longer that sister who ran shirtless with them through the back field on hot summer evenings. No, their big sissy had to wear a ... *bra.* I was an alien.

When I finally did see those first traces of blood on my panties, instead of reaching out, I tried to hide it. I didn't want to be teased by my sisters, and I definitely didn't feel the girls at school deserved to know. It wasn't until months later, when my mother found a pair of my underpants stained with blood, that she came to me. "Monica, did you start your period?" she asked, in front of my younger sisters, who smirked and giggled.

Humiliated, I belted out, "No!"

She looked at me for a moment and then held up the blood-stained panties. "Okay," she said. "Then this has to be one of three things."

My eyes widened when I saw the incriminating evidence.

"One, you started your period. Two, you're bleeding for no reason, and I need to take you to a doctor. Or three, I wore these panties while on *my* period." She tapped her foot. "Well, which is it?"

"I don't know." I could feel my face heat up.

"Well, I know what I *can* tell you." I thought there was a tinge of anger or maybe it was disappointment in her voice. "It wasn't the third choice."

I heard more giggling from my sisters. I shot them a glare and said, "Shut up."

"So, honey," Mom continued. "Do I take you to the doctor, or did you start your period?"

I looked to the floor. "I started my period," I mumbled.

"Okay, then." She walked over and gave me a hug. "I'll buy you some pads."

I ran outside completely horrified and cried for hours in the crook of an ancient bigleaf maple.

Wow! Isn't that a beautiful coming-of-age story? Oh, dear Goddess, how did I ever make it through adolescence?

You know, it wasn't my mother's fault that she didn't handle my blooming womanhood very well. She was raised in a small, backwoods community where no one talked about "the curse." The whisperings concerning a woman's cycle that wafted the woods and valleys of her childhood included neat tips like "Don't touch the flowers or vegetables while on your period, or they'll die." This folk saying derives from a time when a woman's menstrual cycle was seen as something dirty. My other favorite, as relayed by my grandmother: "Don't use a tampon. It will cause you to lose your virginity." No. No, Grandma, it's sex that will cause you to lose your virginity, not a tampon.

When I became an adult and decided to start a family of my own, I promised myself that if I had a daughter, I would not only educate her about the changes that were happening to her body, but celebrate her transformation from beautiful girl to strong, confident, amazing young woman with her. That shame and inadequacy of "the curse" felt by the women of my family for generations would stop with me.

Coming-of-age rites for girls usually happen around the time of their first menses, usually between the ages of nine and fifteen. Many ancient cultures celebrated this passage with a time of isolation and fasting for the young ladies in a hut secluded from the tribe in order to teach them discipline and patience. In some cultures, celebrants were educated briefly by female elders or by their mothers on what would be expected of them as women. They may have been ritually dressed, tattooed, or pierced before being presented to the community as a woman.

The most horrific coming of age rite suffered by young girls is the Maasai practice of female circumcision. Mostly outlawed now, but still practiced by a few nomadic tribes, this form of mutilation, which involves the cutting away of the clitoris, is extremely painful and can be life-threatening for young girls. But through the educational efforts of programs like African Medical and Research Foundation, new rituals have been created to celebrate a Maasai girl's passage into womanhood, which include feasting, joy, and most importantly for the girls, lessons on sex education and human rights.

An example of a modern coming of age ritual for young girls is the *quinceañera*, Spanish for "fifteen-year-old (female)," or *fiesta de quinceañera*. With roots that go back to the Aztec coming-of-age rites when girls entering adulthood were celebrated as future "mothers of warriors," the modern equivalent features lavish parties with Latin and Catholic influences.

From the Victorians we get the sweet sixteen party. This was a way to present your daughter to proper society, in hopes of finding her a husband. Our twenty-first century version can be as simple as pizza and cake with friends or an all-out birthday extravaganza, staged at an event center and costing parents a small fortune. But no matter how you choose to celebrate your daughter's crossing to adulthood, acknowledging these shifts helps open communication about life's inevitable changes.

I have to admit, when my daughter turned ten, I started fantasizing about her first-moon party. I would walk idly along the riverfront, scoping for the perfect branches to drape the yards and yards of red tulle I would use to fulfill my Red Tent dreams. I would imagine the forest floor strewn with rose petals and tea lights hanging from glass jars off of every branch within my reach. I thought about the amazing chocolate buffet we would set up with Chloe's favorite hot cocoa, chocolate truffles, death-by-chocolate cake, and, centered right in the middle, a giant chocolate fountain with plenty of goodies for dipping.

As I washed dishes or worked in the yard, I would let my mind wander to that wonderful evening under a starlit sky with Chloe surrounded by all the women, young and old, who have known and loved her and how electric the night would feel with the energy of those amazing people. I rehearsed the words I would say and would sometimes get so wrapped up in my fantasy, I would actually cry.

Do you know how utterly disappointed I was when she told me she wasn't interested?!

"What?" I choked out. "Why?"

"I don't know." She shrugged her shoulders. "I don't know if I want to celebrate my period with a whole bunch of people."

I clenched my chest. "But, it won't be a whole bunch of people—only women you want to invite."

She shrugged again. "I'll think about it, but I still don't know. I don't like parties that much. I think I would like it better if just me and you went to a movie."

Wow, I thought. Three years of wasted daydreaming.

It was a couple of weeks later that she came to me and said, "Mama, I thought about it."

"Yeah?" I said.

"Well, I don't want to disappoint you, but I really don't want a party."

"That's okay." I smiled. "This is supposed to be about you, not me. If you don't want a first-moon party, we won't have one. I think just me, you, and a giant bag of popcorn at a chick flick would be more fun, anyway." I gave her a hug.

"Well, actually, I still want to do that, but …" She paused. "I thought maybe a first-moon rite with the ladies of the coven and Hannah and Sadie would be really cool."

I smiled. "That's a great idea, Chloe." Yay! I was back to planning!

Whether you throw your daughter a first-moon (or Red Tent) party; plan a coming-of-age rite with your circle, coven, or grove; or choose to celebrate this passage of life with a mother-daughter spa day or movie night, remember that this is a passage that deserves recognition in whatever way your daughter feels comfortable. Enjoy this time together as your little bud blossoms into a beautiful flower.

Here is the first-moon rite we came up with for Chloe. Feel free to adapt it for your special celebrant.

A Witch's First-Moon Rite

Perform this first-moon ritual during the new moon, outdoors if possible.

Before the ceremony, have the celebrant take a ritual cleansing bath. Have the bathroom lit softly with candlelight and maybe a little relaxing music playing in the background. Scent the water with a little orange essential oil; with its uplifting scent and its confidence-building qualities, it's perfect to keep her mood vibrant. This is not supposed to be a time to be stressed out but a time to reflect on the exciting possibilities this new chapter of her life is about to open up to her.

You will need:

Something red for the celebrant: cloak, dress, or whatever she is comfortable with

Pink rose petals (bonding and friendship)

Bowl of salt

Incense

Bowl of water

Red candle (passion and desire)

Red altar cloth

A bouquet of cosmos (feminine energy)

Representations of the Triple Goddess

A white pillar candle

Pretty red dish

Four small gifts that relate to the four elements, plus one given by the mother to represent spirit

A tea light for the celebrant

Cakes and ale (This could be a favorite food of the celebrant. For Chloe it was chocolate! We set up a table of chocolate-covered everything—a little red wine for the adults and hot cocoa for the girls.)

Before the ceremony, scatter the pink rose petals around the diameter of the sacred circle as a representation of the connection of trust and friendship shared amongst coven-mates and the celebrant.

Place the salt, incense, water, and red candle at the points of the corresponding elements, along with the gifts. As an example, the gifts for Chloe included a pretty quartz for earth, incense sticks for air, candles for fire, and a journal for water. Her gift for spirit (from me) was a bracelet that had the quote "She believed she could…so she did." The altar is to be set up with images of the Triple Goddess and a bouquet of cosmos (if possible). Cosmos are a great flower for invoking feminine energy. Place the white pillar candle in a pretty red dish in the middle.

Call the quarters in your usual way. For this ritual invoke the Triple Goddess. Though our celebrant is a maiden "awakening," all three aspects of the Goddess (as in life) have lessons to teach as one journeys into this new phase of life.

Have the celebrant and her mother start at the east quarter and walk the diameter of the circle together (representing their walk together through childhood). When they again reach the east quarter, the mother will stand by the altar as her daughter begins this journey again, this time alone, stopping at each quarter. Waiting at each quarter will be a trusted coven-mate who will bless the celebrant with the appropriate elemental representation (wafting incense, sprinkling salt, etc.). I think it's important that the words spoken be their own and from the heart. After each blessing, the celebrant will be offered her gift.

After she has completed the circle, she will stand in front of the altar with her mother. The mother will then light the tea light and hand it to her daughter, stating,

> This light represents the spark of (fill in the blank with your daughter's amazing qualities) that you have carried with you throughout your childhood. You are no longer just a spark, but a shining star free to light the world with your (fill in the blank). Remember, as you cross this threshold into womanhood, to always keep true to yourself. I present you with this gift of spirit to remind you of this.

At this time the mother presents her daughter with her gift. The celebrant will then snuff out the tea light (representing childhood) and light the pillar candle (representing womanhood). At this time the mother can reintroduce her daughter to the coven, grove, or circle (in whatever matter she would like, maybe with her craft name). Open your circle in your usual way. Spend some time together eating really good food and sharing stories and advice with the celebrant.

Chloe's first-moon rite was a beautiful experience. Of course, I was so emotional, I pretty much blew my lines, but the sentiment was there. No, we didn't have the huge Red Tent party of my dreams, surrounded by her female cousins, aunts, and grandmothers, but I got over it.

For my daughter, more important than celebrating the physical transformation was sharing her "spiritual" transformation with the maidens, mothers, and crones who had advised her and supported her through her journey down the spiral path. That I can respect... from the woman my daughter has become.

Vision Quest: Coming of Age for Boys

"Snips and snails and puppy dog tails." Boy, does that sum up little boys, or what? I was raised with girls. The oldest of four girls, the only male in my household was my dad. He was that tall person in pants with a soft heart who couldn't deny his little girls anything. Our best friends growing up were our female cousins, and in elementary school, I hung out with girls. Boys were those foreign creatures who came to school, licked their snot, slammed bugs in my schoolbooks, and tried to give me mouse legs as a gift.

"I pulled these off just for you, Monica."

I screamed.

So when my son Joshua was born, I wondered about the foreign little wriggling creature. Would he lick his snot and hand me a smashed spider for my birthday? No, but he did lick his snot and give me an eyeball (not real) necklace for my birthday. I still remember his round little face—his cheeks red from play and his eyes shining because he knew he had picked out the perfect gift. And he had. I didn't scream but wore it with pride.

Raising boys brought out the adventurer in me. Through their antics and interests, I became an entomologist, a geologist, a paleontologist, a snake handler, a mountain climber, a sword swinger, a mudslinger, and a circus enthusiast. As they transformed from frog-carrying little boys to gangly young gentlemen—handy with a garden hoe and always willing to keep the wood box full and dishes picked up—I knew I had to do something special to celebrate their transformations from boys to men. I did a little research on adolescent rituals from around the world. I remember reading some of them to Josh, but instead of excitement, he responded with tears. "What's wrong, Josh?"

"I really don't want to be dumped off in the woods alone or have my face tattooed." His voice trembled.

"Do you really think we would do that to you?" I gave him a hug.

It was my husband, Steve, who came up with the perfect idea.

"Well, what is it?" I asked, wondering if it would involve me having to barbecue a large amount of meat.

"That's my secret." He winked.

Now, I love Steve, but sometimes he does things that are just … well, very *boy*-like, and I have to say, I was nervous. And it was under my nervous gaze that the two of them planned their "vision quest" in whispered tones. One morning, as the summer sun rose high above the surrounding hills, Steve came home with a canoe he had borrowed from a friend.

"A canoe trip it is." I have to say I was relieved. Definitely.

"Yep," he said. "In two weeks we will spend three days canoeing and camping on Ross Lake." An impish grin covered his face. He was really excited. They both were.

After the trip, they both came home exhausted but clearly happy. I didn't get to hear about everything that happened, but I know the highlight included waking up before sunrise and skinny-dipping in Ross Lake's frigid waters just as the sun's golden fingers began to reach over the high peaks of the North Cascades.

When Elijah hit thirteen, he had already planned his own coming of age ritual and presented his plan to both Steve and me. "I want to spend a weekend alone living as an ancient Celt along the river," he announced.

"I'm okay with that as long as your weekend alone along the river is on our riverfront property."

His shoulders dropped and he sighed. "Okay."

Elijah spent two months in preparation. He hand-sewed his own clothing using fabric that was as close as he could get to what the Celts would have woven. He made his own fishing pole and gathered food supplies. He and my husband constructed a very tiny round hut; one person could barely fit in sitting down. They thatched it with moss and put an old sheep's fleece in it for the flooring. I ordered woad online and we painted him with Celtic symbols. We pasted his hair with a flour and water mixture to resemble the lime the Celts would have used.

When the day came for Elijah to begin his ritual, Steve dramatically led my boy down to the river property wearing a Green Man mask. He said he watched through the underbrush for a few minutes to make sure that Elijah was set up and admitted that as he walked back to our house (just across the road) he felt a little emotional.

Elijah spent three days and two nights on the river, eating parsnips, nettles, and steel-cut oats. He attempted fishing, did a little journaling, and stitched together a Green Man mask of his own from leaves and a piece of leather he had brought with him. At night, I could hear him rhythmically drumming, which helped me know he was okay.

As the sun set on the third day, Steve emerged with Elijah, our boy who wanted to test himself. Both donned their leafy masks, and Elijah … well, there was a glow about him, a change of spirit. Through his journey, he had awakened, a proud young man.

Coming-of-age rituals for males worldwide have traditionally included a test of spirit and courage, something to answer the age-old question "Are you man enough?" Most of these tests include a physical transformation (circumcision, scarification, or facial tattooing) in which the celebrant must endure a great amount of pain without flinching. Tests of skill could also be asked of the initiate, which usually also included pain—think of the Sateré-Mawé bullet ant ritual or Vanuatu's land-diving ritual. In modern cultures, coming of age for a boy might include getting a driver's license or landing that first job. But what about the inner journey? Isn't it our inner strength that truly characterizes us?

If we are to challenge our boys, let's challenge them to discover if they can be the men who will take responsibility for their actions, demonstrate kindness to all beings, and stand up for what they believe in. Let's challenge them to be self-aware and follow their dreams. And if they choose to walk their path with another, let's challenge them to be the men who walk beside their partner, not over them. For these are the qualities of a true man.

BACKYARD VISION QUEST

"Vision quest," a term coined by twentieth-century anthropologists, was a coming of age initiation for boys entering puberty in some Native American cultures. It included several days of fasting followed by the boy entering sacred land alone in search of his guardian animal spirit. The spirit animal may come in form of a dream or vision and give the boy his life's direction.

A more modern version of this for boys hitting puberty may include an adventure trip that introduces new skills. Adventure trips are a great way to challenge our youth, in turn boosting their confidence and recharging their spirit, while still under the guidance of professionals. Mountaineering, rafting, canoeing, and hiking trips are all great ways of allowing our boys to experience what they are truly made of. Encourage them to meditate on downtime and keep track of their thoughts and visions. What does nature have to teach them?

The problem with guided adventure trips is that they can be very expensive. A solution may be to send your child with a mentor or relative you are comfortable with and have them design their own heroic journey together. New rituals and bonding can be formed from these experiences. For Joshua, it was entering Ross Lake's chilly waters (48 to 50 degrees Fahrenheit) at sunrise with his father. He still talks about the intensity of the moment—the chill of the water under a sky dappled with pink clouds, the fish that jumped, and the stillness just before they hit the water all impacted his transformation.

Maybe your boy seeks to find solace and wisdom within himself. That was Elijah's desire, to reach back to his Celtic roots and experience life at its simplest. For him it was also a way to connect with his ancestors and to reestablish his connection with the Divine—that's where the backyard vision quest comes into play.

We have several acres, including some riverfront property that was "wild" enough for my son to be truly alone but close enough that, if he needed us, all he had to do was literally yell for us or walk across the road and up the path to get back home. But even if you don't have a large backyard or access to private property, it is easy for your son (or daughter) to experience his (or her) own vision quest.

Before your child does this, first make sure this is truly something they are interested in doing. Camping out *alone* isn't every twelve- or thirteen-year-old's cup of tea. Second, make sure they are practiced at any skills they are undertaking. Sending a kid to the backyard to build a fire without the proper knowledge could be a complete disaster. Lastly, they need to have a clear understanding of why they are doing this. As they prepare, have them write down their goals for the experience. These could include self-reliance, deepening their connection with the God and Goddess, or connecting with their spirit guide.

Fasting was part of the vision quest experience, but in lieu of this tradition, I recommend "clean eating" for several days prior to your child's vision quest. Eliminate all refined and processed foods and embrace a diet rich in whole grains, fruits, and veggies.

The most important part of a vision quest is the "solo" aspect of it. If you have access to a large amount of property, that's easy. Just make sure your child can safely and quickly get in touch with you if a problem arises. Help your child set up the camping area and provide plenty of clean drinking water, food, and warm bedding. Have him or her pack a journal, several pens or pencils, and, of course, a really good flashlight. You could walk them ceremoniously to their destination or send them off alone. No matter how you choose to handle this, they may be leaving a little unsure but will definitely be returning with a better sense of who they are both physically and spiritually.

During their stay in nature's classroom, encourage them to spend time meditating and just listening to the lessons that nature has to offer. Have them write down significant stirrings, physical, emotional, and spiritual. Remind them that it's okay to explore their surroundings; lessons don't need to be restricted to the campsite.

Because private property isn't easily available to everyone, another option would be to take your child to a state or county park and camp with them. Give them more responsibilities around camp, including fire building and food preparation. Allow your child time for solo excursions so they can still experience the wonder and sacredness of nature that can only be appreciated when one is truly alone.

Upon returning home, make it a celebration. Have a table set up with a woodsy flair and symbols of the God in his aspect of Green Man or Cernunnos. Serve their favorite meal along with a citrus-filled carrot or lemon cake as symbol of the sun.

Remember, nature has a way of connecting us with our true selves. Unfortunately, these lessons have been almost forgotten, and with modern sensibility, we have replaced the gifts of nature with sweet sixteen parties and new cars. Coming of age is a transition worth honoring.

Handfastings

In December 2012, same-sex marriage was legalized in Washington State, proving that Washingtonians believe love is love and no couple should be denied this rite of passage. One year later my dear friends and neighbors Tom and Nick asked if I would officiate at their wedding, and I couldn't have been more honored.

Plans were made for a summer wedding. The ceremony would be a relatively private affair, with only a few close friends and family members to join them as they exchanged vows under a canopy of bigleaf maple and black cottonwood trees on the edge of the Sauk River. The reception would be a grand party on their property, featuring a local restaurateur's take on barbecue and local beer and wine. While discussing the details of the ceremony, they expressed interest in the handfasting rituals of our family's Pagan tradition. "Really?" I asked. "You would like me to perform a handfasting for you?"

"We would be honored," they both said.

I cried.

What is it about the union of two people that makes us giddy with emotion? It's crazy to think that in the beginning marriage was more like a business contract between two families than a declaration of love and commitment between two people. Marriages provided strong laborers to keep up with backbreaking agricultural needs, children to keep the bloodlines strong, and tight alliances between countries.

It wasn't until 250 years ago, when societies began transforming from agricultural to market-based economies, that love was a consideration in the bonding of two lives. And as far as passion in a relationship—well, up until the Victorian age, most men doubted that women had sexual urges *at all*. We've come a long way.

Practiced since pre-Christian times, a handfasting was an ancient Celtic betrothal rite, and the word "handfasting" is derived from the Old Norse *handfesta,* meaning to strike a bargain by joining hands. In some Celtic regions, that's exactly what it was—a deal between the intended couple, an engagement of sorts, symbolizing the promise to wed. In medieval times, handfastings became a common rite in marriages of mutual consent, the binding of hands by a cord or ribbon, symbolizing the couple's union, and in some traditions the celebrants were kept bound until the marriage was consummated. These rites, often performed in the greenwood without witnesses, were not sanctified by the Catholic Church and therefore considered a "sin."

Today, handfastings can be performed in civil marriage rites (requiring a state marriage license), commitment ceremonies bound as "love shall last," and recommitment ceremonies typically performed on the intended couple's anniversary.

Other ancient traditions that can be added to a handfasting ritual include the following:

- *Jumping the Broom:* In this ancient Welsh tradition, a decorated besom (or broom) is symbolically used to start the newly married couple with a "clean sweep." As family, friends, or witnesses hold the broom low to the ground, the couple jumps over the broom into their new life.

- *Barefootin' It!:* Bare feet touching the earth is a great way of connecting to the element of earth, but in ancient Celtic marriage rites, it was also a way to show humility.

- *Exchanging of Rings:* A Roman tradition and symbol of unity and commitment, the original wedding rings were made from braided grass. Diamond wedding rings didn't come into vogue until the fifteenth century.

- *Gifting of a Tree:* A tradition in Holland was to plant a tree in the newly wedded couple's yard to ensure fertility. A modern version could include a pretty potted shrub or a dwarf flowering or fruit tree for the couple. Most first homes are either apartments or rentals, so this way the couple can take it with them wherever they go.

- *Telling It to the Stone:* The oathing stone is an ancient Celtic tribal tradition in which an object of the earth, typically a stone or piece of wood, was used in the marriage rite to transfer the wedding couple's oaths to the spirits of the land. The stone was then dropped in a sacred pool or other body of water. A modern tradition could include putting the oathing stone in the newly wedded couple's garden.

Handfastings can be incorporated into modern wedding ceremonies as a way of blending religious traditions or adding an Old World flair to a secular celebration, or they can stand on their own. If planning on officiating a handfasting, more important than your ideal of a how a handfasting should be played out is honoring the couple's needs and desires for their perfect day. Both Tom and Nick wanted a ceremony that was short, but still memorable. They wanted Pagan elements, but not too much ritual. They wanted bewitchment, but didn't want theatrics.

Thanks, guys…Way to make it difficult.

The following is the script for the ceremony I put together for Tom and Nick. It was an easy handfasting in the greenwood, simple and to the point. With the greenwood as the backdrop, there was no need for decoration—just a simple altar with a few flowers, candles, and the flower wreaths and handfasting cord for the celebrants, with a besom leaning neatly against the altar for jumping the broom.

Handfasting Ceremony

OFFICIANT: We are here today, on this sacred ground, where leafy tips gently splash upon the water's edge, to celebrate one of life's most poignant moments. We are here to give recognition to the worth and beauty of true love and to cherish the rite that will unite (*insert celebrants' names here*) in marriage. So we ask you, Lord and Lady of the Greenwood, to be present within our circle as (*names*) become one.

If you would all kindly stand as I cast the sacred circle.

Guests stand.

OFFICIANT: Blessed element of air, please join us for this union. Let your cleansing breath be a reminder to (*names*) that with each new sun comes a new beginning.

Blessed element of fire, please join us for this union. Let the fire of desire burn brightly in the hearts of (*names*), reminding them, when darkness falls, to be a light to one another.

Blessed element of water, please join us for this union. Let your healing motion remind (*names*) they are not alone. Guide them to trust one another throughout their lives together.

Blessed element of earth, please join us for this union. Let the soil beneath the feet of (*names*) remind them to always remain grounded and that there is no place like home.

(*Names*), you are declaring your intentions here today before the Lord and Lady and with your family and friends as witnesses, symbolizing your commitment to each other by the ritual of handfasting. Do you come here voluntarily to enter this marriage rite?

CELEBRANTS: We do.

The officiant places the wreaths on the celebrants' heads.

OFFICIANT: These flowers fastened in a circlet symbolize the never-ending power of love. What token have you to represent your love and unity?

CELEBRANTS: (*Simultaneously*) A ring.

Witnesses give rings to each celebrant, who will, one at a time, exchange personal vows and place the rings on one another's ring finger.

OFFICIANT: Would you please join hands? (*Drapes ribbon over celebrants' hands.*)

(*Names*), will you honor and respect one another? Will you support one another in both times of pain and sorrow? (*Wraps ribbon.*)

Will you share each other's laughter and joy and look for the brightness and fun in life and the positive in each other? (*Wraps ribbon.*)

Will you share in each other's dreams and remember to spark creativity in each other's lives? (*Wraps ribbon*).

Will you have the courage and commitment to remember these promises? And always take a step back toward one another with an open heart? (*Ties ribbon.*)

CELEBRANTS: We do.

OFFICIANT: (*Names*), you are now bound together.

A connection, not only of two souls but of the very elements.

You are breath to one another—keep your hearts open and be loving supporters of each other's dreams.

You are spark to one another—kindle the passion of desire for one another and light the way when times grow dark.

You are liquid for one another—able to flow wherever life takes you, trusted soul mates and guides.

You are the foundation for each other—nurturing growth and solidifying a loving environment.

The binding is made. May the Lord and Lady bless you.

So mote it be!

I present to you, (*names*), partners for life!

You may kiss.

The officiant unties the celebrants' ribbon and opens the circle in their own way.

The celebrants' witnesses hold the besom low to the ground, allowing the newly married couple to "jump" into their new phase of life.

notes

Chapter 2

The Power of Family

Dancing in moonlit circles,
the energy rises—bewitching the very air.
The power of family is alive in the greenwood ...

O h, please, Mama. I'm old enough now." Chloe stood in front of
me, eyes closed and hands clasped.

"Sweetie, I know that you're four and that you may feel very grown
up." I couldn't think of anything profound to pass on to my little girl, so
I said, "But you're four."

"Come on, Mama. I promise I'll be good. *Please.*" Chloe looked up
at me with her innocent green eyes. You know that look, the one that
silently tells you "I am so in love with you, Mama" with just a hint of
"but I also know a sucker when I see one."

"Okay," I said. "I will talk to the ladies."

Chloe jumped up and down. "Yay, yay, yay!"

"But," I said, trying to calm her excitement, "I can't promise you
that you can participate in the next esbat. This is a group decision."

As I watched her skip off to ride her imaginary dragon, I thought back to the last time I had attempted to include a young child in ritual. Joshua was three and I was pregnant with Elijah. I decided we would perform a kind of family dedication to the Goddess that was chock full of joyous sentimentality.

Steve and I cast the circle with Joshua on my hip. I put him down to stand beside us—united as family within the safety of the circle. The scent of incense that rode the breeze and the flickering candles that illuminated our surroundings all helped set a mood that was nothing less than bewitching. It was perfect...

But wait a minute, what happened to Josh? Oh, dear Goddess—my son had toddled off.

"Steve, where's Josh?"

He opened his eyes. "Uh-oh," he said.

It was only a few seconds, but in that time a myriad of panicked thoughts went through my mind. First, he left a closed circle ... You just don't do that! Second, my ceremony is ruined. Thanks, Josh! And finally, where is my three-year-old?!

"Joshie!" Steve called out. No answer.

"Come back to Mommy, sweetie." My voice was quavering. Still no answer. We both wavered just slightly before bolting from our circle to search our four-acre farm for our very swift toddler. We separated, each running toward the most dangerous areas of our property: the pond, the field surrounded by barbed wire, and Steve's shop area, full of sharp saws. After only a few moments, I found Joshua on the back porch of our house. It wasn't until after I had hugged the daylights out of him that I noticed he was crunching on something.

"Mama," he said. "What am I eating?"

"I don't know. Let Mama see." He opened his mouth and chewed bits of dog kibble tumbled out. "It's dog food, sweetie."

"It tasted awcky." He wrinkled his nose. I was too relieved to scold him. I just hugged tighter. After that incident, instead of involving our young children in circle, we sang to the moon and made faerie houses and blew horns at dawn at Yule to welcome the newborn sun. We made crafts and wrote plays and spent every second we could in the best temple there is: nature. Our coven also held family events around the sabbats, when our children could celebrate seasonal changes with other like-minded children.

As our children grew a little older, we began with simple rituals full of song and dance. When casting a circle, we used simple rhymes that were easy to remember and packed a much bigger punch for the little ones. By the time they were seven or eight, they seemed to have a pretty firm grasp on what it meant to be Pagan.

This system seemed to satisfy my boys, and it seemed to satisfy the other coven members' children as well. Not once had anyone asked if their child could participate in one of Blue Moon Coven's rituals. But Chloe was, and still is, a very independent girl, her fiery soul longing to stretch itself to the very limits.

I sent out a group e-mail. I know she is four, I conveyed, but would it be okay if Chloe participated in the next ritual? The consensus was yes.

My friend Jean called later that day. "If you want, we could practice with her a little."

"No," I said. "She's been involved in family ritual. I think she'll do fine."

The night of the esbat offered a broken, overcast sky with a trickster moon that peeked at us as it pleased. Chloe insisted on wearing every piece of ritual jewelry I could find, as well as a pink and silver crown and one of my bras under her dress. I obliged; you're only four once.

We gathered at Jean's house. Her ritual space was tucked within a small grove of alder trees on the back of her property. From her back porch Chloe saw the glow of candlelight that flickered amongst the ghostly white trunks and she gasped. "It looks so pretty, Mama."

"It certainly does." I squeezed her.

After some pleasant chitchat and lots of compliments on Chloe's attire, we filed out. Chloe was, of course, familiar with ritual and fell into suit easily. The circle was cast by my friend Felicia, whose quarter calls are always pure poetry.

The aim of the ritual was twofold that night: first, to raise healing energy for a coven-mate who had just had back surgery and was unable to be with us; second, to bless a small Pagan reading/resource room project that we were involved in. As Felicia began our healing ritual with a few uplifting words about our friend, Chloe yelled out, "Can I have a cookie now?"

Felicia smiled and waited for me as I whispered to my daughter that she would have to wait. I nodded my head for Felicia to continue, but just as she began to speak, I heard, "I just want one, Mama. I'm really hungry."

There were a few giggles as I explained to Chloe that they were to be saved until the end and that she needed to be quiet right now. "Sorry," I said to my coven-mates. "This may have been a bad idea."

Chloe began to sob. "Mama, you don't want me here."

Not only was I embarrassed, I was becoming angry. "Right now," I said without thinking, "no, I don't want you here."

Chloe's sobs turned to fits of crying, and there were a few sad sighs from the circle.

I knew instantly what I said was cruel. "I didn't mean that the way it sounded."

She wrapped her arms around my waist and sobbed out of control. I just stared at everyone and shrugged.

It was Marilyn who finally cut the uneasy air. "Well, hell," she said and threw her arms up. "Let's have cookies."

"Yeah," the other eight who had joined us that evening chimed in. "Cookies sound good."

The circle was closed and we sat together under that trickster moon, still ducking behind the clouds. Chloe curled up on my lap and fell asleep before she had finished her cookie. I wrapped her in my cloak, and as she quietly slept, we finished our ritual.

Chloe spent the next six years happy to celebrate the Goddess in ways that were more kid friendly. We made faerie altars and cast simple spells. She enjoyed our coven's summer day camps and sabbat celebrations for the kids and, of course, our own family's worship, for which her responsibilities grew as she did. It wasn't until she was ten years old that she asked for another chance. "Mama, do you think I could try it again?"

"What?" I asked.

"Ritual with your coven."

I laughed. "Of course, but this time you're gonna have to wait for the cookies."

"Ah, Mom."

Making Ritual Fun

Though Steve and I definitely feel that there are many ways to express spirituality and would be fine if our children chose to follow another spiritual path, we still thought it was important to at least lay those first bricks to a sound spiritual foundation. So it seemed natural for us to involve our children in our practices. I had learned the hard way that throwing young children into the proverbial "deep end" of ritual makes for a disaster. My lesson learned: make ritual fun. There is nothing more boring for our little ones than long scripts and expanded spans of time where they have nothing to do.

Ritual should be a playful, joyous act. I know it is for me. A journey filled with joyful moments when creating, singing, dancing, and play are central to our children's teaching ensures an understanding that is far more powerful and more enjoyable than organized instruction. "Why?" you may ask. Because play is a natural act. It is something we are born knowing how to do, like breathing. It is a natural way to communicate our creativity, express our hopes, and work out our anxiety. And creativity, as part of play, is the first step to manifesting magick— foster that innate ability.

Remember, choosing to allow your children to be active in ritual can be a wonderful way to connect spiritually with them, help give them a solid spiritual base, foster deep bonds between family members, and provide structure and security.

Here are some simple ways to make ritual with your children a fun and magickal experience:

- *Incorporate lots of singing and movement.* Kids love songs and movement, be it dancing, drumming, singing, or ringing bells. Shake, baby, shake!

- *Create sacred space in a fun and simple manner.* Casting your circle with simple rhymes makes it fun for younger children and helps impart simple lessons about circle casting, the elements, ritual tools, and so forth.

- *Give your children jobs.* Empower your magickal little ones by giving them a sense of responsibility. Give them a role to play, whether it's speaking a line or lighting a candle. The more active they are in ritual, the better they will understand the sacredness of the event.

- *Keep magick simple.* Don't involve your children in spells that are not age appropriate or that they have little or no understanding of.

- *Incorporate seasonal crafts.* If you have children who love to express themselves artistically, arts and crafts are a fun way to instill spiritual lessons and get them involved with sabbat preparation. My children were big into making masks and acting out plays that they would write to coincide with our sabbat celebrations.

- *Involve older children in planning.* As the kids get older, empower them by having them plan a ritual. You might be surprised at what they come up with. When she was fifteen, Chloe and her friend Hannah planned our Midsummer ritual, and it was absolutely wonderful! It's a real confidence booster for the kids, and as busy adults, it's nice to have the extra help.

- *Serve kid-friendly cakes and ale.* Remember to keep the cakes and ale kid-friendly. Cookies and juice or hot cocoa are nice alternatives. Better yet, turn your little ones into Kitchen Witches by letting them help choose and prepare the cakes and ale.

- *Keep ritual short.* Smaller children have short attention spans. A ritual for a preschooler might include singing and dancing under the full moon, followed by a cookie and some hot cocoa. Speak at your child's level. Nothing bores children more than having to stand still while someone recites pages and pages of script. Let ritual grow as they do.

- *Keep the ritual area safe.* Before involving kids in ritual, make sure all candles are secure in proper candleholders. If performing ritual outdoors, pick up any sticks, rocks, or debris that may be a tripping hazard. Any fire should be built in a fire pit or cauldron and kept small.

- *Hold separate rituals for adults and children.* Especially when your kids are small, it's sometimes easier to have separate rituals, one geared toward the kids and one for the adults. As families grew within my coven, we did just that. As near as possible to the sabbat celebration, we planned events for our kids. On the evening of the sabbat, it was just adults.

- *Let magick happen.* Don't muffle children's natural magickal abilities because it interferes with the script. In fact, when it comes to kids, you might want to throw out the script. Choose a simple outline for your ritual and always be prepared for the unexpected.

Full Moon Family Unity Ritual

This ritual is meant to create a tight family bond. It is a reminder that blood is, indeed, thicker than water. For this ritual we will be invoking the mother goddess Frigg, Queen of Asgard, goddess of marriage, households, childbirth, protection, love, and prophecy.

Since her day is Friday, performing this ritual on a Friday on or closest to the full moon seems appropriate. Decorate your altar with blue, aqua, or gray candles; a representation of Frigg, which may include cat or falcon representations; alder branches; keys; and/or a small spinning wheel.

You will need:

Enough gold or yellow yarn to wrap around everyone in the circle
A key
Cakes and ale (cookies and juice)

Because this is a family ritual, remember to give everyone a job. Maybe have the older children be in charge of altar setup, while the younger children grab their besoms and sweep the ritual space clear of negativity.

Cast your circle in your own way. Remember to keep it fun by using short rhymes that keep the kids' attention.

Starting with the oldest family member, wrap the gold or yellow yarn around his or her waist and pass it deosil to the next family member. As they do this, have them say,

With this golden thread we weave love and unity. There is nothing stronger than the bond of family.

In turn, each family member will wrap the thread behind himself or herself and pass it along until everyone is connected. Once complete, the oldest member will then take the key, hold it up, and say,

The key to family is (fill in the blank).

Pass the key around until everyone has had a turn. Thank the Goddess for the gift of family unity, release the circle, and enjoy cakes and ale together as a family.

Harmony Begins at Home: Sacred Simplicity and Household Altars

When you think of sacred space, where does your mind's eye take you? Maybe to the green fields of the Salisbury Plain in Wiltshire, England, where the great sandstone megaliths of Stonehenge still hold the secrets of its Neolithic past. Or maybe you drift to the Ohio River Valley, where the great effigy mounds lie as silent shrouds, careful not to reveal their mysterious past. How about a grand European cathedral or one of the world's many wonders, such as the Taj Mahal?

When I think of sacred space, I think of my garden and a little bistro table near the pond where I can catch the whiff of heirloom roses and hear the soft trickle of water. There are koi to feed and hummingbirds who threaten to tangle my hair. I let myself go every time I sit in that garden in the presence of the Goddess—and in letting go, I find myself.

It was Joseph Campbell who said, "Sacred space is where you can find yourself over and over again." What better place to experience that kind of tranquility than at home? But it isn't always that simple. Life can be noisy, fast, and chaotic, and no matter how many candles we light, the residue of chaos seems to follow us everywhere … including our homes.

Creating a living space that mirrors nature can help to make our homes a real haven for ourselves and our family, but it's going to take more than changing the paint and hanging a mandala on the wall. It takes a lifestyle makeover.

The Simple Life

Living in harmony with nature and raising your children to appreciate a simpler, more natural lifestyle doesn't have to include moving your family to the middle of nowhere. Here are a few tips that can be incorporated into your urban or suburban lifestyle to help you slow life down and live more harmoniously with nature:

- *Time for a Diet:* From your electronic devices, that is. Our televisions, phones, and computer devices have taken over our lives. I have a friend who was irritated because her daughter was averaging around four thousand texts per month. (That's over a hundred and thirty texts per day!) What? "Take her phone away," I said. "She would absolutely be lost without it" was the reply.

    Limit computer, phone, and television use to only an hour or two per day. Use your extra time to pursue hobbies, enjoy the great outdoors, or play together as a family.

• *Learn to Say NO:* Are you one of those superparents who not only holds down a full-time job but is also on the library's board of directors, coaches T-ball, is president of the Parent-Teacher Organization, and will be making three dozen cupcakes for your daughter's soccer team's annual picnic? Why do we fill our lives with so much added responsibility? Even our kids are encouraged to fill their calendars with activities.

Throughout our lives we are taught that taking on more responsibility will somehow make us better people. Obviously, there are basic things we should be responsible for, such as our finances, actions, and emotions, but when we start taking on too many extracurricular activities, these added responsibilities begin to diminish our own well-being. Limiting social, school, or service obligations will give you and your family more time to really stop and smell the roses.

• *Keep to Nature's Rhythm:* We are a 24/7 world and many of us push ourselves to the very limit to accomplish more, do more, and be more. We need to slow down and listen to what our bodies have to tell us. Just as nature has cycles that determine the seasons and day and night, our bodies too have a cycle that is closely tuned with those of nature.

Remembering to expose ourselves to natural light (go outside!), get enough rest, exercise, and eat properly throughout the day all help us to keep in sync with nature's rhythms. When we push ourselves, we become sluggish and irritable and eventually burn out. Remember, you only have one body. Be good to it.

• *Do You Really Need That?:* We are a society driven by our stuff. We try to fill internal voids with material goods—I will be happier if I have a new phone or a better car or a bigger TV. But as the old saying goes, "Money can't buy happiness." How is happiness attained? Well, according to "The Contagion of Happiness," a study by Harvard, the secret is simple: take care of yourself physically, emotionally, and financially. Spend time doing what you love and do for others. Not so difficult, right?

Well, it shouldn't be, but unfortunately, as Americans, we are slaves to credit cards and to impulse buying. We have to work harder to keep up with the endless circle of debt, which creates stress. This stress makes us unhappy. So how do we remedy this? Are you ready? First, cut up all of your credit cards. Just think about it—the average American has over fifteen thousand dollars in credit card debt alone, according to the "2016 American Household Credit Card Debt Study." Eradicating credit card debt means less time at work and more time with family. Second, only go shopping for what you need. Window-shopping and perusing sites like Amazon and eBay can lead to impulse buying. Make shopping lists and stick to them.

Believe me, escaping materialism is a very freeing experience.

• *Bad Vibes Begone:* This one is tough, but removing negativity from your life is probably the most important thing you can do to simplify your life. Maybe it's a negative relative who makes your chest tighten whenever you're around them, a friend who sucks you into his or her chaos-filled life, or a partner who makes you feel insignificant. Negativity fills our very being with anxiety, which can lead to physical ailments. No matter how difficult it feels, you need to cut negative people from your life and that of your family.

Once that has been done, remember to surround yourself with positive friends, people who are supportive and whose vibrant energy reflects off everyone around them. Do good for others. Whether you and your family help with a beach cleanup or help an elderly neighbor with her snowy walkway, good deeds foster positive thinking. Be grateful for every day. No matter how awful your day was, there is always something to be grateful for—it's a matter of perspective. Look for the little rainbows that color your life. And finally, remember to laugh!

- *Become a Minimalist:* A place for everything and everything in its place. There is something about waking up in the morning to a home free of clutter that relaxes the soul. Too much clutter can give a sense of chaos, and precious moments of free time can be spent looking for items that you know you put "somewhere around here."

  Start with your junk drawers, slowly work your way to the closets, and finally tackle that overpacked storage area. Spend just thirty minutes per day purging yourself of all that *stuff* that you know, deep down, you will never wear, never use, or never look at again. Have the kids do the same in their bedrooms; old toys, clothing, books, puzzles, and crafts they have outgrown can all be packed up and donated. Next, organize your personal workspace so that everything is easily accessed. Believe me, in the end you're going to feel great and you won't miss a thing.

- *Create Time for Yourself:* Even if this means waking up an hour earlier than you normally would, it is important that you create a little me time. Enjoy that hour by doing something that gives you joy. Whether it's having a cup of tea and watching the sunrise, spending a few minutes working in the garden, practicing yoga, or reading a chapter of a favorite book, we all need time to recharge.

- *Redefine What's Important:* Have you ever thought, "I want to, but I just don't have enough time"? Maybe it's not a question of time, but of time management. Make a list of what you do hour-by-hour for an entire day. Did you include television and Facebook?

  Now make a list of things that you would like to do or accomplish. This could include spending more time with the kids or finally finishing that quilt. Maybe you would like to volunteer at your local homeless shelter or just have a quiet night out with your partner. Ask yourself, where can I make changes to fit in what's important to me? Now go back to that first list. Is there anything that could be reprioritized? I'll bet there is. Life can be demanding.

As adults, we have responsibilities at work and home, but by simplifying our routines we can accomplish those goals that define us.

- *Take a Walk:* This is a great way to reconnect with nature and burn off stress as well as calories. If distance isn't an inhibitor, consider walking to work, school, or the store—good for you and for the environment!

- *Stay Home and Play:* Instead of going to the movies this weekend, how about staying home and having some old-fashioned fun with the family? If it's raining, play board games under a blanket fort in the living room and make s'mores in your toaster oven. If it's sunny, have a water fight outside or set up lawn games like croquet and bocce ball. Enjoy a picnic under a shady tree. Believe me, the kids will have a ball and it will cost a whole lot less!

Household Altars

Worship began in nature. Groves, caves, and springs were sacred ritual spaces where priests and priestesses performed their rites. Later, temples were erected where everyday people could visit on festival days to worship whatever god, goddess, or, sometimes, ruler who was being celebrated. Sacrifices were made and augurs were on hand to predict the future for the community. But what about familial worship? For our ancient ancestors, that was easy. It was done at home.

Each household had their own deity whom they worshiped at a designated sacred space or niche set up within the home. These small sacred spaces typically held small statuary, amulets, or paintings representing their deity. Wealthier families could afford ornately decorated altars that took up an entire wall, while a more provincial family may have had a small clay figure tucked humbly on a corner shelf. But no matter the size, these spaces were deemed divine and made for quiet areas for families to gather and worship.

If you haven't already established a household altar, you should really consider doing so. Not because it's a requirement and the gods will strike you down if you don't—oh, dear Goddess, no!—but because it can be a great family activity that everyone can participate in. It can be customized to reflect your family's own personal belief system, as well as the ever-changing Wheel of the Year.

If ritual is to be a joyous, playful act for our children, then altars are a place for reflection and quiet. The very nature of these sacred spaces evokes a sense of stillness and contemplation. And for our children, whose daily lives can be overstimulating enough, altars are a valuable tool to learn to slow down and reconnect to nature's rhythms.

Our family's personal household and garden altars are different from our working altar set up for ritual. They lack the rigidity of layout and direction. They are also free of ritual tools that I feel don't need to be displayed for, and possibly handled by, visitors—especially small children. Can you imagine the neighbor's four-year-old grabbing your athame and running around the living room with it? Not cool.

What is great about family household altars is that you can tuck them just about anywhere in your home, garden, or yard. Some prefer facing an altar north in a home or garden because of its association with power and the element of earth; others prefer east, facing the rising sun and moon, but that isn't always convenient. It is more important that the altar be easily accessible for the family.

When my kids were small, they had a lot of fun planning and creating small elemental altars that they placed at directional points in the garden. Through this project, not only did they learn the value of working together, but they also gained new insight about the Craft on their own, which I love—because sometimes, the best lessons are stumbled upon.

As I worked in my garden, I loved being witness to their magickal treasure hunt. Treasures such as smooth, round stones, feathers, hazelnuts, cones, sticks, and leaves became objects of power or were transformed into beautiful symbolic pieces. Elijah made wind chimes to hang near the altar for air out of wood and stone, Chloe wove a representation of a bowl out of willow for water, and Joshua used natural clay that he dug up near our home and sculpted a representation of Cernunnos for earth.

A potpourri of natural objects, photos of lost loved ones, and representations of the changing seasons, our household altar became a place of enchantment and discovery for our children growing up, a place where they could reflect on the ever-changing Wheel of the Year or commune quietly with the God and Goddess—a place to contemplate the blessings of the earth.

As my children grew older, they designed altars of their own in their bedrooms. The boys' altars reflect their earthy eclecticism, but Chloe's is, and has been for a long time, dedicated to the goddess Artemis. Fierce and adventurous, a protector of nature and goddess of the hunt, for Chloe, Artemis epitomizes feminine power. Symbols Chloe has included are crescent moons; deer, bee, and dog figures; honeysuckle incense; and light blue candles. She also leans her quiver of arrows next to the altar and keeps her long bow hung above it. It's beautiful.

Here are some more great household and garden altar ideas:

THE BASICS

First, you need a place to designate as your altar. And because we can't all afford to go out and buy a really amazing table to suit the purpose, we need to get creative. If your altar is to be indoors, consider clearing a spot on a bookshelf, using a dining room sidebar, or clearing a space in a hutch. If you have a fireplace, the mantel works great too. Another thing to consider is purchasing an inexpensive, round decorative table (they can be purchased for under fifteen dollars) and covering it with a pretty altar cloth.

In the garden, a nice flat stone works perfectly. These can be tucked around foliage or set up in a place of honor, perhaps on a rustic potting table or pretty patio side table.

The basic elements included in most altars are representations of the four elements laid in accordance to their directions and a representation of the God or the Goddess or both. Because this is a family altar, let the kids get involved in the creating. They can draw, paint, or sculpt representations of the elements and deities. Here are some recommendations:

- *Earth:* A bowl of salt, nuts, cones, leaves, or interesting sticks, stones, or gems. Figures that represent animals such as deer, bears, or wolves. Representations of elves or gnomes would work nicely. And, of course, a pentacle drawn, painted, or burnt into wood is also appropriate.

- *Air:* Feathers, incense smoke, or bells. Representations of birds, butterflies, or sylphs. How about hanging wind chimes above the altar?

- *Fire:* Candles or a bowl of sand (desert). Representations of fire creatures, such as salamanders, dragons, or a phoenix. Cacti are a nice representation, as well as chili peppers or a small bowl of a hot spice.

- *Water:* A bowl of water, a chalice, or shells. Representations of water creatures, including mermaids, dolphins, fish, or whales. Hag stones, willow branches, or hazelnuts are nice too.

- *The God:* You can most certainly buy a figure to represent the God. There are some really beautiful ones out there, but because this is attached to family, I feel letting the kids sculpt or draw a figure would be more appropriate—and it will give your altar a special energy that is truly palpable. Representations can be as simple as a wand made especially for the altar from a found stick (oak would be nice) with symbols drawn or painted on it. Maybe a Green Man mask made from felt pieces or a sculptural piece made to represent the God in whatever aspect you choose. The God symbol is typically placed on the right side of the altar.

- *The Goddess:* Once again, I feel it is appropriate to make the representation by hand. Sculptures can be made from anything from salt dough to polymer clay. A classic Venus of Willendorf image is easy, even for little ones, to sculpt. Add magickal symbols of your choice. Or if you're feeling very creative, try your hand at sculpting an image of the Triple Goddess. Other projects could include hand painting a small cauldron or chalice or painting Goddess symbols on a round stone. The Goddess symbol is typically placed on the left side of the altar.

Now that you know the basics, let's add a little flair!

Specializing your household altar is entirely personal. Maybe you want your altar to have an eclectic feel, a cross between altar and nature table. That's great. Pieces can be added and removed, reflecting seasonal change. These altars are guaranteed to hold your child's interest, keeping them coming back to add their own magickal treasures or to see what enchantment you may have added.

Do you have a little one in your life who may be a little fearful? Boost their confidence with a fire altar. This can be set up on a shelf in their room. Make it as simple or as elaborate as you please. Include red embellishments, battery-operated candles (safety first!), maybe a vial of cinnamon oil tightly secured so that it can be handled without spilling, and dragon figurines.

Faerie altars are always popular in the garden. How about dedicating one to the elves? Elves are woodland spirits to call upon for earth's grounding energy. A small altar placed atop an old stump or on a flat stone under a tree or near a fern would be nice. Incorporate amber, pine or cedar chips, and patchouli or sandalwood oil to attract these shy spirits. And remember, keep an eye out at dusk as the moon rises high above the cragged peaks, because you might just catch a glimpse of these elusive woodland spirits.

Shoebox Altar

Here's a fun and portable altar the kids will love.

You will need:

1 shoebox for each child

Enough scrapbooking or colorful construction paper to completely cover a shoebox inside and out (Go for fun patterns that reflect the altar's intention.)

Scissors

Craft glue

Hot-glue gun

Small figurines, toys, stones, charms, and other representations to glue
into the box to represent what your child's shoebox altar is dedicated
to (Example: a faerie shoebox altar may include pretty tumbled stones,
shiny objects, a feather, dried flowers, faerie figurines, and a cotton ball
that has a drop of honeysuckle essential oil dropped onto it.)

1 cotton ball per child

Essential oil of your choice

1 battery-operated tea light per child

First, cut scrapbooking paper to fit all the sides (inside and out) and the
lid of shoebox. Working with one side of the box at a time, use craft
glue to completely cover the side and glue the paper down. Let the box
dry completely (I usually let it set overnight).

When completely dry, use hot glue to tack down objects onto the bottom of the shoebox in whatever way pleases your child; include gluing down a cotton ball in a corner of the box. You will then place a drop or two of essential oil that corresponds with the altar onto the cotton ball. Give each child a battery-operated tea light (do not glue down) that can be kept in the box and turned on when in use. Further embellishments can be added to the shoebox by drawing magickal symbols or gluing on Witchy charms, ribbons, buttons, and so on.

These portable altars can be tucked under the bed and taken out whenever your child chooses.

Our Elemental Babes

There are toads that lumber from under the ferns and upturned pots in my garden as evening shadows begin to creep in, tinting my world with darkened hues. They have startled me on more than one occasion, but instead of being annoyed, I am happy to share my garden with them. They are a sign of a healthy ecosystem and a reminder of our dependence on earth's steadfast soil.

The breeze that rises and falls on dewy mornings moves across the wind chimes. Its song is haunting and stirs within me old stories of long-forgotten ancestors. I wonder if the music is air's way of reminding us of its persistent presence and the knowledge it holds.

After weeks of enduring winter's din, I am joyful beyond words when I can close my eyes under a bright new sun and absorb its warm vitality, reminding me that as long as I believe there is strength in fire, I can take on the world.

But it's my moonstruck soul that is affected most: water's gentle sway ceaselessly pulls on my emotions and taps me into the dreams of others. It constantly reminds me of life's inevitable changes.

We are all elemental beings, part of a web whose silky threads are interwoven with all realms and life forms. From the moment we are born we shift and change, our defining strengths taking on the aspects of one element or a combination of elements. Ideally, we want to have all the elements in perfect balance, but more likely than not, we identify predominately with one element.

In ancient times the zodiac was known as "souls of nature," in reference to the vital forces of the elements that affect us in mind, body, and spirit. The twelve astrological symbols are grouped into "triplicities," or three signs that exhibit the qualities of earth, air, fire, or water.

To help better understand our children's strengths, challenges, and behavioral patterns associated with their predominant element, I have put together the following elemental traits based on astrological groupings. Included are magickal associations, crafts, and play ideas for our elemental babes.

Earth Babies: Taurus, Virgo, and Capricorn

Gods and Goddesses: Persephone, Gaia, Demeter, Rhiannon, Cernunnos, Dionysus, Green Man, and Pan

Colors: Green and brown

Direction: North

Time: Night

Animals: Dogs, horses, and earthworms

Symbols: Rocks, cones or nuts, salt, soil, and sheaves of grain or dried grasses

Herbs: Sage, patchouli, vervain, mosses and lichens, ferns, barley, and oats

Magick: Herb, gardening, crystal and gem, knot, tree, and dirt

You may know this child, the one who can transform a pile of Legos into an architectural wonder. He plays forever in the sandbox, long after the other children have tired of the scratchy sand filling their shoes. She's that little girl willing to help paint the new baby's room and doesn't mind the messy chores, like taking out the garbage or cleaning the litter box. They're the kids in the classroom who tirelessly take on a project and have the patience to see it through until it is finished. They are the practical thinkers—the builders. They are the earth babies whose sun signs are Taurus, Virgo, and Capricorn.

Children whose dominant element is earth are in touch with their physical world. They are steadfast and action orientated. These are the kids who get things done. Don't be surprised if your earth baby is in love with the outdoors. They are great helpers in the garden and work well with animals. They are the kids who don't mind getting dirty and will take every opportunity to literally roll around in the dirt. Remember, physical connection is important to these children. Give them tangible tasks and lots of hugs; they can be very touchy-feely. As ones so closely connected with the earth's vibes, keeping to a natural rhythm is also important to them. Typically mild-mannered earth children may become agitated or prone to outbursts if their schedule is thrown off.

As adults, earth babies easily fit into our modern workaday world. Self-disciplined and persistent, they can easily reach any goal they set up for themselves. At their best, earth babies are loyal, steadfast, patient, practical, and goal orientated. At their worst, they can be bullheaded, unimaginative, and narrow-minded.

Magickally, you may find your earthy little one to be a talented herbalist or Kitchen Witch. As they are attuned with their natural surroundings, they may enjoy making and working with rune stones or working with crystals and gems. They may also enjoy working with earth spirits, such as elves, gnomes, and garden faeries. Don't be surprised if you find your earth baby building elaborate faerie houses and tucking them all around your property.

EARTHY FUN

- Plant a faerie garden.
- Make bread for Lughnasadh.
- Participate in roadside cleanup.
- Build a birdhouse.
- Study crystals and gems.
- Go on a nature hike.
- Make a faerie house.

- Make runes.
- Play with magnets.
- Learn to sew or crochet.
- Make herbal sachets.
- Practice grounding techniques.
- Celebrate Earth Day.
- Create a tea blend.
- Go on an outdoor scavenger hunt.

Clay Rune Stones

Earth babies are naturally hands-on learners, so making rune stones from clay is the perfect project for kids who like to get a little bit messy and have the patience and endurance to see their undertaking through to the end.

In Norse mythology, the god Odin hung from the tree of knowledge for nine days in order to learn the mysteries associated with the sacred runes. In return for the wisdom he gained, Odin gave up his left eye. The Old English word *rūn* means "mystery" or "whispered secret."

I have included the classic Elder Futhark runes and meanings, but you can encourage your kids to get creative and come up with their own designs and meanings, as well.

You will need:

One 2.2-pound package self-hardening clay
Inscribing tool (We use a crochet needle, but really anything that will easily inscribe soft clay will do.)
Paint (various colors)
Paintbrush
Drawstring pouch

Pinch off pieces of clay and shape them to resemble small stones. Encourage your child to make them as realistic as possible. You will need to form twenty-four small stones. When finished, use the following rune list as a reference to carve each of the runic symbols into each stone. Allow them to dry. I like to give them forty-eight hours. After the clay dries, the stones can be painted. When the paint is completely dry, store them in a drawstring pouch.

If your child would like to make rune stones out of real stones, go to a river, creek side, or stony path and gather twenty-four small stones. Take them home and wash off any debris. Pat them dry and paint runic symbols on them.

ELDER FUTHARK RUNES

ᚠ	*Fehu*	Wealth
ᚢ	*Uruz*	Strength
ᚦ	*Thurisaz*	Protection
ᚨ	*Ansuz*	Wisdom

ᚱ	*Raido*	Journey
ᚲ	*Kenaz*	Luck
ᚷ	*Gebo*	Gift
ᚹ	*Wunjo*	Joy
ᚺ	*Hagalaz*	Disruption
ᚾ	*Nauthiz*	Constraint
ᛁ	*Isa*	Standstill
ᛃ	*Jera*	Success
ᛇ	*Eihwaz*	Safety
ᛈ	*Perthro*	Future
ᛉ	*Algiz*	Friendships
ᛋ	*Sowulo*	Self
ᛏ	*Teiwaz*	Victory
ᛒ	*Berkana*	Growth
ᛖ	*Ehwaz*	Trust
ᛗ	*Mannaz*	Self
ᛚ	*Laguz*	Healing
◇	*Inguz*	Fertility
ᛟ	*Othila*	Prosperity
ᛞ	*Dagaz*	Transformation

Born of Air: Gemini, Libra, and Aquarius

Gods and Goddesses: Arianrhod, Nuit, Aradia, Zeus, Mercury, and Thoth

Colors: Yellow

Direction: East

Time: Dawn

Animals: Owl, spider, and bat

Symbols: Feathers, birds, incense, and fragrant flowers
Herbs: Dandelion, lavender, verbena, and dill
Magick: Divination, wind, and visualization

It is air that moves us. It is the element of communication, of movement and ideas. Children born under an air sign tend to be always in motion, as if lifted by the very element that rules them. They are our thinkers, our movers, our shakers. If you have an air child, you may find her leading activities for school or club events. He is that boy who stands up for injustice or shines on the debate team. They are the children who have lofty aspirations and dash about with sylph-like fluidity. They are born of air, with sun signs of Gemini, Libra, and Aquarius.

Children whose dominant element is air see a world full of possibilities. They are analytical, communicate easily, and seek justice. Calm by nature, air children are at ease in social situations and have the ability to draw others to them. With a tendency toward boredom, air kids need a lot of intellectual stimulation—give them thought-provoking or inventive projects. Encourage them to learn to play an instrument or master a new language. Maintaining balance is critical for air children. If their ideas are too lofty, air children may become irrational. Letting their imaginations soar without getting too far off course is the key.

As adults, air children might be found in new business ventures where they can control what's happening from the ground up. They also may be involved with law or negotiations, as advocates for change. At their best, children of air are calm, just, and intelligent. At their worst, they can become flighty, cold, and impractical.

Magickally, your breezy babe may enjoy ritual that includes dancing, singing, or chanting in the wind. As natural poets and storytellers, they should be encouraged to write spells or help with sabbat ritual preparation. Let them try their hand at divination. And don't be surprised if you find your air child interpreting the magick of the skies.

BREEZY FUN

• Make a wish.

• Go bird watching.

- Write a poem.
- Make an origami crane.
- Learn tarot.
- Make and fly a kite.
- Learn to belly dance.
- Sing a song.
- Make incense.
- Collect feathers.
- Make a fan.
- Watch the clouds.
- Raise butterflies.
- Make wind chimes.
- Make a Book of Shadows.

Sylph Wish Kite

Air is the element of imagination, and what better way to let our kids' imaginations soar than by making an old-fashioned kite? By adding magickal symbols and wishes, we are taking the ordinary kite to an enchanting new level.

Sylphs are nature spirits of the air who, it is told, gather around those who seek them for inspiration. So gather the kids and take to the air—let's call on the sylphs with style.

You will need:

1 12 x 12-inch sheet of plastic (Recycle shopping bags.)
Colored permanent markers
2 12-inch barbecue skewers per kite
Kite line (This can be bought by the spool in the toy or hobby section of most stores.)
Twine
Tape
Colorful crepe paper for streamers
Scissors

Before the kite is assembled, we need to decorate it. Lay the plastic out flat and use markers to draw magickal symbols and write wishes and dreams on it.

Clip the sharp edges off the barbecue skewers. Take one skewer and lay it vertically on the unmarked side of the flattened plastic. Now lay the other skewer horizontally across the vertical skewer approximately one-third down its length. This will make the shape of a cross. Use twine to secure the skewers where they cross.

Now take a marker and place a dot on the plastic at each of the four points. Use a ruler to connect the dots and complete the diamond. Now carefully cut your lines. Use tape to secure the plastic to skewers.

Flip the kite over and poke a tiny hole through plastic where the skewers meet. Thread kite thread through and around skewers; tie a knot. Attach a crepe paper tail near bottom of kite.

On a breezy day take your kite out to an unobstructed area. Have the kids say,

As we release these wishes to the sky,
We call upon the sylphs by and by.
Lend us your wisdom as we present you our dreams.

By the power of cloud, wing, and voice,
Let the magick take hold and our intentions gleam.

As you release your kites into the sky, focus on the dreams and wishes you would like to take flight.

Fire Children: Leo, Aries, and Sagittarius

Gods and Goddesses: Brighid, Vesta, Hestia, Arinna, Horus, Lugh, Prometheus, and Helios
Colors: Red and orange
Direction: South
Time: Noon
Animals: Snake, lizard, bee, and scorpion
Symbols: Sun images, candles, and flames
Herbs: Cactus, cedar, garlic, hawthorn, and chili peppers
Magick: Candle, balefire, solar, color, and storm

Do you know a girl with the heart of a dragon? How about a boy who lives life so fully that he leaves a blaze of color in his wake? These are the children of fire, whose enthusiasm, sense of freedom, and confidence radiate unyieldingly. You might find a fire child as captain of the football team or heading up environmental efforts to save unprotected forestland. Whatever fire kids tackle, they do it with a fervent passion and a relentless will that guarantees a job well done. With their lively spirits, the children of fire are those inspirational lights that draw in others like moths to a flame. Their sun signs include Leo, Aries, and Sagittarius.

Children whose dominant element is fire see life as an adventure. Enthusiastic and self-motivated, they are our risk-takers, visionaries, and leaders. They don't mind grabbing the lion by the mane and just going for it! Spontaneous by nature, fire kids are the ones taking the lead on the playground by sparking creative games and inspiring others to step out of their box. But, just as with any flame, too much fuel can cause a fire child to burn out of control. With a tendency to lack self-control, fire kids can become reckless and domineering if their abandon is not tempered. Channeling their fiery spirit can help. Encourage them to join clubs or participate in sporting events that stoke their passion.

As adults, these fiery souls will most likely be experience driven. Whether traveling, adventure seeking, teaching classes, or running corporations, for fire-dominant individuals it's not the destination that matters but the ride itself. At their best, fire children are joyful, honest, and fearless. At their worst, they are domineering, self-centered, and reckless.

Magickally, fire children are intuitive and focused. Encourage them to channel these skills on spells for positive change. Supervised, your little Witchlings can try candle and solar spells. As natural leaders, teens may enjoy starting a circle for like-minded friends. Don't be surprised if their highly attuned instincts make them daring spellcasters, transforming and illuminating everything they touch.

FIERY CHALLENGES

- Go camping.
- Volunteer at a soup kitchen.
- Learn to make candles.
- Make s'mores.
- Compete in a race.
- Learn to make a fire.
- Learn mountain climbing.
- Collect food for a food bank.
- Play red rover.
- Learn about solar energy.
- Go mountain biking.
- Plan and prepare a meal for your family.
- Make a suncatcher.
- Study bees.

Giving Suncatchers

Children whose dominant element is fire are known for their inner strength. Here's a project to allow all of us to gather a little fiery fortitude.

Dažbog was a Slavic solar deity known as the "giving god." He emerged from the arms of dawn every evening to ride his chariot across the sky driven by his three horses, one silver, one gold, and one diamond. His gift to the people was the strength-giving sun that rose every morning and descended to the underworld at night.

These giving suncatchers capture a little of that strength and remind us that we all carry a little fire within.

You will need:

Barbecue grill or toaster oven

1-pound bag translucent pony beads (very cheap and available at any big box or hobby store)

An old muffin tin (do not reuse to cook with)

Drill with ¼-inch drill bit

Heavy thread for hanging (quilting thread works great)

Though it is possible to use your kitchen oven to prepare the suncatchers, due to the fumes I highly recommend doing this outdoors. Preheat a barbecue grill to 425 degrees Fahrenheit. If you don't have one, you could also set up a toaster oven outside.

Take your pony beads and arrange them in a single layer on the bottom of the tin. Try arranging the beads to create symbols that will remind you of strength in your favorite sunny colors. Place the tray in the barbecue for about 10 minutes, or until the beads have melted. If you use a toaster oven, it will take approximately 20 to 25 minutes to achieve the same effect. Let cool a good 1 to 2 hours, invert the pan, and pop them out!

Once nice and cool, drill a hole at the top of the suncatcher. String heavy thread through the hole and hang in a sunny window or out in the garden. Every time it catches the sun, let it manifest its courage and strength-giving rays within you.

A larger version can be made using a cake tin.

Watery Kids: Cancer, Scorpio, and Pisces

Gods and Goddesses: Isis, Danu, Nayru, Aphrodite, Llyr, Neptune, and Osiris

Colors: Blue

Direction: West

Time: Dusk

Animals: Cat, frog, salmon, and eagle

Symbols: Shells, bowls with water, hazelnuts, and hag stones

Herbs: Yarrow, apple, lemon balm, comfrey, and willow

Magick: Dream, moon, mirror, and water

Do you know a little one whose imagination seems endless? That dreamy child who lives somewhere between realities? He is the boy who quietly listens in a group setting, absorbing everyone's thoughts before offering an opinion. She is the empathetic friend who is always there for the other children. They are the kids who seem to know what you're going to do or say, almost before you do. You might find these kids designing the school yearbook or winning creative writing contests. They are the artists, the nurturers, and the dreamers. Whatever watery kids take on, they do it with utmost feeling, making them an unstoppable force. The water signs are Cancer, Scorpio, and Pisces.

Children whose dominant element is water are as flowing and changeable as the element suggests. Secretive and sometimes quiet by nature, these highly intuitive children are highly attuned to their surroundings, so large crowds can sometimes seem overwhelming to them. But with their natural nurturing abilities, watery kids thrive in situations where their focus can be channeled into a single project. Encourage them to foster their passion, whether it's in the arts or an animal project through programs such as 4-H. Because they can be psychic sponges, emotional water signs can sometimes become vulnerable and moody. Use grounding techniques or practice yoga to settle their stormy waters.

As adults, water signs are typically highly prosperous in their endeavors, whether as writers, artists, or small-business owners, and their ability to successfully nurture is not just relegated to the home.

At their best, watery kids are intuitive, empathetic, and creative. At their worst, they are compulsive, irrational, and oversensitive.

Magickally, water children are naturals at divination. Let them try their hand at scrying, palm reading, or interpreting dreams. They may also enjoy learning tarot, and with their artistic tendencies, you might find them designing their own deck. They may also be attuned to spirit guides. Just don't be surprised if your watery kid's intuitive powers keep the magickal undercurrents of your household alive and flowing.

SPLASHES OF FUN

- Write incantations in the sand.
- Look for hag stones.
- Paint a picture.
- Make moon water.
- Go swimming.

- Volunteer at a homeless shelter.
- Play with your pets.
- Keep a dream journal.
- Look for frogs.
- Read a friend's palm.
- Go fishing.
- Make ice cream.
- Learn tarot.
- Make a scrying mirror.
- Sit with a sick friend.

DREAM PILLOW

A perfect craft for our dreamy, watery kids is a dream pillow. Children whose dominant element is water are naturals for dream work, and a dream pillow can help them draw back the veil of their unconscious mind.

Dream pillows have been used to enhance dreams and protect against nightmares for centuries. They are also fun and easy to make!

You will need:

Fabric scraps (size varies depending on pillow size you want)
1 cup peppermint (helps enhance clarity of dreams)
¼ cup lavender (for its soothing qualities)

Scissors
Sewing needle and thread
Polyester fiberfill (enough to fill pillow)

Wash and dry the fabric. Avoid scented detergent or fabric softener, as they will take away from the herbal mix. Combine peppermint (helps enhance clarity of dreams) and lavender (for its soothing qualities) to create an herbal blend called Children's Dream Remembrance Mix. Then select a piece of fabric, preferably cotton or another natural fiber. Cut the fabric into whatever shape you wish. Of course, squares and rectangles are easiest, but don't be afraid to get creative!

With the outer sides of the fabric facing each other, stitch (with a sewing machine or by hand) along the edges, leaving a ¼-inch seam allowance and making sure to leave an open space along one side. Flip the pillow inside out through the open space and fill with polyester fiberfill as well as your herbal blend. Finish the pillow by hand stitching the open area shut. You can embellish it with embroidered moons, spirals, or runes. Sew buttons or add lace—you decide.

Here is a charm to say as you sew your last few stitches:

What night's dark veil has concealed
Through my magick may be revealed.
With these stitches I make, my spell is done,
And as I will it, let it harm none.

Enjoy your dreams!

Chapter 3

Through the Garden Gate

*Go to the place where the columbine mingles with the buttercup
and the air is scented with woodbine. Let the garden's magick take hold,
my child. Here you will find enchantment.*

When Joshua was four years old, I started taking him into the garden with me. I usually gave him busywork like raking a patch of dirt, whether it needed it or not.

One particularly chilly spring morning when the trees were just a haze of green and the air was filled with birdsong, I busily turned compost while Josh played with the red wriggling worms that rose as I worked.

"Mama." Josh wore a quizzical expression. "Does the Goddess live out here?"

Always surprised by my child's observations, I smiled. "Yes, she does," I said.

He breathed in deep. "I can smell her, Mama. She smells good."

I took a whiff of the cool, misty air. It was the sweet, resinous scent of black cottonwood that rode on the breeze. "Yes, I can smell her too, Joshie."

"I like her perfume."

"Yes." I chuckled. "I do too."

One does not follow the spiral path long before feeling that gentle tug to be outdoors. We carry within us a primal need to connect with the very elements of nature—to plunge our hands deep into the earth's soil, to take in every delicious note that is carried by the wind, to absorb the strengthening power of the sun, and to cool our senses with the healing properties of water. But understandably, it's hard to fit in time to get to that perfect mountain meadow or ocean beach to make that connection.

The reality is that most of us now live in urban areas, our lives so busy that our precious time in nature is limited. Sadly, we seem controlled by the mighty ticking of the clock. If only there were more hours in the day!

But there is something we can do right in our own backyards that can bring us closer to the Goddess, and it can be a form of meditation and can involve the whole family. It is something that can be done cheaply and easily, and most of all, it is one of purest and simplest forms of magick. "What is it?" you might ask.

Gardening.

You see, there is magick in a seed. Our ancestors understood this. The very act of planting was magickal for them. In fact, the word "cultivate" comes from the Latin *cultus,* which denoted honoring and adoring in addition to growing crops.

If you think about it, the seed holds within its tiny casing so much power. The power to heal, to nurture and sustain life, or to take life away. These are the lessons I taught my children as I put those first tiny seeds into their hands. And as they placed the seeds in the soil and gently watered them in, I told them of the seeds' deconstruction and fantastical transformation into the plants that we use and enjoy!

Seeds are an incredible gift of the Goddess that can bring magick and provide sustenance no matter where we live. By performing the simple ritual of sowing a seed, we are taken on a mythical journey of the God who with each harvest is cut down, to be buried in the earth and spring forth anew (as is the seed), reborn from the womb of our Mother Earth. These were reasons enough for our family to roll up our sleeves and plunge our fingers into the soil. But if you need a little more nudging, here are a few more reasons (magickal and mundane) to get your family gardening:

- *Gardening can be a great way to wind down.* The repetition of hand to soil, pulling weeds, turning the soil—this is where I feel the greatest connection to earth. I can't tell you how many times I have gone to my garden frustrated about something, and when I am done tearing and digging, covered with soil and sweat, I always feel better.

  A 2007 study published in *Neuroscience* shows that a soil microbe called *Mycobacterium vaccae* has the same mood-enhancing effect as antidepressants. So the saying *is* true—gardening is cheaper than therapy and you get tomatoes!

- *Children who garden grow up to be more adventurous and healthful eaters.* As a Master Gardener I have seen this firsthand in classes I have taught at our local discovery garden. There is no better satisfaction than to watch children exhilarated by the process of growing their own food, from their awestruck expressions as they witness their first seedlings push through the soil to satisfied smiles after their first bite of a juicy little plum tomato they grew by themselves—it's priceless. It leaves them wanting to experience and experiment more with their food choices.

  Across the United States, schools are using this tactic. By starting school gardening projects that incorporate the food grown by the students into the school lunch program, the kids have a better understanding of where their food comes from and the satisfaction of enjoying the fruits of their own labor.

- *Gardening is a great source of exercise.* Simple tasks, such as light weeding and planting, are a great form of low-impact exercise. And if you really start tearing things up—hauling wheelbarrow loads of compost to new beds, heavy weeding and digging—you can burn up to 300 calories per hour.

  This isn't just for the grownups, either. Kids who are active in the garden (or other outdoor physical activities) are not only more physically fit but also score higher on tests and are better able to concentrate at school than their counterparts who spend the same time playing video games or on the computer, according to a 2013 report by the US National Academy of Sciences.

- *You know where your ingredients come from.* Whether I'm making charm bags, casting spells, or making a meal for my family, I want to know that the ingredients I use are fresh, organic, and grown with love and care. Magickally, it is an added assurance to know that my herbs are grown and collected during the appropriate astrological time, giving my spellcrafting a little added kick.

- *You can customize your magickal and nonmagickal gardening needs.* What are your magickal needs? Do you cast a lot of spells for prosperity and success and would like to have more bee balm? Maybe you do a lot of smudging and you require white sage. Maybe you just want something simple like the all-purpose Witch's herb, yarrow. No problem. Growing your own means you can customize your garden to fit your needs.

  It's the same with your food needs. Maybe you can only get your kids to eat Sun Gold tomatoes. Once again, instead of hitting every farmers' market and specialty food store to find these sweet little gems, you can plant one plant in a pot on your balcony and have a summer's supply of healthy snacks.

Remember, the Goddess is alive and magick is afoot for those who seek her. Listen to that primordial voice. With all the distractions of our modern world, it may have been quieted, but it is not silent. It whispers, calling all who listen back into the garden, to that piece of land. Whether it's acreage, containers on an apartment balcony, or a plot at your local community garden, it's time. Gather your family and get reconnected.

A Place for Everything and Everything in Its Place

There is a twisted path not far from my home that leads to the crumbling remains of what was once a small crooked house. The roof was coated with club moss, and licorice fern tumbled over what I assumed were at one time functioning gutters. The woman who lived there was your classic crone. She was also my friend and mentor. She taught me about wild-crafting and natural magick. I treasure the memories of her lessons on herbal lore as we sipped nettle tea under a fading sun.

One of the many remarkable things about her home was that she could grow the most amazing plants in almost anything. Sure, she had the usual succulents in old boots and stumps that tumbled with periwinkle, geraniums that mingled with trailing lobelia in window boxes, and petunias that were stuffed into anything else that could hold dirt. But she also had a lemon tree in an enormous terra-cotta pot and jasmine that clung to the stone surface of an old shed. Every year she would give me armloads of cantaloupe and watermelon and wheelbarrow loads of sweet potatoes that were large and delicious.

What's so unusual about that? Well, I live in Northwest Washington. You know, the land of rain and coffee. As a rule we don't grow lemon trees here, and jasmine is just an expensive annual. As far as the melons and sweet potatoes, they're just plain hard to grow in our climate, and most home gardeners don't even try.

As a novice gardener I would stand in awe and look over her many raised beds that teemed with life. "How do you do it?" I asked her once. "Is there a spell you're using and not telling me about?"

She chuckled. "No, no, my sweet. Not the kind of magick you're thinking of." She went into her house and came back out with an old, tattered journal. As she handed it to me she said, "A place for everything and everything in its place."

What my old friend taught me that day was a lesson on microclimates and plant hardiness. The journal contained notes and illustrations on shade patterns, water access, and wind patterns. She also had sketched out individual plants with notes on each, including maximum height, bloom time, and nutritional, light, and water needs.

To be a successful gardener it's important to first evaluate your property's sun exposure. This can be easily done by watching for a few days and taking notes. Watch for shade patterns from outbuildings and tall trees and jot down how many hours of sun per day your planned planting areas receive. Different plants have different light needs:

- *Direct Sun:* Many fruiting plants require six hours of direct sunlight. These include tomatoes, squash, and cucumbers.

- *Partial Sun:* Root crops can get away with a little less light and only require four to six hours per day. These include carrots and beets.

- *Partial Shade:* Plants that require only three to four hours of light per day are in this group and include your greens: lettuce, spinach, arugula, and chard.

Remember I said my friend was growing a lemon tree in a large pot? Well, that's where plant hardiness comes in. A plant hardiness zone map helps determine which plants might flourish in your area. Zones are determined by the minimum winter temperature in any particular area. You can access a map easily on the web or find one in just about any gardening magazine or seed catalog. In my part of Washington, we are in zone 7. Ideally, lemons are grown in zones 9 through 11. My friend did what a lot of gardeners who want to grow exotic plants do: keep them in pots outside during the warm summer months and overwinter them in a greenhouse or sunroom.

Take note of the wind's movement. Is there a section of yard that always seems to be moving while other sections are relatively undisturbed? How about the slope? Is your property relatively flat or is it steeper at one end? These are all important questions to answer as you evaluate your future garden plot. That place in your yard that receives too much wind might not be the best spot for your pole beans or sunflowers. And if your sloping yard isn't properly terraced, all your precious seeds will just roll off when you water them.

One more thing if your family is new to gardening: start out small and grow as you succeed. A few containers or a small raised bed is all you need to begin. Huge plots can be overwhelming, especially for the little ones.

Remember, you want your family's gardening experience to be gratifying as well as fun. If your child plants his or her first lavender plant under a favorite oak tree, it's going to look pretty for a while. But soon this sun-loving favorite of the mint family is going to reach for whatever light it can find, giving it a leggy and sparse appearance, and eventually it will die. A lot of time, money, and wasted tears can be saved by just doing a little homework.

My lovely friend, who taught me so much about my magickal world, passed on not long after she let me glimpse into that tattered old gardening journal of hers, and it was another year before I could bring myself to visit the crooked little cottage again. I'll admit I looked around for the journal, but her home had been packed up, left only with the lingering smell of dried lavender and a few old canning jars. I took a small start of some periwinkle I found in an old stump. In the Victorian language of flowers, it stands for sweet remembrances. I thought that was appropriate.

The Moon as Your Guide

"Hi diddle diddle, the cat and the fiddle, the cow jumped over the moon," my grandfather chimed as he expertly slipped spinach seeds through his thick fingers.

"Why did the cow jump over the moon, Grandpa?" I asked, as I thumbed through an old wooden crate filled with jars. Each jar was marked and filled with seeds. Some big, some small, and some so tiny you could hold a dozen of them on the tip of your finger.

He thought for a moment and then laughed. "She jumps, dear, because she can!"

I smiled.

"Could you hand me the jar marked 'lettuce'?"

Being eight years old and the only grandchild old enough to help out in the garden, I took my instruction very seriously. But after checking and rechecking the crate and not seeing the seeds he needed, I said, "I can't find the lettuce, but these are cool." I held up a jar containing plump purple mottled bean seeds. "Can't we plant these instead?"

"No, my dear, we will wait a couple of days for those." He walked over to where I was and continued the search. "Aha," he said holding up his prize.

"Why, Grandpa?" I prodded. "Why do we have to wait?"

"The moon's not right," he said as he continued his work.

I played for a moment, drawing figures in the dirt with a small broken alder branch. Scenes unfurled in the dark, rich humus—plants stretching their long tendrils to a moon that was being devoured by a big, plump cow.

"Grandpa," I said, disrupting the quiet morning.

"Yes, my dear."

"I still don't understand."

He chuckled as he sprinkled his lettuce seeds over the lightly turned soil. When he was finished, he wiped his hands on his pants and walked over to where I was drawing in the dirt.

"Well, that's a pretty neat drawing," he said, kneeling down. "I really like the cow."

I smiled and handed him the stick. "Did you want to draw something, Grandpa?"

"Have you ever played school, Monica?"

I grimaced. "I hate school. Why would I play it?"

"Well," he said, smoothing a spot in the dirt. "This will be fun. Let's pretend this is my chalkboard." He pointed to the garden bed. "I will be your teacher, and you, my student."

"As long as we're not learning math." I crossed my legs and settled in.

I watched as he drew a perfect circle. Underneath he drew waves.

"This is the moon." He pointed to the circle. "And these, my dear, are waves."

"You mean like on the ocean?"

"Exactly."

I sat in the garden sifting the soft dirt through my fingers as my grandfather explained to me how the moon's gravity pulls the earth's bodies of water upward, not only creating higher tides during a full moon but also gently pulling the more delicate bodies of water, including the moisture in our garden beds. I was mesmerized.

"For the next couple of days, I will plant my greens. And as the moon grows," my grandfather continued, making a sweeping motion with his hands, "I will plant my crops that bear flowers. And just after the moon is full, I will plant my root crops."

"Does everyone plant like this?" I asked.

He smiled. "No, but they should." He winked as he reached out his hand to pull me up. "Come on. I'll bet Grandma has those sandwiches ready."

"I hope she made egg salad!"

"I have a feeling she did."

After lunch, my grandparents drove me home. I was excited about all I had learned and ran as fast as I could to the backyard, where I found my mother working in our own family's garden.

"Mama, Mama." I could barely get the words out. "Grandpa and I had so much fun. We planted greens and I was in charge of the seed box."

"Whoa!" My mother hugged me. "You're going about a mile a minute. Slow down."

I took a breath. "Grandpa even told me all about how to garden by the moon. Do we do that, Mama? We really should."

My mother sighed. "Oh, honey, Grandpa is superstitious. Don't listen to him." She pointed to our own garden. "You plant a seed and it grows. It doesn't matter if you do it today or tomorrow or next Tuesday. Plants grow."

"Oh." My voice was small. It was hard not to express my utter disappointment.

"I'm sorry, honey." I could tell my mother knew she should have been less harsh. "I think I will have a talk with Grandpa about filling your head with his nonsense," she mumbled as she walked slowly away. Then turning to look back, she said, "I'm getting some lemonade. Did you want any?"

"No, Mama," I said, and plopped myself down in the soil. I took my finger and traced circles in the dirt. I felt sad for a moment, not because of anything my grandfather had said, but for my mother: even at the age of eight I knew she had a mind that was a closed door.

As for my grandfather, I knew—just as I knew the sky shone a brilliant blue and the music that clouded my dreams was the Fae dancing in the forest—that he wasn't filling my head with nonsense. He was right.

Working the land in accordance with the phases of the moon is a practice that goes back to our ancient agricultural beginnings, to a time before calendars and clocks, when people governed their lives and livelihood around the workings of our closest celestial body.

Moon gardening (or lunar gardening) is the practice of working with the moon's gravitational pull. We know the moon influences tides, but it also influences other bodies as well, including the moisture in the soil. Moon gardening is simply working with the moon's phases and timing your garden chores accordingly. Done correctly, it encourages growth and water flow in new seedlings and also adds a special touch of magick and an unbelievable lushness to your garden.

If you're feeling a little anxious because lunar planting might seem restrictive, don't worry. Remember, the moon's monthly cycle is approximately 29.5 days long, with each phase lasting approximately 7.38 days. This gives you a pretty good window for planting in the appropriate phase without the worry of inclement weather or having to miss your child's sporting or after-school event.

- *First Quarter:* As the moon slips quietly into the first quarter she wears a crescent smile. During the time of the maiden moon of Artemis, goddess of the hunt, plant flowering annuals that produce their seeds on the outside and leafy crops such as spinach, lettuce, chard, and kale, as all the energy goes to the leaves. This is also a good time to plant grains.

- *Second Quarter (Waxing Moon):* Zirna, with her half-moon upon her breast, presents us with a time of increased energy. Plant flowering plants that produce their seeds on the inside, such as beans, tomatoes, squash, and cane plants such as raspberries, blackberries, or gooseberries. They will benefit as growth and liquid absorption begin to peak.

- *Full Moon:* Her face is a circle of light that illuminates the night's hushed landscape. During this time of Selene, plant your corn and vining plants—pole beans, peas, and sweet peas will benefit from the full moon's extra light. This is also a great time to gather your magickal herbs and charge moon water to add a little bewitchment to those magickal plants.

- *Third Quarter (Waning Moon):* Cerridwen's transformative powers play softly with the waning moon. During this time when the energy goes to the roots, plant root crops such as carrots or beets, or plants that grow from the same stock, such as asparagus, strawberries, trees, and shrubs.

- *Fourth Quarter (Dark Moon):* The time of Hekate, the dark goddess, is a rest period. Time to work on other gardening chores such as weeding, pruning, thinning out plants, or turning compost.

Fine-Tuning with Astrological Timing

If you want to step it up a little, you can fine-tune your lunar gardening experience by using astrological timing. As the moon travels through the sky, it passes through a different astrological sign every two to three days, and each of the four elements are associated with three signs.

- *Earth* signs are Taurus, Virgo, and Capricorn. These are fertile signs and great for planting (especially root crops) and transplanting your seedlings.
- *Fire* signs are Aries, Leo, and Sagittarius and are typically the best time for weeding and harvesting.
- *Air* signs are Libra, Gemini, and Aquarius and are semibarren and a good time to harvest and cultivate.
- The *Water* signs of Cancer, Pisces, and Scorpio are the most fertile of all the signs and are a great time to plant your flowering and leafy green plants.

My family uses the moon phases for planting our fruit and vegetable gardens and adds astrological timing for magickal herbs and flowers. Personally, I find it really makes a difference in my spellcrafting. If you want to learn more about planting using the phases of the moon, publications like *The Old Farmer's Almanac* or *Llewellyn's Moon Sign Book* are great resources.

Marking the Days of the Moon

Nothing was more exciting for my kids growing up than an art project. I homeschooled them, so I was able to incorporate art (and writing) into every lesson I taught. I loved to watch their faces light up when I pulled out the craft supplies and spread them across the table. Even now with my boys in college and my daughter (still homeschooled) completing high school courses, they all still enjoy the artistic process. My walls are a testament to that!

Making moon calendars was always one of their favorite projects. Not only was it something that they created that could be enjoyed all year, it was their very own guide to our family's agricultural year, a way for them to plan (tentatively) what crops and garden chores they would be responsible for during the growing season.

Because they were small children, I could use it not only to reinforce our Gregorian calendar system, but also to help them learn Goddess and God associations for each month, day, or moon phase.

As my children grew older, we tried a few variations of lunar calendars. These are definitely a little more challenging, as a lunar year is only 354 days as compared to our solar year of 365 days, so lunar calendars usually contain a thirteenth month on a leap year. Different cultures' calendars vary too: Hindu calendars, for example, can vary regionally. Some traditions consider a new moon occurring before sunrise on a day to be the first day of the lunar month, while other traditions believe the next day after a full moon is the beginning. The Chinese lunar calendar begins at the new moon, but the Hebrew lunar calendar's month begins at the sight of the crescent. If you have a child who is up for a stimulating project, researching and creating a lunar calendar is definitely for them.

Moon Calendar

You will need:

A current calendar and/or *Llewellyn's Moon Sign Book* or *The Old Farmer's Almanac*

1 blank calendar per child (You can buy them at most craft stores or print one off the Internet or from your office software.)

Artistic media, which may include one or more of the following: crayons, colored pencils, acrylic paint, watercolors, pastels, glue, glitter, or stickers (Get creative!)

Extra paper

Use a current calendar to help your younger children fill in the months, days of the week, and the numbers for each day of the month. (If they are very young, it's easiest to have this already done for them so they won't get bored.)

Show them how to fill in the days on which each full moon and new moon occur. Let them get creative with this. They might want to just go with the traditional light and dark circles, but sometimes it's fun to give the moon a little personality!

Next, using your guidebook, go ahead and tentatively help your children plan what they want to plant and fill in the spaces during the appropriate moon phase. They can use small illustrations to do this. Maybe your daughter is in charge of the tomato plant. Have her draw a representation of the plant in what would be the appropriate area. In fact, all garden chores can be easily filled in with simple symbols. A raindrop for watering, a basket for harvesting … You get the idea.

Now for the fun part! Twelve fun-filled art activities to accomplish. If using paint, making a collage, or making scratchboard art, it is best to do these on separate pieces of paper and attach them to the blank calendar pages later. If you are using crayons or colored pencils, go ahead and have them draw directly on the blank calendar spaces (always use a light pencil first so that mistakes can be easily erased).

We usually picked a theme as a group. Sometimes it was moon Goddesses and Gods; other times we drew representations of the full moon's names. We have also used faeries, magickal and astrological symbols, and even magickal plants that we could associate with the month or the nearest sabbat. Get creative!

Finish off the calendar by adding important family events, esbats, and sabbat celebrations. When the year is completed, your children will still have the artwork that they can frame and hang in their rooms or add to their Book of Shadows.

What's in a Name?

The moon has a story to tell. It has watched over us since the beginning of time, and we have used its cycles to keep track of our seasons. Almost every culture gave names to the full moons that marked their agricultural year.

By knowing the names, we reach back in time. The names tell us the story. You can almost feel the worry a family went through in a name like Hunger Moon and the jubilation of spring's arrival in Sprouting Grass Moon.

I have listed a few of the many names our lady moon is known by (mainly from Native American tribes, including the Algonquin and Cherokee). What do these names say about our past? Our present? What stories does the moon have to tell about us now? I wonder...

January: The Crone still has a hold on January's dark, silent landscape. Do you think if we listen long enough we could hear the echo of the wolf's lonely call like many of our ancestors did? January can also accumulate a lot of snow. These are the reasons January's full moon was known as **Wolf Moon** or **Snow Moon.**

February: Brighid's mantle has lifted, giving the first signs that winter will indeed come to an end. But in many regions, February's storms can still be brutal, bringing with them more snow than in previous months. For our ancestors it was also a time of hunger. Winter stores were used up and hunting could be challenging. Spring must have felt very far away. For these reasons February's moon was called **Snow Moon** or **Hunger Moon.**

March: The earth is warming and Eostre's warm blessing has brought with it a time of equal light. The soil is softened and earthworms become visible. Animals stir. We can hear the caw of the crow, and the maple branches are red as the sap begins to run. For these reasons the March full moon was called **Worm Moon, Crow Moon,** or **Sap Moon.**

April: Spring has finally arrived and the blush of the maiden can be seen throughout the land in the form of pink blossoms. Birds are laying their eggs and the grass is sprouting green. For coastal tribes it meant the fish were running. For these reasons April's full moon was known as **Pink Moon, Egg Moon, Fish Moon,** or **Sprouting Grass Moon.**

May: The scent of flowers sweetens the lusty month of May. This is a time of preparation and planting. For Native peoples, corn was an important crop and was planted during May. For these reasons this month's full moon is called **Flower Moon, Corn Moon,** or **Planting Moon.**

June: The sun is at its zenith as we celebrate the God. In many regions strawberries are the fruit that is most abundant. The bees are busily at work storing their sweet liquid gold, which would be made into a liquor to be drunk at weddings. The wild rose is abundant and blooming in every hedgerow. These are the reasons June's full moon was called **Strawberry Moon, Honey Moon,** or **Rose Moon.**

July: The sun is a golden mantle upon the fields, whose grasses sway on a warm breeze. The buck is growing antlers now, covered in a velvety sheath, that he will shed come fall. And in some regions thunderclouds bubble and stir among the foothills. This is why July's full moon was known as **Hay Moon, Buck Moon,** or **Thunder Moon.**

August: Time of the first harvest. Grains were ready to be cut and stored or ground into flour. The corn is tall yet still green. In the Great Lakes, Native peoples were fishing for sturgeon. In some regions August's sultry haze gave the moon a red appearance. For these reasons August's full moon was called **Green Corn Moon, Sturgeon Moon, Red Moon,** or **Grain Moon.**

September: Fall is approaching fast now. The shadows are already growing longer. Everyone must work harder now to get the harvest in before winter approaches. For Native Americans, staple foods such as pumpkins, corn, and beans were ready to harvest. These are the reasons September's full moon has been called **Harvest Moon** or **Corn Moon.**

October: The days are becoming shorter as the leaves fade and the veil becomes thin—this was the time of the hunt. This was also a time to butcher domestic animals for the winter as well. Sometimes (when the full moon falling in October is closer to the autumn equinox) the Harvest Moon is in October. For these reasons this month's full moon may be known as **Harvest Moon, Blood Moon,** or **Hunter's Moon.**

November: The days are getting darker and a chilly frost covers the ground. This is the time of year when beavers would have been trapped, their pelts made into warm clothing and blankets. These are the reasons this moon is called **Beaver Moon** or **Frost Moon.**

December: For most regions the nights are very long and the cold has settled in. We keep to the warmth of our hearth fire as we wait for the rebirth of the sun. These are the reasons December's full moon was known as **Cold Moon** or **Long Night's Moon.**

Thirteenth Moon: Sometimes we are lucky enough to enjoy a thirteenth moon within a season. This is known as a Blue Moon, and it occurs about once every two or three years. The name is suggested to be a corruption of the Old and Middle English *belewe,* meaning "betrayer." The first reference to a Blue Moon comes from a 1528 treatise critical of the Church: "Yf they say the mone is belewe, we must beleve that it is true." Here the phrase indicates an untruth, but we now use the term to describe something that rarely happens. These are the reasons the thirteenth moon in a season is known as **Blue Moon** or **Betrayer Moon.**

The moon also tells us a story through the folklore that has arisen from her many brilliant faces. Our ancestors watched the heavens closely to divine the signs of future events. Here are few of my favorites:

- When the moon points up, there will be clear weather.
- To sleep under direct moonlight could cause one to go blind or become mad.
- Seeing a new moon on a Monday will bring you luck.
- A halo around the moon means bad weather is on its way.
- A dark moon on Christmas means a fine harvest will follow.
- A red moon brings wind.
- Marriages consummated during the full moon are the most prosperous.

- If a new moon occurs on a Sunday, there will be a flood by the month's end.
- Two full moons in a month increase the chance of flood.
- To be "moonstruck" means to be chosen by the Goddess, and these people are truly blessed.

I'll have to admit, the last one suits me just fine. I feel privileged to be among the many moonstruck individuals chosen by the Goddess to walk a path that bends and winds through the magickal web of life. And as I always told my children when they were teased because of who they are, just smile and say, "Thank you! I am a little moonstruck." It confuses the mundane!

Moon Water

During the growing season I like to set aside specially moon-charged water for my magickal plants. This will definitely add a little more enchantment to your spellcrafting. I usually start with March's Crow Moon by setting out a bowl to reflect the moonlight and continue the process with every full moon until the end of the growing season.

You will need:

Large bowl (I use a large bowl that holds approximately 1 gallon of liquid)
1 gallon rainwater (I live in Washington State, which makes it really easy for me to collect; if you can't collect it, tap water will do.)

On the night of the full moon place your bowl of water outside. Make sure you can see the moon's reflection in the water. Place your hands over it and say,

Oh, Mother, your brilliant light does shine
Upon this water. Give it energy divine
As I plant with your changing phases in tune.
Let this water make my plants bloom and bloom.
Blessed be.

Go ahead and let the water absorb the moon's energy (you can leave it out all night if you want). The next day transfer the water into a watering can and use a bit while watering your magickal plants.

The Secret's in the Moon!

Every year until I turned twelve and my grandfather had passed on, I gleaned from him as much as I could about gardening. He was the first one to show me how to collect bean seeds and to tell me to always plant pumpkins in a mound (easier for watering after they start to vine). And his most adamant piece of advice was to plant by the moon's phases.

One afternoon, while drinking lemonade with him and my grandmother, I told him that my mom had said he was superstitious, but I believed him anyway. He smiled upon hearing this.

"Ah," he said. "I don't worry about it." I watched as he stirred a little more sugar around in his lemonade. "One day," he continued, "when you're all grown up, if you keep to my lessons, you will have the best garden in the area and then everybody is going to want to know your secret." He patted my hand.

"Then I'll tell them that the secret is in the moon and they'll have to believe me!" I exclaimed.

Grandpa chuckled. "Oh, they'll still think you're crazy, sweetheart. But at least you tried."

It was years later when I was gardening quietly by the moon with my own children that my mother came to my home. She stood and looked over the beds of lush vegetables and brilliant flowers we tended and shook her head. "Okay, what's your secret? My garden isn't growing like this." She pointed to a particularly beautiful group of sunflowers.

I chuckled a little as I wrapped my arm around her shoulder. "Secret's in the moon, Mama." I gave her a squeeze. "Secret's in the moon."

"Ah, you!" she said and laughed.

The Witch's Garden: Magickal Garden Design

What comes to mind when you think of the classic Witch's garden? Is it the dark plants of fairy-tale stories? Maybe it's brooding belladonna (*Atropa belladonna*) that comes to mind, used as an ingredient in the flying ointment of medieval lore. Or how about henbane (*Hyosyamus niger*), believed to be used by Witches to raise storms to blight farmers' fields? And of course, we cannot forget wolfsbane (*Aconitum napellus*), sacred to Cerberus, guardian of the gates to the underworld, and used by superstitious medieval farmers to poison wolves who might be waiting outside their door.

My favorite classic Witch's plant has to be the foxglove (*Digitalis purpurea*). The blooms, as told in Scandinavian folklore, were "rung" by foxes as a warning of approaching hunters. I know it as a faerie plant, with its common name a corruption of "folk's glove," in reference to the nature-dwelling spirits of the land.

When grouped in a garden, these plants lend a Gothic sense of beauty to any yard. They evoke emotions that reach back to a storybook youth where there are still maidens kept in high towers and knights willing to risk their lives for a single kiss. When encountering a Gothic garden, one does half expect a thatched cottage to appear, with a kindly wise woman ready with a cup of tea and sage advice. I have only been to one garden that was classically "Witchy," and it was an experience I will never forget. I was truly enchanted.

But, besides being enchanting, somewhat dark, and alluring, these classic plants are also very *deadly* and should only be grown by experienced gardeners. I do not recommend them for beginners or families with small children or curious pets.

We are going to take a look at another type of Witch's garden, just as enchanting and steeped with folklore and magick. But these Witch's gardens contain edible plants that are also used magickally or medicinally, are a lot more practical, and can still lend Old World charm to any landscape.

I have included a variety of magickal garden designs that can be scaled to suit your planting needs. I have also included some container gardens that can be planted as single species in a variety of containers or all together in one large container. Remember, these are just ideas to help you get started; use them as a jumping-off point and let your creative gardening energy flow.

Kitchen Witch's Herbal Delight

This beautiful little circular garden should be located as close to your kitchen as possible for easy access of gathering herbs as needed. To create a garden that is as much a feast to the eyes as it is to the palate, add a focal point, such as a birdbath or garden statuary right in the middle. My own circular herb bed has a wooden obelisk that I use to support scarlet runner beans and is topped with a gazing ball.

◄ Basil (*Ocimum basilicum*)
  Element: Fire
  Ruling Planet: Mars
  Energy: Masculine

This compact member of the mint family is a favorite at our house in pesto sauce. You can prolong the culinary life of this annual with deep green leaves and white flower heads by continuously pinching back the flower.

According to European folklore, basil was the devil's plant and one was to curse the ground as the seeds were sown. Basil tea has a mild sedative quality and can be used to calm anxiety. Magickally, basil encourages love and can be used in spells for money, protection, exorcism, and peace.

❧ Borage (*Borago officinalis*)

Element: Air

Ruling Planet: Jupiter

Energy: Masculine

This quick-growing herb has soft, cucumber-flavored leaves that are used in teas or as a pot herb. Its lovely blue star-shaped flowers can be candied or used to top off a salad. Borage is known as a bee plant, and its bloom will attract these little pollinators all summer long. Medicinally, borage is known for its anti-inflammatory properties. Magickally, borage is used to increase psychic ability and is used in spells for courage, happiness, and protection.

❧ Chives (*Allium schoenoprasum*)

Element: Fire

Ruling Planet: Mars

Energy: Masculine

A mild-flavored member of the lily family, chives can be added to salads and soups and are also used in Chinese and French cuisine. Medicinally, chives are used to aid in digestion. Chives were once planted in front of homes to ward off evil and disease, and they can be used magickally for protection and spells for lust and healing.

❧ Dill (*Anethum graveolens*)

Element: Fire

Ruling Planet: Mercury

Energy: Masculine

Kitchen Witch's Herbal Delight

With a long history of medicinal and culinary use, dill is a favorite and versatile kitchen herb. Both the fernlike leaves and the seed heads are edible and are used in sauces, in dressing, in fermentation, in pickling, and with fish. The seeds have been used for centuries to ease gas and bloating and to settle an upset stomach. In India, dill was burned to clear thunderstorms. Magickally, dill can be sprinkled around the house for protection or used in spells for jealousy, lust, money, and balance.

◀ Garlic (*Allium sativum*)
Element: Fire
Ruling Planet: Mars
Energy: Masculine

A member of the lily family, garlic is one of the most popular culinary vegetables because of its strong and divine flavor. Garlic bulbs are harvested in the summer months after the foliage has died off; the bulbs are then dried and stored for later use. Medicinally, garlic is known to boost the immune system and reduce blood pressure. Sacred to the Goddess Hekate, garlic was left as offerings at crossroads by ancient Greeks. Magickally, hang garlic to ward off negative energy. Also use it in spells for jealousy, protection, and healing.

◀ Lavender (*Lavandula angustifolia*)
Element: Air
Ruling Planet: Mercury
Energy: Masculine

How can you not love the scent of this shrubby perennial with its purple spiked flowers set atop narrow gray-green leaves? I dry tons of it every summer for sachets, amulets, and holiday cooking. Steep lavender in heavy cream for chocolate lavender truffles, or use it in shortbread recipes for a taste of summer all year 'round.

Lavender is known for its intoxicating scent, and folklore tells us it was the scent Cleopatra wore to seduce Julius Caesar and Marc Antony. Medicinally, lavender can be used in balms for headaches or melancholy. Make lavender tea for its calming effect. Magickally, lavender can be used for faerie magick, peace, sleep, dreams, protection, happiness, and strength.

❧ Rosemary (*Rosmarinus officinalis*)

Element: Fire

Ruling Planet: Sun

Energy: Masculine

This pungent herb is one of the most aromatic herbs in the garden. I keep my rosemary potted and bring it into the kitchen during the winter months. When it's frozen outside and I am in need of a "garden fix," I gently rub my hands over the leaves, releasing its earthy fragrance. Ahh! This Mediterranean herb has pine-like leaves, and its flavor lends itself well to sauces and pork and lamb dishes. Rosemary has long been associated with remembrance and was worn by ancient Greeks to help boost their memory. Magickally, use this herb for remembrance, purification, protection, love, and mental powers.

❧ Sage (*Salvia officinalis*)

Element: Air

Ruling Planet: Jupiter

Energy: Masculine

Sage is a classic culinary herb. This woody perennial shrub has soft grayish-green leaves with a strong savory flavor that lends itself well to Italian and Mediterranean dishes. It was thought that eating sage during the month of May would give a person immortality. Medicinally, it can be taken as a tea or gargled to relieve the symptoms of a sore throat. Magickally, this herb is used in spells for wisdom, purification, intuition, and abundance.

☙ Sweet Marjoram (*Origanum majorana*)
Element: Air
Ruling Planet: Mercury
Energy: Masculine

This lovely perennial herb grows up to two feet high with small ovate leaves and lovely lavender flowers that bloom in the summer. This herb is part of the same family as oregano and can be a suitable substitute in cooking. Known to aid the digestive system, it has long been used as a tea to relieve nausea and improve appetite.

The Romans associated sweet marjoram with love and made chaplets from the herb for betrothed couples to wear. Magickally, use this wonderful herb in dream pillows and for love, happiness, health, and marriage.

Bewitching Gardens for the Little Ones

There is nothing more enchanting for kids than a truly interactive garden. A place of their own to grow, learn, dream, and play. Children who are included in the design, maintenance, and harvesting of a garden are more likely to become adults who have a positive relationship with the land. And by adding fun elements such as a mud-pie station, bird and butterfly feeders, and comfy seating, you are guaranteeing your children many fond memories of fun and exploration.

For a magickal touch, mark the quarters of the garden with appropriate statuary or natural treasures, such as cones, feathers, stones, or shells. You could also dedicate your children's garden to your favorite deity. How about one of the many harvest deities, such as Demeter, Cerridwen, Hestia, Pomona, or Ceres?

CHILDREN'S GARDEN HIDEAWAY

Who doesn't like a little secret hideaway? Punctuated with a large leafy teepee covered with green beans and nasturtiums (both edible), this whimsical little garden plan is sure to enchant your little ones. You may never get them back in the house!

For this garden I have included a few climbing plants that can be grown over a "teepee" trellis set wide enough for the kids to crawl into. These inexpensive trellises can be made with 6 to 8 bamboo stakes 7 feet in length that can be picked up for around a dollar each at any DIY or garden center. A trellis can be put together by sticking the bamboo stakes 2 to 3 inches into the ground, bringing them together at the top (like a teepee), and tying them securely with twine. Plant your seeds at the base of each bamboo stake. There is no set diameter, but remember to make it large enough for the kids to crawl into and snack on beans or play in their own private hideaway.

❧ Sunflower (*Helianthus annuus*)
1 seed packet (American Giant)
Element: Fire
Ruling Planet: Sun
Energy: Masculine

Native to South and Central America, easy-to-grow sunflowers were cultivated for their seeds and oils, which are a good source of vitamin E. The sunflower was sacred to the Aztecs and was used to crown priestesses of the sun temple. Medicinally, sunflowers were used for treating coughs and bronchial infections.

The seeds can be eaten fresh or roasted in salads and breads. The oil is also used in dressings and margarine. Folklore tells us that sleeping with a sunflower under your bed will allow you to know the truth on any matter. Magickally, sunflowers can be used in dream work or in spells concerning wisdom, health, or fertility.

Children's Garden Hideaway

❦ Green Bean (*Phaseolus vulgaris*)
1 seed packet (Blue Lake pole bean)
Element: Air
Ruling Planet: Mercury
Energy: Masculine

Nothing says summer like fresh, crisp green beans! Originating from South and Central America, green beans were introduced to the Mediterranean by Columbus. Though low in calories, green beans are a great source of vitamins and minerals. According to folklore, you could rub a green bean on a wart, and as long as there were no witnesses, the wart would disappear. In magick, green beans can attract money.

❦ Radish (*Raphanus sativus*)
1 seed packet (Cherriette or Red Globe)
Element: Fire
Ruling Planet: Mars
Energy: Masculine

The simple radish has a long history. First cultivated in China, this small member of the cabbage family was a prized root crop throughout the ancient world. It was brought to America by early settlers and has been a garden mainstay ever since. High in vitamin C and potassium, radishes make a great addition to salads, soups, and stews. They are also used in Chinese cooking. According to folklore, radishes, when carried, help protect one from the evil eye. Magickally, radishes can be used in spells for lust and protection.

❦ Lettuce (*Lactuca sativa*)
1 seed packet (loose-leaf blend)
Element: Water
Ruling Planet: Moon
Energy: Feminine

There are many varieties of lettuce, and they are descendants from wild lettuce that was native to Asia and Europe. Wild lettuce was used as an aphrodisiac and was associated with the god Min in Egypt. Medicinally, it was dried and drunk as a tea to promote relaxation and as a sleep aid for restless children. As a culinary herb, it can be used in salads, wraps, and grilling recipes and has a subtle effect on the digestive process. Magickally, use lettuce in love charms and spells for protection, divination, and sleep.

◀ Tomato (*Lycopersicon esculentum*)
1 plant (Sun Gold cherry)
Element: Water
Ruling Planet: Venus
Energy: Feminine

Once known as *pomme d'amour,* "love apple," in France, this delicious beauty originated in South America, where its seeds were regarded as an aphrodisiac. Americans believed tomatoes to be poisonous and grew them only as a decorative plant until 1830 when, according to folklore, Colonel Robert Gibbon Johnson stood on a courthouse step in Salem, Massachusetts, in front of a jeering crowd with a basket full of tomatoes and announced he would eat the entire basket and survive. He ate them all and, of course, lived.

There are hundreds of culinary uses for tomatoes and many great varieties to choose from. For a children's garden, I recommend Sun Gold cherry tomatoes. They are easy to grow, sweet and flavorful, and a great way to introduce fresh garden flavors to picky kids. Magickally, tomatoes are a great protective plant; also use in spells for love and prosperity. Because tomatoes are a member of the nightshade family, use tomatoes in place of the more dangerous belladonna.

◀} Pot Marigold (*Calendula officinalis*)

1 seed packet (Oktoberfest or Pacific Beauty mix)
Element: Fire
Ruling Planet: Sun
Energy: Masculine

A traditional potherb whose uses go back to ancient times, pot marigold is a sunny favorite in gardens today. This annual daisylike flower of the Asteraceae family is native to the Mediterranean and grows fifteen to twenty inches tall. Its bright yellow to orange blooms can be used topically, as a dye, or in foods. We infuse calendula in olive oil to use in a soothing anti-inflammatory salve for scrapes, scratches, and itchy skin. According to European folklore, to offer protection from robbers and thieves, strew calendula under your bed. Magickally, use marigold for protection, prophetic dreams, legal matters, and physic powers.

◀} Nasturtium (*Tropaeolum majus*)

1 seed packet (climbing mix)
Element: Fire
Ruling Planet: Sun
Energy: Masculine

This easy-to-grow plant is not only edible but also great for attracting hummingbirds to your garden. The nasturtium is a perennial in its native home of South America, but for most North American gardeners, it is considered a half-hardy annual. There are many cultivars of nasturtium, including low-growing and climbing, but all varieties have trailing stems that reach about ten feet. Blooms are singular and range from bright yellow to orange and red. Nasturtiums are known for their peppery flavor and have been a popular salad green since the seventeenth century. In magick, use nasturtiums to garner spiritual strength and for purity.

☙ Strawberry (*Fragaria vesca*)

4 everbearing plants (Ozark Beauty)
Element: Water
Ruling Planet: Venus
Energy: Feminine

Whenever I bite into a juicy strawberry, I am taken back to my family's garden and summer afternoons gorging on those sweet red gems. There are two types of strawberry plants: June-bearing, which produce a large quantity of fruit for approximately three weeks in late spring or early summer, and everbearing, which produce berries sporadically throughout the growing season.

For a children's garden I recommend an everbearing variety for two reasons. First, unless you plan on making preserves, everbearing varieties provide continuous snacking for the kids. Second, an everbearing strawberry plant produces fewer runners (small clone plants attached by a stolon, or shoot, that extends from the mother plant) that can easily overtake the garden.

Strawberries are most definitely the fruit of love and have been used as an aphrodisiac and in love spells for thousands of years. In Bavaria, strawberries were gathered and hung in baskets from the horns of cattle as a gift to the nature spirits for healthy calves and an abundant milk supply. Use strawberries in preserves, desserts, salads, and sauces. Goddesses associated with strawberries include Freya, Aphrodite, and Venus. Magickally, use strawberries for love and luck.

FAERIE GARDEN

For adults, faeries are rarely seen with naked eyes. They are sensed. Their singsong voices are caught up in a spring breeze. The sounds of their nightly revelry are tangled in the chirp of tree frogs or interwoven in the splashing of rain. They are the flicker of movement under the lilac or a shadow wound in a scurry of dry leaves that tumbles swiftly across footpaths. Communication is easiest when the veil is thin (Beltane and Samhain) or at the "between" times of dawn, dusk, noon, and midnight.

For children, it is different. Faeries are tangible. I was very close with the Fae as a child, and I remember wistful afternoons spent in their presence. Faerie music haunts my dreams to this day.

My children, too, have had interactions with the Fae. Chloe, more than anyone, seemed deeply connected with these nature spirits. As a natural empath, she feels deeply for the earth and the spidery web that connects us to the otherworld. As a child, she talked about them freely, as if they were her dear friends that lived just down the lane ... And they were.

If you'd like to truly connect with nature spirits, a faerie garden can be an enchanting addition to your backyard. Of course, the Fae are pleased when we cultivate our backyards lovingly and with a tender hand. Be good to your soil by providing it with lots of rich organic compost. Think of the birds, butterflies, and bees by adding a water feature and plants to entice our pollinators and feathered friends. Lastly, let the faeries know they are welcome with a small altar and a garden blessing.

The plants included for this faerie garden can be tucked in a partly shady nook on your property.

❧ Honeysuckle (*Lonicera caprifolium, L. japonica*)
Element: Earth
Ruling Planet: Jupiter
Energy: Masculine

This amazing climber, which can grow up to twenty feet, is beautiful trailing along a fence, trellis, or arbor. The trumpeted flowers are a favorite to hummingbirds, who teach us to delight in beauty and appreciate life and laughter. Use honeysuckle in spells for prosperity and psychic powers.

❧ Maidenhair Fern (*Adiantum* spp.)
Element: Air
Ruling Planet: Mercury
Energy: Masculine

Ferns are our most ancient plants and have been around for 300 million years. There are thousands of varieties that grow in many different habitats. Maidenhair ferns are an enchanting choice and add faerie charm to any garden. It is said if you sit next to a fern bed in the evening, you will entice the faeries to come near you. There are 250 varieties of maidenhair fern, the most common being the northern or American maidenhair fern (*Adiantum pedatum*), which grows up to 16 inches high and will grow in zones 3 through 8, and the southern maidenhair fern (*A. capillus-veneris*), which thrives in zones 7 through 10.

In magick, fern can be used in spells for protection, luck, prosperity, and rain making.

❧ Columbine (*Aquilegia canadensis*)

Element: Water

Ruling Planet: Venus

Energy: Feminine

This old-fashioned perennial is a faerie favorite. It is easy to grow, but while it is a short-lived plant (two to three years), it self-seeds prolifically. Columbine can grow up to three feet tall and is loved by pollinators. One of its folk names is "jester's cap," as the blooms resemble the cap and bells of a jester and to receive a columbine symbolized foolishness. The essence of this magickal plant is said to help people find their true identity. In magick, use columbine concerning love and courage.

Note: columbine seeds are toxic.

❧ Forget-Me-Not (*Myosotis scorpioides*)

Element: Earth

Ruling Planet: Mercury

Energy: Masculine

These sweet little beauties grow well in a shady, moist environment and are a perfect addition to any woodland garden. Growing anywhere from six to twelve inches tall, they are self-seeding and spread easily. Their tiny flowers grow in clusters, and it's not uncommon to find blue, white, and pink flowers on the same cluster.

Faerie Garden

My favorite legend about the forget-me-not is of a knight who was walking with his lady near the banks of the river Danube. Seeing the pretty blue flowers, he bent to pick one for his love. As he bent down, he slipped into the river and the swift current soon pulled him under. Sadly, he knew he wasn't going to survive, so he threw his beloved the flower, and his last words to her before being taken by the river were "Forget me not."

Long used in spells for love and devotion, the forget-me-not is also a favorite of the Fae and, according to folklore, has the power to unlock secret treasures guarded by the spirits of nature.

☙ Foxglove (*Digitalis purpurea*)

Element: Water

Ruling Planet: Venus

Energy: Feminine

Yes, I have already established foxglove as a poisonous plant, but it is also a classic faerie plant that I felt should be included. Foxglove grows wild around our area and pops up everywhere on our property. Even with dogs, baby goats, and small children running amok, I personally have never had a problem. That being said, if you have pets or children who you think might ingest this powerful plant, use discretion.

Covered with bell-shaped flowers, this dramatic spiked biennial planted in your garden or by your front door will attract the Fae and provide protection for your home. As a plant of the underworld, it can be used in divination. Foxglove can grow up to five feet tall and is self-seeding. In magick, use foxglove for protection and divination.

☙ Pansies (*Viola tricolor*)

Element: Water

Ruling Planet: Saturn

Energy: Feminine

In floriography pansies represent merriment, and believe me, that is exactly what these hardy annuals add to the garden. Low growing (six to nine inches), they make a great border flower and will bloom continuously throughout the growing season. It is said these pretty little flowers attract parades of trooping faeries, and as their leaves are heart shaped, it is said they are able heal a broken heart. In magick, use pansies for love and focus.

Dream Garden

Everyone needs a place to dream. A little place in your yard or on your balcony where the scent of lavender and thyme beckon you to sit and relax. A place where jasmine seeps into your sleeping senses and induces prophetic dreams. The idea of a garden as a resting place goes back to the beginnings of gardening. Pliny the Younger wrote of a resting place in his own garden, an alcove with a couch, in amongst the springing fountains.

Considering the pressures and chaos our modern-day lives offer us on a daily basis, it is more important than ever to include a place for quiet contemplation in our own garden. Fill your little section of paradise with sensory elements that promote restfulness. Consider aromatic plants and maybe a water feature to include the soothing sound of trickling water. How about statuary and mementos that reflect pleasant memories from your past? Don't forget to add a comfortable lounge chair or hammock.

Here is a list of plants to get you started. If you're a city or apartment dweller, these plants can be easily planted in containers.

◄ Lemon Balm (*Melissa officinalis*)
Element: Water
Ruling Planet: Moon
Energy: Feminine

The green leaves of this plant have the scent of lemon with a hint of mint. This clumping herb grows two to three feet tall and tends to spread profusely if not contained. Its sunny fragrance helps relieve depression and aid in memory. It can be used to make tea and sachets and to add a little zest to soups, sauces, and seafood. In magick, use lemon balm for love, healing, memory, and success.

Dream Garden

◄ German Chamomile (*Matricaria recutita*)

Element: Water

Ruling Planet: Sun

Energy: Masculine

This low-growing (twelve-inch) annual flowers from June to July. The young sprigs can be used for seasoning, while the flowers are dried and used in tea to induce sleep. Magickally, use this traditional herb of the summer solstice for money, sleep, dream, children's magick.

◄ Catnip (*Nepeta cataria*)

Element: Water

Ruling Planet: Venus

Energy: Feminine

This member of the mint family is adored by cats! Catnip typically grows in spreading clumps two to three feet tall. It has erect, branched, square stems clad with aromatic ovate leaves. The flowers bloom in summer and are fragrant. This herb was used for centuries to ease stomach ailments and support digestion. A tea made from the dried leaves helps to induce sleep. This is a great herb to use in dream pillows for prophetic dreams and to add to incense blend for astral travel. In magick, use catnip for spells concerning cat magick, dreams, sleep, love, beauty, and happiness.

◄ Jasmine (*Jasminum officinale*)

Element: Water

Ruling Planet: Moon

Energy: Feminine

This sprawling deciduous shrub grows best in zones 7 through 10. If you live in a colder climate, it can be potted and overwintered indoors. The blooms are white or pale pink and are very fragrant from early summer through autumn. And with its delicious scent, most fragrant in the evening, it encourages nighttime enchantment. Jasmine oil is one of the principal oils used in perfumes; its honey-like fragrance promotes confidence and optimism. Magickally, use jasmine for spells concerning prophetic dreams, money, and love.

◄⟩ Polyantha Rose (*Rosa polyantha*)
Element: Water
Ruling Planet: Venus
Energy: Feminine

This rose blooms nonstop from June until frost, with double rosette-shaped blossoms of light pink. It grows two to three feet high and wide. According to mythology, Cupid accidently shot an arrow into a rose garden because he was stung by a bee, causing the rose to grow thorns. Well, thorns have not deterred this plant from a long use in love spells, mixtures, potions, charms, and elixirs. Besides love magick, rose hips and petals are also used in healing spells. Use roses in spells for luck, love, protection, healing, and divination.

◄⟩ Creeping Thyme (*Thymus serpyllum*)
Element: Air
Ruling Planet: Venus
Energy: Feminine

This easy-to-grow plant tucks neatly between stones and bricks on paths. It has small, dense leaves and grows about two to four inches high. In folklore, thyme was worn to attract good health, and when tucked under a pillow, it ensured pleasant dreams. In magick, burn this herb to purify ritual space or use it to aid in psychic powers. It can also be used in spells for sleep, healing, love, and courage.

Enchanted Patio Gardens

If you live in an apartment, have a small yard, or maybe have just a few sunny patches in a shady yard, container gardening can provide beauty and produce a wide variety of plants and herbs to suit your family's food and magickal needs.

Even with several acres to work with, I love containers. They help give interest and create focal points in large gardens. Containers are also a nice way to get the kids excited about gardening. First, they are small, so children don't feel overwhelmed when caring for their garden space. Second, since a container is anything that holds dirt, they can fill up an old wagon, shoes they have outgrown, or a discarded sand pail and feel good about keeping these items out of the landfill and repurposing them to make our world a better place. Here are three container gardens to inspire you to plunge your Witchy hands into the soil!

CULINARY CAULDRON CONTAINER

This container contains herbs to add a little bit of culinary zing to your dishes.

❧ French Tarragon (*Artemisia dracunculus*)

Element: Air

Ruling Planet: Venus

Energy: Feminine

Tarragon is a member of the daisy family and originated in western Asia. This herb has shiny green leaves that grow on slender stalks from one to three feet high and a bittersweet peppery flavor that lends itself well to seafood and egg dishes. It is one of the four *fines herbes* of French cuisine and a main component in Béarnaise sauce.

Its genus, *Artemisia*, derives from Artemis, the Greek goddess who fed tarragon to Chiron, the centaur. In medieval times it was

believed that carrying tarragon would keep you safe from dragons. Use tarragon in magick concerning confidence, courage,
strength, and passion.

❧ Parsley (*Petroselinum crispum*)

Element: Air
Ruling Planet: Mercury
Energy: Masculine

Don't let parsley's mild flavor fool you. This little herb packs a
vitamin-C punch that is among the highest of any food, and it
has a notable amount of iron, calcium, and fiber. It is used often
in soups, stews, and sauces to enrich the background flavor and
can also be added to pestos and marinades. Medicinally, parsley
aids digestion and relieves gas and bloating.

In both Greece and England, parsley was connected with
death, and the term "to be in need of parsley" was said of people
near death. The Romans had a slightly different outlook on this
nutritious herb: they wore parsley wreaths to ward off intoxica-
tion during feasts. Magickally, use parsley for protection, spirit
work, fertility, lust, and purification.

❧ Fennel (*Foeniculum vulgare*)

Element: Fire
Ruling Planet: Mercury
Energy: Masculine

This graceful, aromatic perennial can grow up to six feet tall.
The leaves and seeds go well with fish dishes as well as rice and
stir-fry. The bulbous root can be used cold in salads or cooked
as a vegetable. Medicinally, fennel soothes the stomach and increases breast milk production in nursing mothers. Grow fennel
near your home for protection. Magickally, use fennel in spells
for protection, healing, and purification.

◀ Lemongrass (*Cymbopogon citratus*)

Element: Air

Ruling Planet: Mercury

Energy: Masculine

Lemongrass is a stiff grass native to India that grows in clumps from one to four feet tall. The light citrusy flavor of lemongrass has always been a mainstay of curries, but it is also used in soups, salads, marinades, and stir-fries. Medicinally, lemongrass has been used to soothe the stomach and for fever and depression.

Lemongrass, when grown near your home, wards off evil. Use lemongrass to increase psychic powers and in spells for lust and divination.

◀ Dill (*Anethum graveolens*)

See pages 104–106.

MAGICKAL HAPPENINGS CONTAINER

To the mundane they are just pretty flowers—but we know better! Add these plants to a container and conjure up some real garden magick.

◀ Mugwort (*Artemisia vulgaris*)

Element: Earth

Ruling Planet: Venus (Moon)

Energy: Feminine

This legendary Witch's herb has accumulated many legends and superstitions. It was thought to protect one from poison and wild beasts and was one of the ingredients purported to be used in the Witch's legendary flying ointment. Roman soldiers placed the herb in their shoes to prevent aching feet.

At one time it was a common ingredient in stuffings, sauces, and poultry dishes, but because of its rather bitter taste, it has fallen out of favor. Before hops, it was used in the production of ale. Mugwort is a member of the daisy family and can grow up to three feet tall. Its leaves are a gray-green with white on the underside. The flowers are inconspicuous and bloom in the summer.

Sacred to Artemis (as are all plants in the genus *Artemisia*), mugwort is associated with the moon and to the cycles of womanhood. It was thought that tying a branch of mugwort to a laboring woman's left thigh would help ease labor. As a tea it has been used to both induce labor and relieve menstrual cramps. Mugwort has been used to stimulate the appetite and in Chinese medicine, it is used for rheumatism.

Magickally, drink mugwort tea to encourage lucid dreaming and use mugwort-infused water to cleanse ritual tools. Use mugwort for divination, astral projection, prophetic dreams, protection, and psychic powers.

☙ Patchouli (*Pogostemon cablin*)

Element: Earth

Ruling Planet: Saturn

Energy: Feminine

Because patchouli is native to tropical climates, it doesn't overwinter in many regions, so it is perfect for a container. Patchouli is a member of the mint family with large green serrated oval leaves and small lavender flowers. Used in India to repel moths, it was layered between the creases of fabric, perfuming the cloth with its distinctive woodsy, sweet scent.

Medicinally, it has been used externally in its distilled form to increase one's libido and as an antidepressant. Its antiseptic properties make it an excellent choice in treating wounds and minor infections.

Patchouli is an excellent herb for connecting with Mother Earth and for fertility magick. Patchouli is a wonderful choice to use for prosperity, sex, and earth magick and for grounding.

❧ Peppermint (*Mentha ×piperita*)

Element: Fire
Ruling Planet: Mercury
Energy: Masculine

A cross between watermint and spearmint, peppermint is a twelve- to eighteen-inch hardy perennial that self-seeds easily. As with any member of the mint family, peppermint can easily take over a garden, so grow with caution.

The active ingredient in peppermint is menthol, an organic compound that produces a cooling sensation. Used medicinally, it reduces inflammation and eases bloating, gas, and nausea. Peppermint is also used to soothe skin and scalp irritations, freshen breath, and whiten teeth.

Scent a cotton ball with a little peppermint oil and tuck it near your work area to aid concentration. Fresh mint can be added to water and used to cleanse and purify your ritual tools. Sprinkle peppermint around your house to ward off negativity. Use peppermint in spells for love, healing, purification, money, and clarity.

❧ Lavender (*Lavandula angustifolia*)

See page 106.

TEATIME CONTAINER

How delightful it is to create your own tea blends. These amazing plants can help get you started.

❧ Bee Balm/Bergamot (*Monarda didyma*)

Element: Air
Ruling Planet: Mercury
Energy: Feminine

Also known as bergamot for its scent, which was found to be similar to the bergamot orange, bee balm is a favorite of bees, butterflies, and hummingbirds. I can't get enough of its aromatic scent so I grow this stuff everywhere. The blooms of this eastern

North American native are red to mauve whorls that grow on solitary terminals. This twelve- to fourteen-inch hardy perennial tolerates damp soil and partial shade, which makes it a perfect addition for bog or waterside gardens.

Medicinally, bee balm is high in vitamin C and A, and when drunk as a tea, it may help soothe a sore throat. It was bee balm that was used by European settlers of the Oswego River, near Lake Ontario, as a suitable replacement to their own tea, and oil of bergamot is added to black tea to give Earl Grey tea its distinctive flavor. Crush the leaves of bee balm to release its oils for an excellent insect repellent.

Carry a leaf of bee balm in your wallet for attracting money. Use in spells for clarity, peace, success, contentment, and happiness.

◀} Lemon Balm (*Melissa officinalis*)

See page 119.

◀} Spearmint (*Mentha spicata*)

Element: Air
Ruling Planet: Jupiter
Energy: Masculine

Another tenacious member of the mint family, spearmint is best confined to containers. Less pungent than peppermint, spearmint is popular with chefs and works well in both cold and hot drinks. Rich in antioxidant vitamins, spearmint is a soothing herb that can be made into a tea to settle nervousness, headaches, fatigue, and stress. It can also be made into a salve to relieve dry skin or hives.

In mythology, Minthe was a lovely river nymph who caught the eye of Hades, god of the underworld. Persephone, none too happy about her husband's wandering eye, turned Minthe into a crawling plant. Hades, unable to reverse the spell, gave Minthe the gift of a bright scent so she would always be noticed.

In magick, use spearmint for healing, love, clarity, and purification.

◗ Valerian (*Valeriana officinalis*)
Element: Water
Ruling Planet: Venus
Energy: Feminine

Valerian has been the go-to herb to support relaxation and sleep for hundreds of years. This lovely perennial is native to Europe and grows up to two feet tall. It has lovely, scented, umbrella-like seed heads of tiny pink blooms. Both the leaves and the roots can be used to create a tea that has a mild tranquilizing effect.

In magick, the powdered roots can be used in sachets for protection or love. It is said if a woman pins a sprig of valerian to her clothing, men will follow her anywhere. Hang valerian in your house to ward off negativity. Use valerian in spells for sleep, love, protection, and purification.

◗ Violet (*Viola odorata*)
Element: Water
Ruling Planet: Venus
Energy: Feminine

Don't be fooled by this modest little flower. It has been connected to the trials and triumphs of love since ancient times. It is said that Zeus fell in love with a nymph named Io and changed her into a white heifer to protect her from his wife's jealous rage. Io was sad and cried because of the coarse grass she was forced to eat, so Zeus changed her tears into sweet violets that only she was allowed to eat.

Violets are a low-growing hardy perennial with dark green heart-shaped leaves and pretty little drooping purple or white flowers that bloom in the spring. Both leaves and flowers can be used to make a sweet tea to soothe coughs and colds. The blooms are pretty in a salad or can be candied, made into jams and jellies, or added to vinegar.

To ease the pain of unrequited love, carry a violet with you. Plant them in your garden to bring peace and harmony to your home. Magickally, use violets in spells for lust, love, peace, protection, healing, and death and rebirth.

Everything Old Is New Again

When I think back to my youth growing up in the sleepy Skagit Valley foothills, there are three things that stand out: the scent of black cottonwood perfuming misty spring mornings, summer afternoons exploring lush fairy-tale forests, and the taste of heirloom tomatoes straight off the vine.

As a child, I didn't care whether we grew heirloom or hybrid—I wouldn't have known the difference. All I knew was that there was nothing sweeter than homegrown, and no matter how many store-bought tomatoes were placed in front of me the rest of the year, they never compared.

Even in my early twenties, as I tested my gardening wings with those first pots of Early Girl tomatoes I purchased and lovingly nurtured to state-fair perfection, I couldn't replicate the old-time goodness of my mother's (and grandmother's) tomatoes. One day, I finally called my mother. "What was the name of the tomatoes that you and grandma used to grow?"

"Oh." She thought for a moment. "Well, let me see. I believe they were called Cardinal tomatoes."

"Do you know where I could buy the starts?"

"Oh, honey, I don't think there are any stores around here that sell Cardinal tomatoes. You might try calling around to some of the specialty nurseries."

"I don't understand why," I said. "I remember those being so good, and mine—well, they're pretty good, too, but …" I sighed. "Not as good as the ones I remember from our garden."

"Those were heirloom tomatoes, and you just can't find them in any old gardening center. Your grandmother always gave us a few starts when she kept a large garden."

"By heirloom, do you mean old-fashioned?"

She paused. "Yeah, old-fashioned is one way of describing them."

It wasn't until a few years later when I began a large garden of my own that my interest in heirloom plants was further piqued, so I did a little research. For a plant to be considered an heirloom, it must be open pollinated, meaning pollination occurs by natural methods (bird, insect, wind, etc.), and it must be from seed developed more than fifty years ago.

What fascinated me the most about these old-fashioned favorites were the names and stories behind them. The Cardinal tomato, grown by grandmother and mother, was a commercial variety introduced in 1884 by Washington Atlee Burpee (yes, of Burpee Seeds). Look at Dr. Wyche's Yellow tomato—Dr. Wyche was a circus owner who dabbled with plant development in his own amazing garden. His secret: he fertilized his plants with elephant and tiger manure. And what about the Mortgage Lifter tomato? During the Depression, a man called Radiator Charlie had a radiator repair business that fell on hard times, leaving him six thousand dollars in debt. Charlie turned to his garden and within a few years had developed a tomato that was large (averaging two and a half pounds), meaty, frost and disease resistant, and a beautiful pink-red in color. He sold the starts for a dollar each and eventually paid off all his debts.

What really fascinated me was that the people behind the plants being developed weren't horticultural scientists—they were average Joes doing the best they could with what they had. Wow!

Heirloom plants lend history and a touch of romance to a garden. They are a testament to a long-ago way of life and to the seeds that were lovingly passed down through the generations, providing sustenance, beauty, and a continuance of family tradition.

Heirloom versus Hybrid

When looking through the rows and rows of seed packets every spring, it's easy to become overwhelmed. There are heirloom and open-pollinated seeds and there are F1 hybrid seeds. You might see a package marked non-GMO. What does all this mean, and which is the right seed for you and your family?

HYBRID (F1 HYBRID)

Hybrids, also known as F1 hybrids, are plant varieties resulting from pollination between genetically distinct plants to create a desired trait. Because the seed is created for the first generation of plants to produce higher yields and demonstrate more vigorous growth, gardeners must purchase new seeds every year. Great hybrid seeds to start with include peppers, eggplant, cabbage, broccoli, and cauliflower.

Pros:

- They produce a larger yield, typically up to 25 percent more.
- Hybrids are often more vigorous and show more plant growth over a season, great for gardeners with a short growing season.
- The yield is more uniform.

Cons:

- Because hybrid plants are designed to be used for one season, second-generation plants will yield less or no fruit and may have physical characteristics that vary greatly from first-generation plants. Saving seeds from a hybrid plant is a no-no.
- They have lower adaptability to stresses such as pests or disease.
- There is lower genetic variability in food plants.

OPEN-POLLINATED PLANTS

Open-pollinated plants (OPs) are stable plant varieties resulting from the pollination between the same or genetically similar parents. Great open-pollinated seeds to start with include peas, beans, leaf lettuce, and tomatoes.

Pros:

- Open-pollinated plants are more genetically diverse.
- Greater variation within plant population means plants can slowly adapt to local growing conditions.
- Seed saved will stay true to its type year after year, so you can save your own seed with open-pollinated varieties.

Cons:

- They are not always able to produce uniform fruit.
- Some plant varieties need to be separated to avoid cross-pollination.

Heirlooms

Heirlooms are open-pollinated plant varieties that have been nurtured, selected, and handed down for many generations. Most sources agree that a variety must be over fifty years old to be considered an heirloom, but there are some who suggest over a hundred years and still others who believe the plant variety must predate World War II as the starting point. Great heirloom vegetables to grow are beets, beans, cucumbers, and tomatoes (remember to look for varieties that grow best in your region).

Pros:

- Heirlooms are adapted to their growing regions, which makes them more disease and pest resistant.
- They yield plants that are true to the plant that produced them. This is great for saving seed.
- They have hands down the best flavor!
- By growing heirlooms, you are keeping part of our agricultural past alive.

Cons:

- Because they are open pollinated, heirlooms may naturally cross-pollinate with other varieties, creating plants that are not original to the heirloom.

- For best results, most heirlooms should be grown within their region of origin, so you need to do your research when growing heirlooms.

Genetically Modified Organisms (GMO)/ Genetically Engineered (GE)

Genetically modified organisms or genetically engineered foods have been genetically engineered to make plants (or animals) more resistant to insects and herbicides, grow faster, and stay fresh longer. In 1994, there were no genetically modified crops planted in the United States; now there are over 165 million acres planted each year. According to Oslo-based online newspaper Forskning.no, a 2009 study by the Norwegian School of Veterinary Science found that GMOs may contribute to weight gain and liver and kidney failure in rats. Sixty-four countries around the world have strict restrictions or bans on genetically modified foods. The United States has none. I recommend choosing only seeds that are marked "certified organic" or "non-GMO."

Seed Saving

Saving seed is a fun and inexpensive way to preserve not only a bit of family history, but also the genetic diversity of our heirloom food and flowering plants.

For thousands of years, people saved seeds from their largest and most vigorous plants, replanted them, and then passed the seeds from one generation to the next. This process created cultivars that were well adapted to their region's growing conditions.

In 1900 we had over 1,500 varieties of food crops, but with the onset of modern farming, farmers began to rely on seed companies for their crops and soon the slower selling seeds were dropped, translating to lower genetic variability. Today, 90 percent of our calories are provided by fewer than thirty varieties of food crops, and the top four (wheat, rice, soy, and corn) supply 75 percent of the calories we consume.

Most of today's commercial seeds are bred for different reasons than the seeds of our grandparents were. Unlike heirloom or open-pollinated seeds that carry within their casing the ability to withstand stresses, such as pests and disease, hybrid seeds are bred to improve shipping quality, uniformity, and the ability to be stored for long periods of time.

Saving your own seed is relatively easy, but there are a few things to consider before you start. First of all, hybrid seeds (look for the word "hybrid" or "F1 hybrid" in the description on the seed packet) do not always breed true to type, so it's best to avoid them. Also, many common vegetables (such as cabbages, root vegetables, brussels sprouts, and parsley) are biennials (plants that require two years to complete their life cycle) and won't go to seed until their second year. The last thing to consider is cross-fertilization, which can take place when pollen is exchanged between flowers on different plants of the same genus. You can minimize the process by planting only one variety of the plant at a time.

The first seeds I saved were flower seeds, and this is a good place to start, especially if you are introducing seed saving to your children. Instead of pinching off all the spent flowers after they have bloomed, let a few develop seedpods. When the seeds are dry, shake them into a bag. Now, wasn't that easy?

Here's a list of some of my favorite flowers to save:

• Foxglove (*Digitalis purpurea*)

• Hollyhock (*Alcea rosea*)

• Nasturtium (*Tropaeolum majus*)

• Sweet pea (*Lathyrus odoratus*)

• Bee balm (*Monarda didyma*)

Vegetable and fruit seeds take a little more finesse. Here are a few to get you started:

Beans, Peas, and Other Legumes: Leave a few pods on your legumes until they are "rattle dry." Pick the pods and remove the seeds when they are completely dry. If needed, pull up the entire plants after they have died back and hang them upside down in a garage or shed.

Pumpkins and Squash: Cut squash open when they are fully ripe and scrape the seeds into a bowl, and then wash, drain, and dry them. Seeds are dry when they break and no longer bend.

Cucumbers: When the cucumber has started to yellow on the vine and get a little mushy, cut in half and scrape seeds into a bowl. Remove their slimy coating by rubbing them gently around inside a sieve while washing them. Rinse and dry. Seeds are dry when they break and no longer bend.

Peppers: Select a mature pepper and cut open. Scrape the seeds onto a plate and let the seeds dry in a non-humid, shaded place. Seeds are dry when they break rather than bend.

Eggplant: Leave eggplant on the vine until it is yellow and hard. Cut eggplant in half and pull the seeded area away from the flesh. Dry on a plate for one to two weeks.

Now that we have dried a few varieties of seed, it's time to store them until the spring. Seeds need to be kept in a place that is dry and cool. Humidity and warmth will shorten a seed's shelf life. I keep my seeds in paper envelopes tucked into mason jars in the pantry. Your refrigerator is also a good choice. Don't forget to label and date your seeds and try to avoid opening the container until you are ready to plant. Stored seeds will retain their viability for different lengths of time depending on the type of seed, but most seed is good for about two years.

Now that you have saved some amazing seed varieties, it's time to make a difference in your community. You can donate some seed to the local food bank or senior center or have the kids pass them out at your local farmers' market. This is a great way to encourage more people to grow their own food and preserve heirloom varieties so they won't disappear. Seeds, along with a terra-cotta pot and a bag of potting soil, make a great gift for friends and family too!

Feel satisfied and more connected to the earth by cultivating and sharing seed, and empower yourself with the knowledge that you are in control of what you grow and feed your family!

Getting Back to Our Roots

As the sun begins to set, casting a lovely pink glow over my garden, I sit and think of the gardeners before me. My mind drifts to my own parents, who looked to the land to provide their girls with nutritious food, planting within me the seed of sustainability. I think of my grandparents, who quietly and successfully marked their agricultural year by the moon and her cycles, teaching me to value the old ways. And I can't forget my dear old friend Stella, who taught me how to find the magick in every bud, leaf, and flower. She taught me patience and reminded me of the Goddess's lessons whispered gently on the breeze. And I am proud to pass these seeds of wisdom on to my own children.

So as you plunge your own hands into the dark, loamy earth, think of your ancestors, who tirelessly worked the land to provide sustenance for their families and seed so that the next generation might thrive. Remember the wise women and cunning men who gleaned medicine and magick from their gardens, meadows, and hedgerows, and recall the tales of magick and metamorphosis in the gardens of myth and lore. For a garden does transform us. In the garden a troubled soul finds solace, a hungry mind finds fulfillment, and a spiritless heart learns to beat anew.

Garden Blessing

I hope you have enjoyed our magickal romp through the garden. Is there dirt under your fingernails? Are there scratches on your knees? Good—it means you have been working hard. How about the kids? Is their hair tangled with leaves and debris? Are there holes in the knees of their britches? I hope so. It means they're having fun. Now that you have planted your new garden, it's time to bless it. You can perform the blessing I have included below or use it as inspiration for your own garden blessing. Enjoy the delights of your new garden!

We are calling upon Cerridwen to bless the garden and its transformative powers.

You will need:

Flat stone or tile
Small cauldron or fireproof pot
Green tea light or small candle

Take the family into the garden. On a flat stone set a small cauldron or fireproof pot with a green tea light or small candle in it. Light the candle and say together,

> *Cerridwen, we call upon your transformative hand to bless this space.*
> *A haven for bird, bee, and faerie, this garden now to grace*
> *With the power of earth, air, fire, water, and spirit—divine.*
> *Bless this garden and all that who enter it with solace there to find.*
> *Blessed be!*

Let the candle safely burn out.

Chapter 4

Fire Burn and Cauldron Bubble

Gather round the hearth, my children,
and let me tell you tales of the old days,
when life was simple and everyone believed in magick ...

In the bleak of midwinter, when I sit huddled up to my woodstove, I think back to my years as a river guide during the cold, dreary days of January and February, a time when the eagle population in the upper Skagit Valley is at its peak, and there are hundreds of eager tourists willing to pay money and fight the cold for a four-hour tour in a self-bailing raft just to catch sight of an American bald eagle.

I remember bumping down the river, my guide stick firmly planted in the river's frothy folds, as my frozen hands maneuvered the boat on its proper course. The rain that fell in icy pellets stung my face and slowly seeped through my layers of wool, finally soaking my skin with a cruel chill that went straight to the bone.

Hour after cold hour, I floated with tourists down Skagit River's watery byways, which gave us an extraordinary glimpse of a Pacific Northwest rarely seen by most. Teeth chattering, the tourists pointed stiff fingers to snags high in the cedar, fir, and hemlock forests that trace the river's banks. "One hundred fifty-one," someone keeping count called out. "One hundred fifty-one eagles."

"Remember," I said, trying to sound cheery, though I wanted nothing more than to be back in front of my warm fire. "When we get to the takeout, we ask the other groups how many eagles they saw. If their number is larger than ours..." I flash a frozen grin. "We add one to their count." Even when I'm miserable with cold, the competitive side of me shines on.

When the day was over, I would climb into my old Toyota truck and beat furiously at the dash. "Come on, fan," I would curse. "Blow one more time for me." But more often than not, the fan wouldn't spin and I would shiver as I counted the minutes to my home. As I slowed to cross the single-lane bridge that connected me to Concrete Sauk Valley Road, my heart would begin to race. "Almost home" was my mantra. "Almost home."

Through skeletal branches that lashed and creaked, I would finally spot the soft, yellow glow of my home, arousing an excitement in me like that of a schoolgirl who had been away for weeks at camp and couldn't wait to breathe in the familiar scent of pillows and blankets, even though I had just left ten hours earlier.

The door would open and my children would greet me. The scent of wood smoke and cinnamon candles and hot soup would all beckon to me at once.

At last, I would be in my favorite robe and snuggled up in front of my fire. Steve would bring me homemade clam chowder and sourdough toast. The kids would gather around me and tell me stories about their day. Who did what to whom and who had a great idea to make this or that would tumble from everyone all at once. I was tired and would close my eyes just for a second. "Yes," I would hear slip from my lips, followed by cheers. I knew I was going to kick myself for whatever I had agreed to, but it was okay … I was warm, nourished, happy, and home.

Hearth Song

If our homes were living entities, then the hearth would be the heart. For our ancestors, fire was more than a pretty flickering flame to lend a cozy feel around the holidays—fire was life.

Social life, in a way, began around the lapping flames of the communal fire. For this was a place of safety and warmth where all would gather to listen to the stories told by elders as they shared a nourishing meal. Within the plumes of smoke rose the wispy shadows of the ancestors and spirit guides that protected the clan. And if one listened closely, their ancestral wisdom could be heard in the cracking and popping of the coals.

The smoke hole in the peak of a dwelling was known as a gateway to the otherworld. Siberian shamans used notched birch logs as "shamanic trees" to climb to the top of the smoke hole and ritually enter the spirit world.

As fire rings became hearths, magickal symbols were carved into chimneys, so no evil could unintendedly slip through. The bones of loved ones were buried under fireplaces as their souls lived on through fire's transformative flames. Images of house spirits were placed near the hearth where scraps of food, a bit of butter or a little bread, were fed to the flames to appease the spirit's good nature.

House spirits came in many forms. To the Romans they were *lares*, or protectors of the household. "House brownies" helped with the household chores in northern England and Scotland. In Korea, *gasin* were a collective group of household deities. For Slavic people, it was the *domovoi* who took up residence. *Bwbachod* was a Welsh household spirit who could become mischievous if not appeased, and the *nisse* was a protective household spirit in Scandinavian countries.

Coaxing the Flames and Rekindling the Hearth

When a woman was married, she was first taken to greet the fireplace, for it was women who tended the hearth. She was the one who stoked the coals throughout the night, and before the rest of the household awoke, she was the one who whispered her dreams into the flames and chanted words of protection for the day. The lady of the home knew well of fire's transformative forces. And she knew precisely what wood to feed it for her desired effect. It was a woman's job to know the smoke of hawthorn would chase away evil spirits and that fir burned long and hard enough to cook a pot of stew. She knew to burn willow for someone with fever, as it gave off a cooler heat, and that ash was the best wood of all to burn, as described in the classic "Firewood Poem" written by Lady Celia Congreve in 1930.

The Firewood Poem
Beechwood fires are bright and clear
If the logs are kept a year,
Chestnut's only good they say,
If for logs 'tis laid away.
Make a fire of Elder tree,
Death within your house will be;
But ash new or ash old,
Is fit for a queen with crown of gold

Birch and fir logs burn too fast
Blaze up bright and do not last,
it is by the Irish said
Hawthorn bakes the sweetest bread
Elm wood burns like churchyard mould,
E'en the very flames are cold
But ash green or ash brown
Is fit for a queen with golden crown

Poplar gives a bitter smoke,
Fills your eyes and makes you choke,

Apple wood will scent your room
Pear wood smells like flowers in bloom
Oaken logs, if dry and old
keep away the winter's cold
But ash wet or ash dry
a king shall warm his slippers by.

For our Celtic ancestors, the fire was only extinguished to initiate new phases of the year (Samhain and Beltane) and then rekindled from a central sacred fire. For them, there was no separation between their spirituality and their daily lives. Magick was woven into the seams of the most mundane tasks, infusing their lives with the sacred, and this was especially true with the hearth. Herbs were routinely thrown into the fire: handfuls of nettles were fed to the flame to conquer fear, juniper berries encouraged a loving environment, and lavender was tossed in to promote peace. Acorns placed upon the mantel were said to protect the inhabitants, and olive branches were hung on the chimney to prevent lightning strikes.

My favorite folk custom, and the one that demonstrates the hearth's true importance in ancient culture, was that when one was visiting another's home, one must take a bow at the hearth before paying respects to the hosts.

As Pagans, fire is still an important element in our magickal lives. Its transformative powers are used to cast spells of empowerment, to ritually destroy bad habits, and for purification, but the power of the hearth has become lost in our mundane lives. Hearths that once held status in our homes, as they offered comfort, heat, nourishment, and fellowship, have now been replaced with central heating, electric ranges, and microwave ovens. Our personal lives are so completely filled that sitting down to a family meal is almost impossible.

So how do we rekindle the power of the hearth in a modern world? It's simple. We get back to that room in our house that Carl Jung suggested, in his book *Memories, Dreams, Reflections,* represents potential in our dreaming minds, where ideas are transformed and new discoveries are kept in drawers and cupboards. What is this room? The kitchen.

Really, I am not trying to set women back fifty years. I promise. I am only trying to reawaken the wise woman spirit within us all—the keeper of the flame. We need to erase the image of the 1950s housewife, teetering behind her husband with a martini glass and a Jell-O mold, and embrace the hearth keeper as a role of empowerment, for the hearth keeper knew the secrets held in plants that grew among the hedgerows. She was a counselor to those in need. She was a midwife, bread baker, brewmaster, and healer. The hearth keeper was the teller of magnificent tales and the keeper of ancient knowledge. And it was she who passed her secrets on so the next generation would thrive.

Though in the past the hearth keeper was traditionally a women's role, men too are helping to keep modern hearths alive. Most families today require both partners to work, so household responsibilities are divided. In our home, it is Steve who does the laundry, and I take care of the lawn. And though I prepare the majority of the meals, he is responsible for weekend dinners. Since 2001, the number of stay-at-home dads has doubled in the United States from 1.6 to 3.4 percent according to the US Census data. Though the look of the hearth keeper may be changing, the role is no less important.

The best examples of hearth keepers are the hearth goddesses themselves.

- *Caca:* Caca was an ancient Roman hearth goddess who betrayed her brother, Cacus, a fire-eating giant shepherd who was much hated for his bullying and cattle thievery. Caca reported his deeds to one of his victims, and her lover, Recaranus. Recaranus killed Cacus and recovered his stolen cattle. Locals were so pleased that they worshipped Caca with a perpetual fire tended by virgins.

- *Vesta:* Also known as Hestia to the Greeks, Vesta was the Roman goddess of the hearth, home, fire, and state. When asked by her brother, Jupiter, on his ascension to Mount Olympus what wish he could grant her, she requested her eternal virginity. Her temple was situated at the *Forum Romanum*, where it was the duty of the priestesses, known as Vestal Virgins, to keep the eternal flame lit and keep the sanctity of the sacred pledge of safety for Rome.

- *Brighid:* A Celtic triple goddess and daughter of the Dagda, Brighid rules over the hearth, poetry, and childbirth. Most likely beginning as a sun goddess, for she was born at sunrise with rays of fire beaming from her head, Brighid's holy temple was situated at Kildare, where a perpetual flame was tended by nineteen virgins. With the coming of Christianity, this beloved goddess was quickly turned saint.

- *Frigg (Frigga):* Norse Goddess of the hearth, home, childbirth, fertility, marriage, and destiny, she spun the clouds of fate upon a spinning wheel that represented female wisdom. Frigg was known as a nurturing and tender goddess whose sacred animal was the goose. In Germany she was worshipped as Bertha or Holda and was the inspiration for Mother Goose.

It's time to wake up your inner hearth keeper. Take the kids into the kitchen and bake up something wonderfully outrageous on a rainy Sunday afternoon. Practice a little Kitchen Witchery by adding herbs and spices to your recipes that correspond to your magickal needs—heat up your spells with cinnamon, use black pepper for protection, or divine your future with tea leaves.

The kitchen is a great place to reconnect with our families too. I don't know how many times one of my kids has come into the kitchen while I was preparing a meal and asked, "Mom, can I talk to you about something?" By the end of the conversation, not only had we worked out the problem, but they had typically joined in the cooking as well.

Some of my most cherished memories have occurred in a kitchen: years spent cooking with my mother and sisters in my parents' kitchen during the holidays, laughing with my husband and children in our own kitchen as they take another picture of one of my birthday cake "fails" (please stop with the Martha Stewart cakes, family … it's killing my ego!), esbat plans and coffee with my coven-mates at Jean's kitchen nook, and playing Cards Against Humanity with Tom and Nick at their kitchen table.

I consider myself a strong twenty-first-century individual; I am no one's fading violet. But part of that strength was forged by the fiery embers of the wise women of our past. Those strong individuals who kept hearth fires burning through the cold winter nights, who healed the sick and fed their families when it seemed there was nothing left. The ones who foraged for food and weaved the cloth that provided protection from the weather. These were the women who whispered to the moon and entwined the magickal with the mundane. These were the great-granddaughters of the druids and priestesses who kept the Goddess's eternal flame lit. And to them I am thankful.

Hearth and Home Cleansing

This is a great home blessing for a new home or for the old homestead that's been in your family for generations. A smudge stick is used to ritually cleanse the house of negativity and draw in peace and harmony.

You will need:

Cedar and lavender smudge stick
Heat-proof container or abalone shell

For this blessing I chose a cedar and lavender smudge bundle. Cedar repels negative energy, while the lavender draws peace and harmony.

Open your front door. Light the end of your smudge stick until it begins to smoke. If it begins to flame, shake gently or use your shell or fire-proof container to press the stick into until there are only embers and smoke.

Starting at the front door and working deosil, use your hand to direct the smoke in every corner, doorway, and nook and cranny of your home until you have once again reached the front door. As you do this, repeat,

This is a home of love,
This is a home of peace,
This is a home of joy.

When you once again reach the open front door, use your hand to make a pushing gesture through it and say,

Negativity is not welcome here.

Shut the door. Snub out your smudge stick.

You can follow this up by thanking the goddess of the hearth (or house spirit of your choosing) for their protection by lighting a small yellow tea light and leaving a bit of milk and bread near your family's gathering place.

Cooking through the Seasons

One way to reinforce the importance of hearth and home to our children and keep them in tune with the earth's powerful rhythms is by teaching them to eat and cook with what is fresh and available seasonally in your family's region. Eating locally grown seasonal foods benefits us on so many levels:

- *Buying local produce that is in season adds variety to our meals.* Do you ever get in a rut in the produce aisle? It's too easy to grab what's familiar and easy week after week. A bunch of half-ripe bananas, a couple heads of broccoli, a few tasteless tomatoes, and a bag of spinach. Sound familiar? Switching to new foods seasonally helps break up our diet monotony and encourages us to try new fruits and vegetables that we may not have realized grew in our areas.

- *Fresh, local foods add a nutritious punch to our diets.* Produce found in the grocery store has been picked unripe, has been transported over great distances, and then sits in storage before being placed in the produce section of the grocery store. Eating produce that is grown locally means your fruits and vegetables have been picked at their peak of freshness and spend a lot less time in transportation. This equates to approximately three times more nutrition than out-of-season produce.

- *Buying locally helps the environment.* It cuts down on the amount of fossil fuels used in the transportation of produce and cuts our carbon footprint on our fragile earth.

If you planted a garden, this is a perfect place to start. Gather ripe fruits and vegetables and plan menus accordingly. Shop for produce at local farmers' markets or take advantage of Community Supported Agriculture programs (CSAs) offered by farmers. A CSA box is fresh produce that can be purchased directly from local farmers, cutting out the middleman. And don't forget about wild edibles. If you know what you're looking for or have access to a knowledgeable guide, foraging for early greens, such as stinging nettles, or local edible mushrooms is a lot of fun. Let's get to know a few seasonal favorites as we cook through the seasons.

Winter

During the cold, dark days of winter, we look to our larder for sustenance. Jars lined, shelf upon shelf, remind us of summer's glory—jams and jellies, canned vegetables, and sauces all hold the taste of what was and what will be again. But what about fresh vegetables? Availability of fresh foods varies from region to region, especially in the winter months. Obviously, someone in Minnesota, New York, or Idaho will not have the same offerings as someone in Florida, California, or Texas. Some of what we may find in the local farmers' market, greenhouses, or your own backyard winter garden may include brussels sprouts, kale, endive, collards, leeks, squash, carrots, and sweet potatoes. Look for fruit such as passion fruit, oranges, cactus pear, dates, and grapefruit.

❥ Winter Squash

Element: Fire

Ruling Planet: Sun

Energy: Feminine

A versatile vegetable that keeps well long into the chilly winter months if stored in a cool, dry place (up to six months), winter squash is a favorite in our family. Of the over twenty varieties of winter squash and pumpkins, my favorites include butternut squash, for its sweet, nutty flavor perfect for soups and stews; Blue Hubbard squash, with its gray-green skin, offering a sweet orange flesh that tastes similar to sweet potato; and spaghetti squash, which has a stringy flesh when cooked, similar to spaghetti pasta, with a mild flavor that goes well with sauces.

Magickally, squash dishes are a great meal to share with family and friends during the bleak days of winter—they are powerful for deepening relationships. Also use seeds in spells for prosperity, spirituality, and protection.

Roasted Herbed Butternut Squash

1 large butternut squash (peeled and cubed)

3 sprigs rosemary (finely chopped)

3–4 sage leaves (finely chopped)

2 cloves garlic minced

3 tablespoons olive oil

Salt and pepper to taste

Mix cubed squash, herbs, garlic, olive oil, and salt and pepper until well coated. Spread on a baking dish and bake at 400 degrees Fahrenheit for approximately 45 minutes or until the squash is fork-tender and caramelized.

Spring

Spring bursts upon us with wild delight. This is the time for greens. Farmers' markets and backyard gardens are alive with different varieties of lettuce, radishes, asparagus, snow peas, spinach, and chives. You may also find rhubarb, fennel, artichokes, and fava beans. Look to the green-wood for wild edibles, such as fiddlehead ferns, cattail, morel mushrooms, watercress, wood sorrel, and stinging nettle.

☙ Stinging Nettle

Element: Fire

Ruling Planet: Mars

Energy: Masculine

Stinging nettle was considered a spring tonic to our ancestors. This green, which grows abundantly in shady and moist areas all over North America, can appear as early as February and is a powerhouse of nutrition. Packed with vitamins A and C, magnesium, calcium, protein, iron, and potassium, nettles help kick-start your immune system, and, best of all, they are free for the taking. When collecting any wild edible, it is extremely important that you know exactly what you have harvested before you ingest it. The best way to do this is to go with a knowledgeable companion who can show you exactly what to look for. Stinging nettle is one of the easiest wild edibles to identify. If you can't identify it by its straight stems and dark, toothy, heart-shaped leaves, just brush against one. If you didn't feel the prickly sting that can last up to twelve hours, it wasn't a nettle.

Harvesting nettle is best done in the early spring when their shoots are less than six inches from the soil. Wear gloves and use scissors to cut off the tips (the top four leaves).

Nettles must be cooked to release the formic acid that is contained in sacs on the hairs of the leaves. This can be done in two ways: by dehydrating the leaves or cooking them. Nettles are a great replacement for spinach in any recipe and make a comforting tea.

Magickally, sprinkle nettle around your house for protection or wear it as an amulet to ward off negativity. Use nettles in spells for protection, exorcism, lust, or healing.

NETTLE PESTO

This delightful pesto, with its earthy undertones, is a true family favorite at our house. Give it a try, and don't be surprised if you like it better than traditional basil pesto.

3 cups nettles
3–4 cloves garlic (depending on how much you like garlic)
½ cup olive oil
1½ cups parmesan cheese
½ cup pine nuts (I have also used walnuts and sunflower seeds)
Salt to taste

First, blanch the nettles in a saucepan filled with water. Over medium heat, bring water to a boil. Wearing gloves, drop the nettles into boiling water and push them around with a spoon so they are all submerged. Let them sit approximately 30 seconds or so, just long enough to get the sting out. Drain nettles in a colander and cool.

In a food processor, chop garlic cloves, cooled nettles, and olive oil. Next, add parmesan cheese, nuts, and salt to taste, and process until smooth. Makes approximately 1 quart of pesto.

Use in your favorite pasta recipes, on pizza, or as a dip, or substitute it in whatever recipe you would use traditional pesto.

Summer

The air is alive with the hum of bees, and the garden is alive with color. Summer rewards us with lush treasures that are a feast to not only our eyes but also our palates. Farmers' markets and backyard gardens are at their peak, so take advantage of summer's bounty, which may include tomatoes, lettuce, carrots, tomatillos, onions, garlic, beets, and summer squash. Also look for summer fruits, including berries, figs, cherries, apricots, peaches, and melons.

❧ Heirloom Tomatoes

Element: Water

Ruling Planet: Venus

Energy: Feminine

Heirloom tomatoes are absolutely divine during the summer months. With their lovely array of colors, sizes, and shapes and wonderful rich flavor, they epitomize the Norman Rockwell summers of our grandparents.

Heirloom tomatoes can be used to replace hybrid tomatoes in your favorite tomato-based dishes, but to truly appreciate their fabulous flavor, I recommend eating them cold. I like them fresh off the vine or in a salad. Magickally, tomatoes can be used in spells for love, prosperity, and protection.

Heirloom Tomato Caprese Salad

1 large ball mozzarella cheese

4 large heirloom tomatoes

½ cup fresh basil leaves

Olive oil

Balsamic vinegar

Slice mozzarella and heirloom tomatoes approximately ½ inch thick and arrange with basil leaves on a platter. Drizzle olive oil and balsamic vinegar to taste. Serves 4.

Autumn

The countryside parades colorful hues, and the scent of apple and wood smoke perfume the air. It is time to prepare ourselves for the winter's long reign. But wait—the garden still has so much to offer. This is the time to look for okra, corn, eggplant, zucchini, bell peppers, ginger, kohlrabi, and potatoes. Apples, pomegranates, pears, kiwi, quince, dates, pineapple, and kumquats may also be found in local farmers' markets.

☙ Apples
Element: Water

Ruling Planet: Venus

Energy: Feminine

Autumn wouldn't be the same without the sweet taste of apples. For straight-out snacking, I suggest Honeycrisp apples. Their sweet crispness has made them very popular in the last couple of years. My favorite baking apples are Jonagold apples. These juicy little gems are crisp with a tart, fresh taste that can't be beat. When cooked, they hold their shape and retain some of their tartness.

Medicinally, apples have been used to treat gout, headaches, high blood pressure, and heart problems since ancient times. Who hasn't heard the old saying "An apple a day keeps the doctor away"? Magickally, use apples in love spells, for health, for immortality, or in garden magick. This favorite tree of Witches (I know it is one of mine!) is popular for making wands. Also known as the "food of the dead," apples are typically seen on altars at Samhain.

APPLE BREAD PUDDING WITH SALTED CARAMEL SAUCE
For the pudding:

1 cup brown sugar

1¾ cups half and half

¼ cup butter

5 cups cubed crusty bread, such as French

3 cups sliced apples

2 teaspoons ground cinnamon

3 eggs beaten

½ teaspoon vanilla

For the sauce:

1 cup brown sugar

½ cup heavy cream

6 tablespoons salted butter

Pinch of sea salt per serving

Preheat oven to 350 degrees Fahrenheit and grease a 9 × 13-inch baking dish.

In a saucepan, combine brown sugar, half and half, and butter. Cook over medium heat until melted. Set the mixture aside to cool. In a large bowl, combine bread, apples, and cinnamon.

Whisk eggs and vanilla into the cooled half and half, butter, and sugar mixture and pour over bread and apples. Transfer the mixture to the baking dish and bake for approximately 40 minutes or until a knife inserted into middle comes out clean.

While the bread pudding is baking, make the salted caramel sauce. Combine brown sugar, heavy cream, and butter in a saucepan. Bring to a boil over medium heat. Turn heat to low and cook several minutes until thickened.

Serve the sauce over the bread pudding with a pinch of sea salt. Serves 6 to 8.

Stocking Up: Food Preservation 101

Around the turn of sixteenth century, no country manor was complete without a special room tucked near the kitchen or sometimes the dairy, where the lady of the manor could be found concocting rose water to freshen her complexion or medicinal syrups to ease a sensitive stomach. This was also the room were preserves and cordials were prepared, flower essences were distilled, and herbs could be found hanging from racks, their scent clinging to the rafters long after their use. What was this room you might ask? It was the stillroom; part kitchen, distillery, and storage area all wrapped into one, the stillroom was set aside for the lady to perform her housewifely arts.

Tucked behind the jars of aromatic spices, vinegars, and bundles of dried herbs, there was bound to be the lady's "receipt book." Among the tattered pages you could find how much was spent on dry goods for the month or the price of a new horse, but you would also find old family recipes that had been passed down from mother to daughter for generations.

Yes, you could find a wonderful recipe for a Christmas pudding and the perfect cherry cordial, but dig deeper and you could find steadfast herbal remedies for a cough or gout, maybe a poultice for a sprained arm or a tea to calm the nerves. Keep turning the pages and you might be surprised, for sometimes strewn among the recipes were other formulas. You might find a spell for banishing negativity or a list of ingredients for a love charm. The word "receipt" is derived from the Latin *recipere*, "to receive," so a receipt book was a book of "things received" and, in some ways, can be compared to our modern Book of Shadows.

Stillrooms began to die out in the early part of the twentieth century. Modern pharmaceutical practices, commercial food preservation, and mass-produced cosmetics all helped lead to its demise. At best, our modern pantries are a suitable replacement. My own isn't as romantic as the stillrooms of yesteryear. It does have shelves lined with jewel-toned preserves, pickles, fermented veggies, sauces, and dried mixes. I have a shelf dedicated to magickal herbs and another for salves, soaps, and lotions. Depending on the time of year, you may also find braided garlic and bundles of drying herbs—but you will also find my modern washer and dryer, a chest freezer, and two sagging coat racks, weary from the weight of too many coats, sweatshirts, and heavy sweaters.

Although, I have to admit I long for a room of my own for concocting my lotions and potions, creating charm bags, and preserving my own food, one that resonates with the scent of dried rosemary and bergamot, it's probably not going to happen. And that's okay. The important thing is that I keep the tradition of the stillroom alive by practicing the home arts and magickal crafts of those amazing women of the past.

One of my most cherished memories is that of my mom, grandma, and aunt in my grandmother's large kitchen chopping, smashing, stewing, stirring, and sweating as they happily prepared quarts and quarts and quarts of food that we would enjoy all winter long. That was another time, though, right? Why should we preserve our own food now? We're busy and it's much easier to just run to the store and buy a bag of frozen green beans or a jar of jam. The answers—and reasons for preserving food—are the same as reasons for eating seasonally. Locally grown food is more flavorful, contains more nutrition, is less expensive, supports our local farmers, and is good for the environment. And the great thing about preserving your homegrown or locally grown fruits and veggies is that the fresh taste of summer is available to you and your family all year long! So whether you're a dabbler, interested in experimenting with a couple of jars of jam, or you want to go hard-core, supporting most of your family's food needs from your own stores, here is a little Food Preservation 101 to help get you started.

Some of the most common forms of food preservation include:

- *Canning:* This is a great way to preserve your food through pasteurization. High-acid foods, such as tomatoes, fruits, and pickles, can be canned through a method known as water-bath canning. This involves placing your prepared jars in a canner (or large kettle), and making sure water covers the jars by 1 to 2 inches. A lid is placed on the pot as it is brought to a rolling boil. The jars are then left to set in boiling water for the time indicated on the recipe you are using (typically 10 minutes). The jars are then removed and left to sit on the counter, untouched for several hours. You will know if the jars are properly sealed if you press on the middle of the lid and it does *not* spring back. If it does, process the jars again.

    If you are canning non- or low-acid foods like green beans or corn, you must use a pressure canner to kill bacteria that thrive in low-acid foods (botulism, anyone?). These canners can be a little tricky, so if you're new to canning, I suggest starting with the easier water-bath method.

- *Drying:* What's great about drying food is that the finished product takes up a lot less space in the pantry. It's also really easy! I own a food dehydrator, which I absolutely love, but you can dry foods in the oven, set on a low temperature, or air dry them if you live somewhere that gets a lot of sun. Steve found the plans for an outdoor solar dehydrator in a DIY magazine. It turned out great, but we live in Washington State ... I tried to tell him. I store my dehydrated food in sterile, dry glass jars. You can also use zip-top bags that you place in small tins or try vacuum sealing.

- *Pickling:* This is a method of processing fruits and vegetables that involves creating a brine from salt and vinegar. The best-known pickled vegetable is the cucumber, but if you can dream it, you can pickle it. There are tons of amazing recipes out there. Just remember to keep them in the refrigerator or process them with the water-bath method of canning to make sure they are safe.

- *Fermentation:* There is something about the fermentation process that absolutely fascinates me. This is a process in which you are ageing a food with the use of yeast, bacteria, or fungi. Some easy fermentation foods to start with include sauerkraut (cabbage), yogurt (milk), and soft cheeses.

- *Cellaring (Root Cellar):* When I think of "cellaring" food, my mind takes me to episodes of shows like *Little House on the Prairie*, with Pa bursting through a wooden trap door that leads to underground food stores. Truth is, you don't need to literally dig out a cellar. This food preservation method is basically a form of climate control so that foods such as squash, pumpkins, potatoes, and carrots retain their freshness longer. A cool, dry place in the garage or a shed will work just fine.

- *Freezing:* This method is very easy and can really preserve the flavor of your fruits and vegetables. The problem with freezing is space limitation. The freezer above the typical refrigerator-freezer unit in the average kitchen is quite small. Chest freezers that can fit into a pantry or garage are a nice solution but not always feasible. There are also a few tricks to know when freezing foods: blanch greens before storing them, never freeze anything creamy, and freezing food with a high water content is a no-no. Foods that freeze well include berries, peas, cauliflower, broccoli, asparagus, corn, and beans.

Recipes from the Stillroom

Enjoy my version of recipes that may have graced a receipt book in your own family's past.

Rhubarb Earl Grey Tea Jam

Rhubarb (*Rheum rhabarbarum*) is a plant of protection and fidelity. The leaves of this cool-season perennial favorite are toxic, but the stalks are tart and full flavored. There are dozens of rhubarb varieties and everyone has an opinion on which is the best.

I grow two varieties, a red-stalked Valentine rhubarb and a green-stalked variety (the name has been lost) that came from a start from my great-grandfather. Green-stalked varieties are typically more prolific than red varieties, but they have similar flavors, so what it comes down to for most cooks is appearance. When green rhubarb is cooked down, it tends to look a little like … vomit, whereas red rhubarb has a pretty, jewellike quality. My remedy for ugly rhubarb jam: I throw in a few handfuls of red raspberries.

You will need:

1 cup Earl Grey tea (make sure to steep it for about 15 minutes)
10 cups chopped red rhubarb stalks
6 cups sugar
Juice of 1 lime
1 pinch salt
1 1.75-ounce packet pectin
2 tablespoons pure vanilla extract

First, sterilize your jars, lids, and rings in a large (nonreactive) pot of boiling water for about 10 minutes.

In a large kettle, add Earl Grey tea, rhubarb, and sugar. Bring to boil. Add lime juice and a pinch of salt and let it bubble for another 10 minutes.

Add pectin and stir until well combined. Continue to cook for another 3 to 5 minutes.

You can check your jam by dipping a spoon into it. If it coats the back of the spoon evenly, it's ready. Stir in vanilla extract.

Pour into sterilized jars, wipe away any spillage, and apply lids and rings. Process the jars in a water bath for 10 minutes.

Makes approximately 2 quarts.

Raspberry Lemon Balm Jam

In magick, raspberries (*Rubus idaeus*) are used in spells for protection and love, so this jam is the perfect gift for a magickal friend. Though there are many varieties of raspberries, we will be using the common red raspberry that is easily found in farmers' markets everywhere. Note in the instructions below that the lemon balm and sugar mixture should be made the day before; the sugar will absorb the oils of the herb and infuse it with a lovely lemony flavor.

You will need:

2 cups lemon balm leaves

5 cups sugar

6 cups raspberries

Juice of 1 lemon

1 1.75-ounce packet pectin

Crush the lemon balm and place it in a bowl with the sugar. Toss until lemon balm is well distributed. Cover and let set for at least 24 hours.

Sterilize all jars, lids, and rings.

In a large (nonreactive) pot add raspberries and cook on low heat for 10 minutes. As the raspberries simmer, use a spatula to press berries and release their juices.

If you want a seedless jam, remove from heat and strain your berries through a sieve. Then add the strained mixture back to the pot. If you don't mind the seeds, skip this step.

Remove the lemon balm from the sugar and add the sugar and lemon juice to the mixture. Bring to a boil and let the mixture gently bubble for approximately 5 minutes.

Add pectin and combine well. Let the mixture return to a boil and bubble for another 5 to 6 minutes. When jam coats the back of a spoon evenly, it's ready.

Pour into sterilized jars, wipe away any spillage, and apply lids and rings. Process in a water bath for 10 minutes.

Makes approximately 2 quarts.

Strawberry Basil Freezer Jam

Strawberries (*Fragaria vesca*), in magick, are used in spells for love and luck. Well, lucky is the person who samples this delightful jam. With a hint of basil, this jam just tastes Witchy somehow. Use your favorite strawberry variety for this recipe. I usually use a June-bearing berry called Shuksan, but check your local farmers' market for the berry that grows best in your region. This recipe is a no-canning recipe, which keeps the flavors fresh and makes it easier for the little ones to help with the food preservation.

You will need:

4 cups fresh strawberries (2 pounds)

2 cups sugar

5 tablespoons instant pectin

⅓ cup chopped basil leaves

Prepare berries by "hulling," or removing the stems. I use my thumbnail, but you can use a commercial hulling device.

Combine sugar and instant pectin in a bowl. Set aside.

Place strawberries in a large bowl. Use a potato masher to smash up those berries to release their wonderful juice. Add your sugar and pectin mixture and keep stirring for approximately 3 minutes or until sugar is dissolved. Add chopped basil. Ladle jam into freezer-safe containers and let stand for 25 to 30 minutes before placing in the freezer. Makes approximately 2 quarts.

Now how easy was that?

Refrigerator Fire Pickles

Adding the fire element to these easy pickles will empower you with the confidence to take your pickling to the next level! Like I said before, if you can dream it, you can pickle it. Experiment with different vegetable and spice combinations. Omit the peppers and add mint to pickled carrots. How about a little added cumin with pickled cauliflower? The sky is the limit. Refrigerator pickles are easy and last for approximately two months in the refrigerator.

You will need:

12 3–4 inch pickling cucumbers
4 cups water
2 cups apple cider vinegar
10 garlic cloves
2 tablespoons kosher salt
1 tablespoon granulated sugar
1 teaspoon mustard seed
1 teaspoon dill seed
1 teaspoon peppercorns
2 bay leaves
½ cup chopped dill
2 whole red chili peppers
2 grape leaves (optional)
4 sprigs dill

Sterilize jars, lids, and rings.

Clean and cut cucumbers into spears or chips.

In a medium saucepan add water, vinegar, 2 cloves of garlic, salt, and sugar and bring to a boil. Reduce heat and simmer for another 5 minutes. Set aside to cool.

Divide spices, garlic cloves, chopped dill, and chili peppers evenly between two 1-quart jars. An old-fashioned method of retaining crispness was to add a grape leaf to each quart. Crispness was secured by the release of tannins from the grape leaves. I do this and I find it helps, but it is completely optional.

Add prepared cucumbers to each jar and tuck 2 sprigs of dill in each jar. Pour your cooled brine into each jar, covering the cucumbers. Here's a fiery little blessing to say as you pour your brine over your pickles:

Bless this Kitchen Witch with the power of strength.
Blessed element of fire, use no restraint.
I ask for abundance from the Goddess divine
As I mix up my magick in this spicy brine.

Secure lids and rings. Refrigerate for at least a week before indulging in these marvelous pickles. Makes approximately 2 quarts.

If you would like to process your jars in a water bath for added shelf life, do so for 10 minutes. They will store on a shelf for a year.

Pickled Honey Beets

In magick, beets (*Beta vulgaris*), thought of as an aphrodisiac, were used in love spells. So why not add a few pickled beets to recipes for a Beltane supper with your consort!

Once again, this pickling recipe can be prepared with a no-canning method by refrigerating the finished product for at least a week. Pickled beets will keep for approximately 2 months under refrigeration. Or you can you use a water-bath canning method and store them in your pantry for a year.

You will need:

6–7 pounds small whole beets (large beets are fine; cut into quarters)
4 cups water
4 cups apple cider vinegar
2 cups honey
1 tablespoon kosher salt
1 teaspoon ground cloves
2 teaspoons ground cinnamon

Clean and trim the greens from the beets. Leave approximately 1 inch of stem and root. Put the beets into a large pot of water and bring to a boil. Let simmer for approximately 25 minutes or until the beets can be pierced with a fork. Let cool. Once cool, the skin should peel easily away from the beets. You can place whole small beets in jars or slice up larger ones and fill jars.

In a medium saucepan, add water, vinegar, honey, salt, and spices. Bring to a boil, then let simmer for approximately 5 minutes. Cool before adding to beets. Secure jars with lids and rings. Refrigerate for at least a week before tasting, or process for 10 minutes in a water-bath. Makes approximately 2 quarts.

Dehydrating Fruits and Vegetables

Dehydrating fruits and vegetables for snacking or adding to your favorite recipes is fun and easy. As you slice and dice, let the kids fill the trays, allowing them to be a part of the food preservation process. Not only is it a confidence booster, but it will also help entice them to try new flavors.

Here are a few tips to get you started:

• Use fruit that is ripe but not bruised or mushy.

• Yes, you can dehydrate frozen fruits and vegetables.

• Make sure all fruits and vegetables are properly cleaned and are sliced in a consistent thickness to ensure even drying.

• Nonacidic fruits, like apples or bananas, can be coated with lemon, lime, or orange juice to keep them from turning brown.

• Vegetables such as fresh broccoli, cauliflower, carrots, and peas should be blanched before dehydrating to speed up the process.

• Cool all dehydrated fruits and vegetables completely before removing them from trays.

• Before storing your dried treasures, condition them first by storing them in open containers for approximately 3 to 5 days. Give them a shake once in a while; this will ensure enough moisture has evaporated. If condensation begins to appear, put them back in the dehydrator.

• Store dehydrated fruits and vegetables in airtight containers and leave in a cool, dark place.

- Oven drying takes about twice the amount of time to dry fruits and vegetables as a dehydrator. This can be expensive, can heat up the house, and can be dangerous if you have very small children. A food dehydrator is definitely worth the investment. You can pick up a decent one for under fifty dollars.

- Using the power of the sun is another option. Unless you buy or make specialty equipment, it's only a viable option if you live in a region that has continuously high summer temperatures and relatively low humidity.

Favorite Fruit Mix

As summer wanes, we are blessed with an abundance of apples, blueberries, and cherries. One of the ways we enjoy them is dried and put together with walnuts that I purchase from a local farmer. This is a great mix that we add to yogurt and granola or just snack on. If there is any left at Yule, I soak it in rum and add the mix to a very boozy fruitcake.

You will need equal parts of each fruit (dried):

Dried apples
Dried cherries
Dried blueberries
Walnuts (to taste)

To prepare apples, peel, core, and slice into ⅛-inch slices (an apple peeler and corer work great). Coat apples with lemon juice to keep them from turning brown (optional). To prepare cherries, halve and remove pit from each cherry. Prepare blueberries by quickly blanching them in boiling water just until the skins start to crack.

Set the temperature on your food dehydrator to 135 degrees Fahrenheit.

Place the fruit on trays evenly and so that they are not touching one another.

Dry apples for approximately 5 hours or until leathery and pliable. Cherries and blueberries need to dry for approximately 10 hours.

Once all fruits have been dried and conditioned for 3 to 5 days, mix equal parts together and add walnuts to taste. Store in an airtight container in a cool, dark place.

Dried Bean Mixes
Element: Air
Ruling Planet: Mercury
Energy: Masculine

I like to grow and dry my own shelling beans, not only to save seed for later plantings, but also for use in spellcrafting and to enjoy in soups and bean dishes all winter long. Magickally, dried beans can be put in a mojo bag to ward off negativity and used in rattles to frighten away evil spirits. Use dried beans in spells for exorcism, protection, and love.

Here are a few of my favorite varieties:

❧ Scarlett Runner Beans (*Phaseolus coccineus*)

With their lovely scarlet flowers, these quick climbers are a hummingbird favorite. The lovely mottled pink and purple beans are large and darken when dried. They are a thick-skinned bean that I soak in cold water for approximately twelve hours before cooking. They have a mild flavor and are wonderful when mixed with other bean varieties in baked bean dishes.

❧ Black Coco (*Phaseolus vulgaris*)

This is a nice bush variety that doesn't require staking. You can prepare them as you would a snap bean or let them mature for drying. They have a rich flavor that is perfect for soups and, my favorite, black bean burgers.

❧ Burt's Soup Bean (*Phaseolus vulgaris*)

This is a fairly rare heirloom climber. I was introduced to this wonderful variety through a seed exchange held at a nearby organic farm, and I love it! Burt's Soup Bean is a fast grower that has beautiful showy purple blooms. Each eight-inch purple pod holds within it approximately eight brown beans that have a nice meaty flavor. We enjoy them slow-cooked with a little smoked paprika and sea salt. The only place I found online that sells them is Victory Seeds, who specializes in rare and heirloom seeds.

Growing and drying beans is easy and fun. Cooked beans are an excellent source of protein, not to mention vitamins and minerals such as magnesium, folic acid, iron, and zinc. No wonder they are considered a superfood!

Kitchen Witchery Rhyme

Here's a fun Kitchen Witchery rhyme for the kids to say as they help stock the family's stillroom:

I slice and stir and chop and sift.
Learning to cook is an ancient gift.
With a dash of magick and a pinch of love,
As the Goddess wills it—cooking is fun!
Blessed be!

notes

Chapter 5

Into the Greenwood

We are at home among the dog rose and bramble
and feel the tendrils of the otherworld tug gently at our souls.

"Are you missing a child?" A tall man in his fifties, whom I vaguely recognized as a neighbor, was standing in my yard.

"What? No, I don't think so." I was covered in dirt and held a handful of weeds that I had found creeping between my rows of garlic.

He was dressed completely in green with a branch of elderberry sticking out from the brim of his hat. He bore a striking resemblance to a picture I had seen once of Jack in the Green, and that's probably why I hadn't noticed my six-year-old daughter standing behind him. A coy smile swept across his face and he stepped aside, exposing Chloe, who ran to me sobbing.

The green man smiled widely. "I'm Pete," he said. "Your neighbor from up the road."

I was dumbfounded. Pete ... Chloe ... Lost ... I didn't know how to process what he was saying.

"I was working on the water," he said. "Glad I was too. I may not have heard her cries from the house."

My heart was pounding in my throat and tears filled my eyes. I clung to my daughter.

"I didn't even know she had left the yard," I said, feeling like the worst mother ever.

He chuckled quietly. "It happens," he said, and turned to leave.

It happens? I thought. No, it doesn't just happen. How could I be so damned negligent? I held her tighter.

It wasn't until after she had completely calmed down—cookies in one hand and apple juice in the other—that I asked how she had managed to get to the back of Pete and Claudia's 150 acres.

She pointed to the bluff that rises on the south side of our property. "I was Hedge Witching," she said. "I wanted to get some lady fern so I could become invisible."

"Why didn't you tell me? I would have taken you out later this afternoon," I said, failing in my attempt to not sound like I was scolding her.

"I wanted to surprise you by being invisible. There's a perfect spot on the hill for lady fern." She paused. "But then I heard some crows crying out and I went to see what they were doing." She took another drink from her juice.

"What were the crows up to?" I asked, trying to hide how completely terrified I was becoming the more the story unfolded.

"They were chasing a raven. Mama, they were beating the poor raven up, and I had to do something! So I followed it."

"Oh, jeez!" I dropped my head.

Chloe furrowed her brow. "I was just trying to help," she said, then looked to the ground.

"I'm not mad, sweetie. I'm just a little shocked."

"Well, I wouldn't have gotten lost if the stupid raven would just have listened to me. I told him to fly to me and that I would keep him safe and that he could live in my room."

"Well," I interjected. "I don't know about that."

She sighed and took another bite of her cookie. "I guess I wasn't paying much attention because I looked around and I was lost." Tears filled her eyes. "And that stupid raven just took off. Mama ..." She looked at me. "I called for you, but you didn't hear me." She fell into my arms.

My heart lurched and I closed my eyes. And though I knew deep down that it wasn't my fault, I felt that in some way I had failed my daughter. "Well." I swallowed back my pain. "Pete heard your call and now you're home."

"I know," she said. "I thought the raven would have liked my help. Why did he do that, Mama? Why didn't he trust me?"

"The Goddess gave creatures instinct to help protect them in the wild. Besides ..." I kissed her head. "It sounds like he was up to some mischief."

"The crows were the mean ones."

"No, sweetie. The crows were protecting their nest." I tickled her and she began to giggle. "That big ole raven was going to try to steal their eggs."

Chloe became serious again. "I was scared too, Mama. Was that instinct?"

"Yes," I said. "You knew you were lost and you called for help."

She smiled. "And the Goddess sent me my very own Green Man to help me out of the forest."

I gave her a hug. "Pete the Green Man," I mused.

"Oh," Chloe said and dug deep into her jeans pocket. "I forgot something." She pulled out a bit of mangled fern. "I found the fern. Do you want to be invisible with me?"

I laughed. "Yes! Let's be invisible together."

The Hedge Witch

You will hear me talk a lot about a dear friend of mine who lived between the worlds. Choosing to release a life of monetary gain, she came to the Upper Skagit Valley to walk the path of the Hedge Witch.

Through exploration, experimentation, and observation, she became a skilled herbalist, midwife, and magickal practitioner. It wasn't uncommon to find her walking near the dog roses at the river's edge, her head tilted up to let the breeze touch her cheeks; she wore a lithesome expression that reflected a life at peace. And if someone stopped to say hello, she would smile bright-eyed, with an offering of wild chamomile to aid in sleeplessness or chickweed for swelling. Stella was a hedgesitter, or one who teeters between the mundane and magickal worlds.

In Norse mythology these wise women were known as *vǫlur*. They were the clan mothers who provided courage to warriors, wisdom to leaders, inspiration to poets, and healing to the sick. As both midwife and undertaker, she was a fragile link to life and death.

Under the lacy branches of hawthorn or in the cool shadow of the bramble, the wise woman would sit. This is where the spirits of the vegetation approached her in the guise of a furry woodland creature, bird, or insect. It was to her that the secrets of the nine sacred herbs were whispered. It was to her that the healing power of roots, buds, and twigs were revealed. And it was to her that the magick of the elements was shown. The hedgesitter was always grateful for her visions and would return with an offering of a bowl of milk or oatmeal in gratitude.

Modern Hedge Witches may no longer be traipsing about the forest's edges foraging for herbal supplies, but they are exploring herbalism by growing culinary, medicinal, or magickal herbs and applying their uses accordingly. They may not be whispering inspiring words into poet's ears, but they are inspiring friends, family, and coworkers with an infectious spirit and sage advice. They may not be providing courage to the warrior class, but they are encouraging others to believe in themselves and are a spiritual guiding light to seekers of the Craft. The hedges of today's magickal practitioners are no longer a physical boundary between the wilderness and the homestead but a metaphorical border that connects us to the otherworld, its tangled roots helping to hold our connection to the magick and wisdom of the wise women and cunning men of old, steadfast within our souls.

A Hedge Witching We Shall Go!

Hedge Witching is a term our family uses when gathering magickal supplies from wild areas. In eastern Skagit County, nature holds true to her wild abandon, and many gardeners work nonstop to keep her tangled fingers from overtaking their yards and gardens.

Stepping off our back porch, one can easily find hazelnuts for wisdom and yarrow to repel negativity. Along the riverbank I find dog roses for love and willow for healing. Near the roadside is columbine for courage and foxglove for faerie magick. We have learned we are not separate from nature here but just one of the delicate threads that make up the earth's glorious tapestry. So practicing respectful gathering methods is a must. Here are few dos and don'ts when gathering magickal supplies:

- Never, ever take from a plant whose identity you are not 100 percent sure of.
- Never pick plants that are endangered or protected.
- Try to connect with the spirit of the plant and ask nicely for a bud, twig, or leaf—and don't forget to say thank you.
- If at all possible, take nuts, twigs, leaves, and so on that have already fallen.
- Don't be greedy. It doesn't take an armload of St. John's wort to make a tincture.
- Avoid roadside picking where chemicals may have been used.
- Stick together, especially with your littlest Witchlings. If you do get separated, advise them to sit tight and call out so you can find them.
- Make it an educational romp. Ask your kids key questions about local flora and fauna. Be prepared with a well-illustrated plant guide.
- Bring snacks and plenty of water. Enjoy being in nature's classroom.

An Herbal Medicine Cabinet

The Hedge Witch was not only a knowledgeable herbalist, midwife, hearth keeper, and magickal practitioner, she was also an alchemist! Practice a little modern alchemy with these basic recipes for lotions, potions, tonics, salves, and soaps. Experiment by adding herbs and essential oils for your magickal, medicinal, or beauty needs. Most are easy enough to involve the kids in the making, and they make great gifts for any occasion.

Dandelion Vinegar Tonic

> ◀ Dandelion (*Taraxacum officinale*)
> *Element:* Air
> *Ruling Planet:* Jupiter
> *Energy:* Masculine

Never, ever curse the bright, smiling yellow faces of the dandelions that seem to pop up every spring, much to the chagrin of most gardeners. Magickally, dandelions can be used in wish spells, for divination, or for calling spirits. Medicinally, they have been used to stimulate the digestive system, restore the mineral balance to the kidneys, and detoxify the liver for hundreds of years. Dandelions are packed with potassium, calcium, and high amounts of vitamins, which make them a highly nutritious spring green.

To capture a bit of their health benefits all year long, steep the dandelions (root and all) in apple cider vinegar. It can be taken as a tonic or used in place of other vinegars in your favorite recipes.

You will need:

Dandelion greens and roots

1-quart jar

Apple cider vinegar

Plastic lid or wax paper and a rubber band

You will need to dig enough dandelions to completely fill a 1-quart jar (approximately 10). Make sure to thoroughly rinse the greens and scrub the roots until they are free of dirt. Pack the jar with dandelions and pour the apple cider vinegar until it completely covers the dandelions. Cover the jar with a plastic screw-on lid or wax paper and a rubber band (vinegar reacts to metal lids). You may want to label and date your jar. This helps if you are making multiple batches of herbal vinegars over a matter of days or weeks. Place in a dark place in your pantry or in a cupboard for at least 6 weeks. After 6 to 8 weeks, use a sieve to drain your vinegar. You can leave it in the quart jar or use a decorative bottle to store your vinegar.

Plantain Healing Spell

◀ Plantain (*Plantago* spp.)
  Element: Earth
  Ruling Planet: Venus
  Energy: Feminine

This plantain is not related to the *Musa* ×*paradisiaca* plantain, a less sweet member of the banana family. It is a common weed that can be found in Europe, North America, and parts of Asia, and if you check, you will most likely find this in your own backyard. Its folk names include ripple grass, snakebite, ribwort, waybroad, and Patrick's dock. Medicinally, plantain can be taken as a tincture or tea to relieve indigestion. Externally, use plantain to relieve rashes, stings, and snakebites. Its anti-inflammatory and antibacterial qualities make it great for healing minor wounds. Magickally, use plantain in spells for protection, healing, and strength. Folklore dictates that if you carry a plantain leaf in your pocket, it will protect you from snakebites.

For this spell, we will be focusing on sending out healing energy. You will need:

1 tea light
1 small cauldron or fireproof container
Ground dried plantain

Light the tea light and place it in a small cauldron or fireproof container. Whether you're sending positive healing vibrations for a sick friend or using this as part of an earth-healing ritual, focus clearly on the fruition of your intent. Can you see your friend clearly healed or a sky clear of pollution? Good.

Now, as you sprinkle the ground plantain over the flame, say,

Healing energy within the power of plantain,
We ask for renewal and a release from pain.
Wholeness and light surround us, three times three.
As I will it, so mote it be.

Let the candle burn out in a safe place.

Green Man Salve

This is a great salve that combines the healing powers of comfrey, known for its quick healing qualities on superficial wounds; yarrow, for its properties as a mild pain reliever and antispasmodic; and plantain, for its anti-itch and anti-inflammatory qualities. With the addition of lavender essential oil's microbial properties, it's wonderful for stings, abrasions, rashes, and chapped or dry skin patches.

The best time to gather these herbs is around midsummer when everything is in full leaf and concentrating their healing properties to their parts above ground. Dried herbs can also be purchased through herb craft–supply companies.

To infuse oil, gather enough plant/herbal material to fill a quart jar. Bruise and tear herbs to help release their healing oils, and pack them into the jar. Pour olive oil (you can also use other oil, such as grape seed, sunflower, etc.) in the jar, cover it with a lid, and place it on a sunny window for three weeks or more. You may want to give it a shake once in a while. When your infusion is ready, pour it through a cheesecloth-lined sieve. Make sure to squeeze every bit of the oil out of the plants. Keep infused oil in a cool, dark place until ready for use.

To make the Green Man salve, you will need:

1 cup coconut oil
1 cup infused olive oil (comfrey, plantain, and yarrow)
½ cup beeswax
15–20 drops lavender essential oil

On low heat, use a double boiler to slowly heat coconut oil and olive oil. Stir in beeswax. When melted, take off heat and let set for approximately 10 minutes. Add lavender essential oil. Makes approximately 16 ounces of salve, which will make 4 4-ounce containers.

Antifungal Salve

From athlete's foot to ringworm, fungus is most definitely among us! Anyone with active kids will find this to be true. Here is a salve to help combat this pesky little problem. The secret is in the black walnut hulls, which are antiparasitic, antifungal, antibacterial, and an antiseptic. You can find them through any herbal craft–supply company. Infuse black walnut hulls in olive oil in a small container for at least three weeks before preparing salve.

You will need:

½ cup cocoa butter

1 cup olive oil infused with black walnut hulls

½ cup beeswax

50 drops tea tree essential oil

50 drops lavender essential oil

20 drops lemongrass essential oil

On low heat in a double boiler, mix cocoa butter, infused olive oil, and beeswax. Once the ingredients have melted, let the mixture set over the heat for approximately 15 minutes. Take off heat and add essential oils. Store in a cool, dark place.

Use on affected areas twice a day. If problems persist, see your physician.

Basic Creamy Milk Soap

The day before you make your soap, measure out your milk and freeze it in ice cube trays for 24 hours.

You will need:

4.3 ounces lye (sodium hydroxide)

10 ounces milk (goat, cow, hemp, almond, coconut, soy)

10 ounces coconut oil

10 ounces olive oil

5 ounces sweet almond oil (or substitute with hemp, avocado, sunflower, or grape seed oil)

Additives such as essential oil, oatmeal, honey, etc.

Rubber gloves

Goggles

Digital scale

Dust mask or other mouth covering

Two glass bowls (one smaller that will nest into the larger bowl)

Potato masher

Stainless steel or enamel-lined pot

Immersion blender (stick blender)

Cooking thermometer

Soap molds

Wearing rubber gloves, goggles, and a mouth covering, measure out your lye and set aside.

Place the premeasured frozen milk in a bowl and splash it with just a bit of water, which will help to kick-start the lye solution. Create an ice bath by placing ice cubes and water in the larger bowl, and place the smaller bowl containing the frozen milk inside it.

Slowly sprinkle about ¼ of the lye onto the frozen milk. Be careful to avoid contact with skin. Use a stainless steel potato masher to work it into the mixture. Continue this process until all the lye is incorporated. Replace ice cubes in the ice bath as they melt. It is important to keep the mixture cold and that every bit of lye is dissolved, so don't rush this step. As the lye dissolves, it will most likely turn bright yellow to orange. That is normal. If the mixture turns dark brown, the lye has scorched the milk and the process must be started over. Once lye is properly incorporated, set aside.

In a stainless steel or enamel-lined pot melt the coconut oil on low heat until liquefied. Add olive and sweet almond oil and heat until 90 to 100 degrees Fahrenheit.

Add your milk and lye mixture to the oil mixture and use a stick (immersion) blender to bring the mixture to "trace," when the soap is thick enough to hold an outline when drizzled across the surface.

Add any additional ingredients, such as essential oils, oatmeal, honey, and so on. Quickly pour the mixture into molds and let rest for 24 hours. Unmold and let cure for 4 to 6 weeks. Yields about 2.5 pounds of soap.

Lip Balm

This one is easy enough for the kids to help with! You will need:

3 tablespoons cocoa butter

3 tablespoons coconut oil

3 tablespoons beeswax pastilles (or grated beeswax)

10 drops essential oil of your choice (Peppermint is a good one to start out with.)

Lip balm tubes or small containers

In a double boiler, on medium-low heat combine cocoa butter, coconut oil, and beeswax. Heat until melted. When completely melted, immediately take the mixture off heat and quickly add essential oil. Fill containers and let them firm up on the counter or in the refrigerator. Makes approximately 15 tubes of lip balm.

Calendula Body Butter

This wonderful cream is infused with the healing properties of calendula. You will need:

½ cup cocoa butter

¼ cup calendula infused olive oil (see page 177 for infusing instructions)

¼ cup sweet almond oil

20 drops lavender essential oil (optional)

In a double boiler heat cocoa butter, infused olive oil, and almond oil over medium-low heat until melted. Add essential oil (optional) and mix. Transfer to a bowl and let cool approximately an hour or until the oil just starts to solidify. With a hand mixer, beat the mixture until it resembles whipped cream and stiff peaks form. Transfer it to a container and use within 3 months. Makes approximately 8 ounces.

Orange Bergamot Sugar Scrub

Use this orange bergamot sugar scrub to give your skin a soft glow and to promote peace and tranquility.

You will need:

1 tablespoon dried orange peel
1 cup granulated sugar
½ cup coconut oil
1 drop jojoba oil
10 drops bergamot essential oil

Mix orange peel and sugar. Add the oils. Mix well. Pour into container and enjoy. Makes approximately 12 ounces.

Easy Laundry Detergent

This is an easy and very inexpensive way to deal with laundry. And because this is a low-suds detergent, it can be used in both standard and high-efficiency washers.

You will need:

4 cups borax
4 cups washing soda
2 bars organic soap (How about your own homemade?)
1 cup baking soda
25–30 drops essential oil (optional)
Cheese grater
1-gallon container with lid

Grate the soap and set aside.

In your container, mix borax, washing soda, and baking soda. Add grated soap and thoroughly mix. Add essential oil if desired; mix thoroughly. Makes about 84 ounces. Use 1 to 3 tablespoons per load.

A Witch's Dozen of Magickal Herbs

In my pantry, tucked neatly on shelves near the lavender soap, salves, and balms, are jars of herbs that have been grown according to astrological timing, lovingly tended, dried, and stored for magickal purposes. When curious friends find our family's personal "magickal apothecary," they tend to be disappointed.

"Where's the eye of newt and toe of frog?" I am asked.

I laugh. "Well, the eye of newt is in the kitchen spice cabinet and the toe of frog is presently trying to take over my pond." I point toward my garden.

The looks I get are puzzling, but I am very familiar with old folk names for plants and can be pretty quick with the Witchy comebacks. "Eye of newt," I know, was once a name for mustard seed, and "toe of frog" was buttercup—a plant that thrives in our temperate Pacific Northwest climate.

Since I am also a practical Witch, I only store what I know I can grow myself or what will be used consistently in my spellcrafting. So you will probably not see sorcerer's berry (belladonna) or brain thief (mandrake) in my larder, but you will find plenty of elf leaf (lavender), ground apple (chamomile), and knitback (comfrey) that all work wonderfully for my magickal needs.

Here are a few tips and tricks for gathering and drying your own magickal herbs:

- There are many practitioners who use a ritual knife called a boline for harvesting magickal plants. You can do this, but it is not necessary. I have an old pair of scissors I have used for years.

- Most definitely use moon phase or astrological timing for gathering herbs. The full moon is a great time for harvesting magickal herbs, as are the fire signs of Leo, Aries, and Sagittarius.

- Gather your herbs in the morning just after the dew has evaporated to minimize wilting and capture essential oils.

- Pick your herbs when the blooms are budding out, but not yet in full bloom.

- If you will be gathering large quantities of plant material, keep harvested plants covered with a cloth to prevent sun damage.

- Never dry your herbs in the sun. This will damage the color, flavor, and magickal strength of your herbs.

- Less tender herbs such as lavender, rosemary, and sage can be bundled and hung indoors upside down. I hang my herbs in the pantry.

- Food dehydrators work great for drying tender plants such as basil, mints, and lemon balm. Follow the instructions on your food dehydrator.

- Tender herbs can be bundled and hung to dry, but protect their leaves by putting the bundles in paper lunch bags, open at the bottom, so air can still circulate around them.

Time to take a peek at the magickal herbs we have lining our shelves. Mind you, we do look to wild sources as well, but those are only gathered as needed. All of the herbs listed were chosen for practicality and reliability. No need for exotic plant material that requires special handling; in my experience these tried-and-true herbs that can be easily grown in most regions do the trick just fine.

❧ Basil (*Ocimum basilicum*)

Element: Fire

Ruling Planet: Mars

Energy: Masculine

This annual used in many Italian dishes was once known as "witch's herb" because it was once believed that witches drank the juice of the basil plant before flying on their broomsticks. When carried in a pocket or purse, this herb attracts money. Use basil in incense blends for astral travel and for spells concerning protection, wealth, love, and exorcism.

✦ Borage (*Borago officinalis*)
Element: Air
Ruling Planet: Jupiter
Energy: Masculine

This happy herbaceous annual, with its lovely star-shaped flowers, is easy to grow and spreads like wildfire. Tuck borage into your pocket when you're in need of a little courage, or sprinkle the dried herb around your home for protection. It's great for increasing psychic abilities when drunk in tea. Place a bouquet near you when doing divination. Use in spells for happiness, psychic powers, protection, peace, happiness, and courage.

✦ Chamomile (*Chamaemelum nobile*)
Element: Water
Ruling Planet: Sun
Energy: Masculine

This low-spreading plant with daisy-like flowers is most definitely a plant of calm and relaxation. Use in tea and dream pillows for restfulness and prophetic dreams. This is a great herb to add to a bath before ritual and for attracting peace and love. Place chamomile in your purse to promote wealth, and sprinkle around your property to remove curses cast against you. Use in spells for wealth, rest, love, purification, balance, and dreams.

✦ Comfrey (*Symphytum officinale*)
Element: Water
Ruling Planet: Saturn
Energy: Feminine

Also known as boneset for its long history as a medicinal plant, this hairy-leafed plant that grows in abundant masses is known for offering protection to travelers. Comfrey is a nice addition to charm bags for aid in healing and drawing people together. Use in spells for travel, money, bringing together, healing, and protection.

◄ Lavender (*Lavandula angustifolia*)
Element: Air
Ruling Planet: Mercury
Energy: Masculine

I truly love this perennial shrub, a favorite of the Fae. With a scent to die for, it's no wonder it is a successful herb in love spells. Use in smudge sticks to bring peace to your home or use in a bath for its calming effect. To see ghosts, it is said, carry lavender with you, and it can also be worn to protect you from the evil eye. Make a faerie besom from the stems! Use in spells for faerie magick, love, protection, peace, calm, happiness, purification, and longevity.

◄ Lemon Balm (*Melissa officinalis*)
Element: Water
Ruling Planet: Moon
Energy: Feminine

I love this perennial of the mint family, but if you don't want it spreading everywhere, pot it. Use in sachets and in tea for its calming effect and to relieve the blues. Sacred to Diana, use this herb in spells for animal healing. Also use lemon balm for happiness, love, success, compassion, fertility, depression, healing, and memory.

◄ Mugwort (*Artemisia vulgaris*)
Element: Earth
Ruling Planet: Venus (Moon)
Energy: Feminine

A traveler's herb, mugwort can be placed in shoes to retain strength on long walks or carried in a pocket to bring one safely home. Drunk as tea, it aids in astral projection. Burn mugwort before divination practices or rub the herb on divinatory tools to increase power. For vivid dreams, add mugwort to a dream pillow or hang near your bed. Use mugwort in spells for psychic powers, protection, dreams, strength, travel, and cleansing.

◖ Rosemary (*Rosmarinus officinalis*)

Element: Fire
Ruling Planet: Sun
Energy: Masculine

Grow rosemary near your home to attract elves to your property. Put it in sachets or tuck it near a desk or study area to allow rosemary's distinctive earthy fragrance to enhance your power of thought. Before a healing ritual, rinse your hands in rosemary-infused water. Add rosemary to incense to rid negativity. Use rosemary in spells for youth, memory, purification, dreams, sleep, lust, love, and cleansing.

◖ Rue (*Ruta graveolens*)

Element: Fire
Ruling Planet: Mars
Energy: Masculine

The presence of rue in the garden is a clear indication of protection. This woody evergreen, which produces yellow flowers, can be potted and brought indoors to denote sacred space. Use rue in healing spells. It is said that placing rue on your forehead can relieve headaches. Add this herb to your bathwater to break hexes against you, or hang above a doorway to ease anxiety. Use rue in spells for anxiety, health, clarity, protection, and balance.

◖ Sage (*Salvia officinalis*)

Element: Air
Ruling Planet: Jupiter
Energy: Masculine

Thought of as the insurer of long life, sage has long been connected to healing and wisdom. To cleanse your ritual space or home, smudge with sage. Carry sage in your pocket to promote wisdom, and write wishes on sage leaves and tuck them under your pillow. Use sage for spells connected with healing, wisdom, wishes, purification, and longevity.

◄ᠯ Spearmint (*Mentha spicata*)
Element: Water
Ruling Planet: Venus
Energy: Feminine

This protective member of the mint family can be stuffed in sachets or dream pillows for protection during sleep and to promote vivid dreams. Its cooling qualities aid in healing spells. Put in a charm bag for protection and wealth, or leave a few sprigs at your altar to aid in your magick. Use spearmint in spells for lust, money, protection, sleep, clarity, and healing.

◄ᠯ Thyme (*Thymus vulgaris*)
Element: Water
Ruling Planet: Venus
Energy: Feminine

This sweet, low-growing woody herb is a longtime garden favorite. The Romans washed in thyme-infused water to enhance their attractiveness and carried it around to ward off snakes. Burn thyme to attract good health or to purify ritual space. Use thyme in dream pillows to ensure a good night's sleep. Use in spells for courage, healing, purification, sleep, psychic powers, love, and peace.

◄ᠯ Yarrow (*Achillea millefolium*)
Element: Water
Ruling Planet: Venus
Energy: Feminine

This feathery perennial with lovely heads of tightly packed pink to white flowers is one of my favorite magickal herbs. It was used medicinally for thousands of years for treating external wounds and was drunk as tea for melancholy. It was hung as wedding decor to ensure the couple's happiness for seven years. Yarrow is an herb of attraction and can be used in spells to attract love, courage, or friendship. Drink yarrow tea to improve psychic powers, and grow plenty in your garden to attract the Fae. Use yarrow in spells for courage, love, faerie magick, psychic powers, divination, and attraction.

Tea Blends

Whether you want to relax, feel invigorated, or create a unique gift for someone special, creating your very own tea blends is a great way to get the benefits of healthful herbs, and it's a lot less expensive.

The trick to creating your own tea blends is as simple as three, two, one.

Three: Discern the action of the tea you want to create. Are you looking for a tea to help you prepare for ritual? Maybe you want to ease an upset stomach, aid in dream work, or help calm your nerves. Use approximately three parts of this herb or herbs.

Two: Now choose an herb or two that complement the action of your primary herb or herbs. Blend two parts of this herb or herbs to your blend.

One: Time to add a little pizzazz to your blend. Use one part of an herb or herbs to increase the potency and enhance the flavor.

Homemade tea blends can be very simple or as complicated as you please. The three-two-one method is just a guideline. Enjoy experimenting with herbs and spices for their taste, health benefits, and magickal benefits. And letting the kids create their own tea blends is a fun, hands-on approach to introducing herbalism. We love to create personalized tea blends for our magickal friends at Yule. A small bag of tea, along with a pretty mug and a tea ball, makes a lovely gift. Your tea blends will keep six to twelve months in an airtight container. Here are a few simple blends to kick-start your creativity:

Love Spell Tea Blend

This tea blend was created to promote love and tranquility.

3 parts peppermint
2 parts rose hips
1 part licorice root

Place 2 tablespoons per serving in a tea ball or bag. Add boiling water and let steep for 10 minutes.

Let Me Sleep Tea Blend

Try this blend to shut down an overactive mind and lull you back to sleep.

3 parts vervain
2 parts chamomile
1 part lavender

Place 2 tablespoons per serving in a tea ball or bag. Add boiling water and let steep for 10 minutes.

Moon-Time Tea Blend

A comforting blend to ease the symptoms associated with menstrual cycles. Makes a great coming-of-age gift for a moon ritual or Red Tent party.

1 part cramp bark
1 part marshmallow root
1 part spearmint
½ part skullcap
½ part passionflower
¼ part ginger root
¼ part chaste tree berries

Place 2 tablespoons per serving in a tea ball or bag. Add boiling water and let steep for 10 minutes.

Dream Traveler Tea Blend

Want to know where your dreams are taking you? This blend promotes active dreaming.

2 parts mugwort
2 parts chamomile
1 part calendula
1 part spearmint

Place 2 tablespoons per serving in a tea ball or bag. Add boiling water and let steep for 10 minutes.

Chapter 6

"Green" Witchery

Can you feel her pain, my child?
We must learn from the mistakes
of our grandfathers ... before it's too late.

Living in the foothills of the North Cascade Mountain Range in the
Pacific Northwest, my family and I spend a lot of time in nature.
How could we not? The Goddess has blessed us with the cragged,
snow-capped peaks of the Cascade Mountains that reach high into our
eastern skies; the Salish Sea, dotted with the beautiful San Juan island
chain, to our west; and, standing sentinel among us like the Ents of
Tolkien's realm, giant conifers softly draped with moss and lichen.

Here, nature is an extension of ourselves. It is our classroom, our
pantry, our medicine chest. It is a place to relax, to explore, and to discover the magick within everything that lives and grows in this lush
landscape. I have taught my children to look upon our environment as a
gift, a living, breathing entity that has been entrusted to us to take care
of, and to pass on the knowledge of its care to the next generation.

But, sadly, somewhere along the line we have forgotten our inter-connectivity with the earth and that we are neither above nor separate from the rest of nature. In doing this, we have failed Mother Gaia. We have exhausted her resources, polluted her skies, and poisoned her waters. We have become greedy and wasteful, and if change doesn't happen quickly, we will lose everything.

Green Habits to Live By

If we all do our part, no matter how small, we can make a difference. I'm not talking about grand gestures—no need to sell your house and catch a Greenpeace ship to protest whaling or live in the top of a three-hundred-foot Redwood tree to save forestland (though that would be amazing, and I really wish I had the guts to do that). Small gestures are just as important. Remember, one small pebble can cause a mighty ripple. Here are a few habits to live by:

Be a Resourceful Sorceress

Whether you need school clothes for the kids, are looking for a creative gift, or need a few magickal supplies, get to know your local thrift shops, clothing exchanges, consignment shops, flea markets, and junk and antique stores. Don't forget websites like Craigslist and apps like FreeShare as well. Shopping and donating to businesses that sell repurposed goods is a great way to keep our landfills free of debris, support small, local businesses, and save a little money.

At thrift stores I have found several cauldrons, fabric that made lovely altar cloths, clothing I repurposed for ritual wear, and tons of crafting supplies that the kids and I have used for magickal crafting and for use at our Greenwood Day Camp.

I have made some fabulous purchases at thrift stores, but my over-exuberance has, at times, led me to make a few blunders. So remember, before getting too excited about the amazing velvet dress or awesome Doc Martens boots, make sure to check the item over carefully to make sure all seams are intact, all zippers are working, and there are no major stains, cracks, or holes. Thrift and junk shops sell everything as is, so when you get your treasures home, wash them. I like to go a step further when purchasing secondhand items that will be repurposed for ritual by giving them a good psychic cleansing as well. I don't need someone else's negative energy clouding my magickal treasures.

When donating items, don't include things that you know are broken or beyond repair. Wash all clothing, bedding, pet, and bath items. Attach items to be purchased as a pair or those that have remote devices by tying or taping them together. If donating computers, remember to erase the hard drives.

Part of being a resourceful sorceress is learning to repurpose items that you may have otherwise discarded at home. Containers, glass jars, buckets, gadgets, and discarded tins can live on to fulfill other purposes. I've seen some pretty creative items, including cheese graters made into lighting and old doors transformed into garden gates. We made an old desk into an island for our kitchen, a greenhouse from glass sliding doors intended for the landfill, and a swimming pool from a trout-rearing freestanding pond that the Department of Fish and Wildlife was discarding. So before throwing away the unwanted pallets or collection of keys, take another look at them. With a little ingenuity, you can transform trash into treasure and help save the planet to boot!

Be a Recycling Wizard

One day, not too long ago, I found Elijah in the kitchen, hands on his hips and a scowl on his face. "Mom," he said, "we need to talk."

A nervous ripple ran up my spine. He stood with three glass containers and two tuna cans lined up on the kitchen counter.

"What did I do?" I felt like I was twelve.

"I was going through some of the recycling containers and I found these. I think some people in this family are getting lazy." He pointed to the glass jars that were coated with a greasy film that hinted to their past contents. The tuna cans still wore the paper labels, and their odor gave away that they had not been properly rinsed.

"Uhh, that wasn't me. It was probably your father." I completely threw Steve under the bus, but in all honesty, he is our laziest recycler.

"We need to be a little more attentive, Mom." He added, "And I noticed that you came home with groceries in a plastic bag."

"I had washed the cloth bags, Elijah, and forgot to put them back in the car." I was waiting to have to explain why I was up so late and why the pile of dirty clothes was still on the floor in my room...Geesh.

Recycling practices have been ingrained into my children. It is as natural to them as breathing, and Elijah is the fiercest of my eco-warriors. At family get-togethers, held at homes of members who do not recycle, he packs our contribution of the trash to take back to our home, where it can be recycled. He has rigged up his mountain bike to hold a small trash bin on the front of it for roadside cleanup and he makes sure our own recycling containers are properly separated and cleaned. Does he get a little militant at times? Yes, but I will forgive him that.

Teaching our children to be recycling wizards is essential to our overburdened earth, which supports over seven billion people, and I believe it is a crucial part of our practice as practitioners of an earth-based religion. Here are few ways to instill habitual recycling practices:

- *Creatively mark recycling containers.* This can make separating recyclables enjoyable. Let the kids design the containers and don't forget to put pictures on them so that your smallest Witchlings know what goes where.

- *Combine play with cleanup* by participating in park, beach, trail, or roadside cleanup events. These could be part of a planned community or coven effort or just a family affair!

- *Host trash-to-treasure parties.* Have the kids collect items such as toilet paper rolls, bottle caps, cardboard, and fabric scraps, and invite their friends over to get creative.

- *Tour your local recycling center.* This is a great way for the older kids to get a handle on how and why recycling works.

- *Be a role model.* Recycling isn't something to be done around Earth Day, only to be forgotten a couple of weeks later. Habitual recycling practices ensure that your children will continue recycling into adulthood.

Be a Composting Alchemist

When most people think of recycling, they tend to think of colorful bins full of plastic bottles, aluminum cans, or flattened cardboard boxes. I like to think of eggshells, coffee grounds, yard waste, and vegetable scraps as well.

Almost 30 percent of our landfill waste is made up of organic material that, as it breaks down, releases methane gas (global warming, anyone?). Proper composting of organic material not only keeps a substantial amount of green and brown matter out of our landfills but also helps create new soil that returns much-needed nutrients to our earth.

For the property owner, composting can be done cheaply and easily in a shady area of your lawn or garden. For urbanites there are other options. Take advantage of free compost drop-off points and community gardens that will take your food scraps. Some cities are experimenting with curbside food-waste pickup. There are also some full-service companies who, for a fee, will pick up your yard waste for composting.

If you always wanted to try composting but felt intimidated by the process, here are a few things you need to know:

- For composting to work successfully, you need to have equal parts brown matter (leaf or yard debris), which produces carbon, and green matter (kitchen scraps or grass clippings), which produces nitrogen, along with a little water to help it all break down.
- Never include dairy or meat scraps with your kitchen scraps. They will attract rodents and slow down the composting process.
- Kitchen scraps may include eggshells, coffee grounds, tea bags, vegetable and fruit scraps, rice, noodles, grains, corn husks and cobs, potato scraps, and old bread products.
- Layer your brown and green matter equally and keep it moist by adding water and covering.

- Add kitchen scraps to your compost bed by burying within the compost pile.

- Routinely turn your compost with a pitchfork or shovel. This keeps air circulating and helps it break down.

- Compost piles that smell bad are most likely out of balance. You may need to add more brown matter or water. It might not be getting enough oxygen and needs to be turned more often.

Making Energy Conservation Fun

On those nights when the moon's glow seems especially bright, lighting the yard with an ethereal glow, and the honeysuckle seems especially sweet, we turn off the breaker that attaches us to the rest of world. The quiet that accompanies this action changes our perspective on our natural world.

When Joshua was little, he would say, "Do you hear that, Mama?"

"No, I don't hear anything," I would answer.

"It's the sound of silence, Mama."

Silence in its purest form is an odd experience. At first it's deafening, as if no other sound can penetrate its insulating grip. But then you begin to hear things, things you may have not noticed before—a branch swinging softly in the breeze, the hum of bees in the comfrey, the sound of children playing in a yard across the river.

On these nights, when we disconnect from the modern world, I feel a deep connection not only to my family, but also to the natural world we are so tightly woven with. I am sister to the deer that lies just beyond our periphery and to the crow that coos in the hemlock on the bluff. I am one with the elements, who stir my every emotion.

We light a fire in the small fireplace in the gazebo, and by the light of a dozen flickering flames we partake in a meal that is enjoyed at a slower pace. The fruits of our labor are truly enjoyed on these nights. We play games until the lemon balm has lost its power and we are bombarded by the hum of a thousand mosquitos.

"Time to get back to reality?" I ask as I swat my face.

"I think so," Steve says and points to our sleepy kids.

I am always the last to go in, savoring the night's beauty. I stand beneath the silvery moon. "Thank you, dear lady," I say. "Thank you for my family and for the night and especially for the beauty of silence."

That's about the time I hear the click of the breaker box. The modern world comes roaring back, full of hums and beeps and pings. But as I return to the modern world, I am transformed every time by the sound of silence.

Turning off the modern world for even a couple of hours is one way to conserve a little energy and enjoy time with the family. Light candles safely and have some games and snacks at the ready. Listen to the sound of silence. What sounds do you hear that are typically drowned out by the hum of appliances and the drone of the television?

Here are a few more simple things, recommended by the Environmental Protection Agency, that you can do to cut energy costs:

- *Plant trees or shrubs.* Who knew! But planting trees and shrubs on your property can help cut cooling costs up to 40 percent. The rule of thumb is to plant taller deciduous trees on the eastern and western sides of your home. Why not the southern side? Because it is the roof and the western and eastern walls that are affected by the summer's high rising and setting sun.

- *Change those bulbs.* Simply changing to energy-efficient compact florescent bulbs can save you money. CFL bulbs last about ten times longer than an incandescent bulb and use approximately 75 percent less energy.

- *Add insulation to your home.* Heating and cooling costs can be cut considerably just by making sure your home is properly insulated. Check attic and floor spaces to make sure your insulation is up to par. The amount you need depends on the climate in your region.

- *Take it easy on the water.* A long hot shower in the morning is a nice way to wake up, right? But what is it doing to your water and electric bills, let alone to the environment? By taking quick showers and being mindful of water usage during meal preparation and cleanup, you can put money back into your pocket. You are also conserving a finite resource that is becoming scarce in some areas.

• *Just unplug it.* Did you know that 75 percent of the electricity drawn from our electronic devices and appliances happens when we aren't using them? I know … shocking! The best way to eliminate "phantom load" is by unplugging appliances and devices when you are finished using them. You can make it easier by plugging multiple devices into power strips and just hitting the switch.

Trash to Magickal Treasure

Upcycling your clothing is a great way to extend its use. Here are a couple of projects to get you started.

Felted Wool Faerie Hat

This is a fun way to reuse those wool sweaters that have been accidently shrunk or felted. If you don't have a felted wool sweater, go to a thrift store and buy an inexpensive 100 percent wool sweater. Take it home and wash it in hot water, followed by drying it in a hot dryer. You will know if the wool is felted because you will no longer see the knit pattern, and it won't unravel when cut. I made these fun faerie hats for quick dress-up pieces for my kids when they were growing up.

You will need:

1 felted wool sweater
Matching thread
Hot glue or fabric glue
Buttons, silk flowers, bells, or ribbon for embellishing (optional)

Measure the circumference of your child's head along the middle of the forehead and then add an inch for seam allowance. Divide this number by 2.

Draw a right-angled triangle on a folded sheet of newspaper or scrap paper using the number you came up with as the base, the folded edge representing the height (figure A). Make it as tall or short as you please, as long as it fits on your sweater.

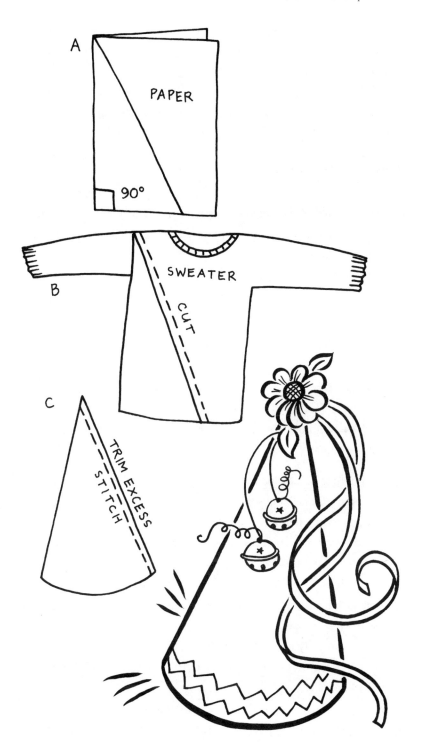

A

PAPER

90°

B

SWEATER

CUT

C

TRIM EXCESS

STITCH

Lay the pattern along the bottom ribbing of the sweater, keeping the right angle against the seam on either side of the sweater (figure B). Cut along the diagonal side (the hypotenuse).

With wrong sides together, sew the hypotenuse side and trim excess felting close to the seam (figure C). Turn the hat right side out, and using hot glue or fabric glue, embellish with bells, ribbon, flowers, etc.

Bleach Pen Altar Cloth

If you have T-shirts, jeans, or anything made from a natural fiber that has been stained or damaged—or maybe you're just bored with them—don't toss them. Transform them with bleach gel pens (or a little bleach on a cotton swab).

I used a bleach pen and a yard of plain black cotton fabric I found at a tag sale to create a fabulous altar cloth.

You will need:

1 yard of a solid-colored natural fiber
A neutralizing solution (10 parts water to 1 part hydrogen peroxide in
    large pan)
White towels
A bleach pen (or cotton swab and a small bowl of liquid bleach)
Stencils (optional)

Cut and hem seams of altar cloth to desired dimensions.

Mix your neutralizing solution. This is what you will use to stop the bleaching action when you reach your desired shade. Set aside.

Lay down white towels over your workstation and lay your altar cloth on top. Now for the fun: use your bleach pens to create amazing Witchy designs, Celtic knots, or symbols of your choosing. If you don't feel comfortable doing this freehand, there are a lot of great stencils to choose from.

Watch carefully as the bleach takes effect. Bleaching action timing varies depending on fabric and color fade, but do not leave it on longer than 15 minutes.

When you have achieved proper fade, put the altar cloth in the neutralizing solution and agitate for at least five minutes. Wash as usual.

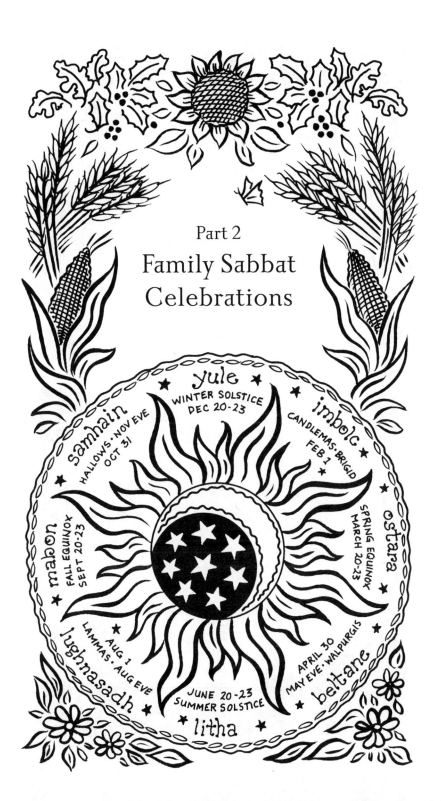

Part 2

Family Sabbat
Celebrations

yule
WINTER SOLSTICE
DEC 20-23

samhain
HALLOWS · NOV EVE
OCT 31

imbolc
CANDLEMAS · BRIGID
FEB 1

mabon
FALL EQUINOX
SEPT 20-23

ostara
SPRING EQUINOX
MARCH 20-23

lughnasadh
AUG 1
LAMMAS · AUG EVE

litha
JUNE 20-23
SUMMER SOLSTICE

beltane
APRIL 30
MAY EVE · WALPURGIS

notes

Chapter 7

Samhain

The last of the leaves cling to shadowy branches
and wood smoke rises in long tendrils to a tired sky.
Ancestral voices can be heard just above the wind's lonely song.
And magick is electric for those who believe…

Chloe was three the day my grandmother passed away. It was a dark, dreary day just before Yule, and we had spent the morning with my sisters at my parents' house, preparing it for what we knew would be a somber Christmas holiday.

My grandmother lived next door and, when not being cared for by my mother, had a hospice nurse at her side.

So that afternoon, while we unpacked the holiday china and wrapped last-minute gifts, we received the call. I gathered my daughter from in front of the TV and, with my parents and sisters, solemnly walked to my grandmother's home.

As we gathered around her bed and watched her last exasperated breath, Chloe played with her doll under the caring eye of the hospice nurse in the living room.

Calls were made, and though we were sad, it was truly a relief. My grandmother had put up a good fight, and it was time for her to be at rest. I took Chloe home before the coroner arrived.

I was quiet as we drove the winding road to our home. I wasn't quite sure how to explain to my three-year-old daughter what had just transpired.

But as the skies darkened and released a pelting rain, Chloe spoke up. "Grandma feels better, Mama."

I was surprised. "What do you mean, sweetie?"

"I saw Grandma and she told me."

"Did you see her in her bed?" I prodded.

"No, Mommy. She came in the living room."

I could feel the anxiety drain and my eyes filled with tears. Grandma was truly free.

The Wheel of the Year continued to turn. Spring brought riotous greens and plenty of garden chores. Summer's warmth enveloped us with fun-filled days picnicking on the river, and autumn arrived bejeweled in fire and scented with wood smoke. All the while, Chloe continued to tell me about her talks with Grandma.

"Grandma said she likes your flowers," she would casually say while walking with me through the garden. Or sometimes, "Grandma said you were very helpful when you were little."

As October came to its glorious crescendo, we set up our family's Samhain altar. Chloe clumsily situated the picture I had of Grandma in its pretty gold frame, and I added a glass hummingbird, my grandmother's favorite, beside it. For several days Chloe would stare at the picture, sometimes mumbling something or just letting out a little giggle.

We celebrated Samhain privately, as we always do under October's brilliant Blood Moon, and more than a few tears were shed as we celebrated my Grandmother's extraordinary life. The night of Halloween found us in town with an array of little rain-soaked ghouls, whom my own costume-clad children called friends. And after an exhausting night of trick-or-treating, haunted garages, and hot apple cider, we drove our little monsters home to pass out in front of the television while watching *The Nightmare Before Christmas*, completely buried in candy wrappers.

It was past midnight when I heard whisperings from my room. I silently walked to the living room, and watched my little girl as she talked at the altar.

"I will miss you, Grandma," she said. "Take these." She pulled out some of her Halloween candy, placed it on the altar, and then continued. "One Snickers for you, Grandma. Two for me." She put one fun-sized bar in front of my grandmother's picture and two other chocolate bars back in her bag. "One sucker for you. And two licorices for me." She continued this until her pile was gone. "Goodbye, Grandma." She ended her conversation and began to walk toward me.

"It's late, sweetie," I said, not meaning to startle my daughter. "Did you have a fun night?"

Chloe sighed. "Grandma went away." She continued to walk toward her bedroom.

"Did she say where she was going?" I asked.

Chloe shrugged. "I don't know, but I gave her some of my candy." She smiled.

"That was nice, sweetie." I gave her a hug.

"Night, Mama."

"Good night."

I stood for a moment enjoying the rare stillness of my usually noisy house. The rain pounded against the roof, and I thought in the distance I could hear the haunting call of a coyote. I turned to go back to bed but stopped when I heard something fall near the altar. I walked over to find the glass hummingbird had been knocked to the floor. I picked it up and placed it near my grandmother's picture, then smiled.

"Goodbye, Grandma," I said. "Enjoy your new adventure."

The Celtic Connection

For many Pagans with children, it's hard to know where Samhain begins and Halloween ends. Our American Halloween is truly a secular holiday that is more than slightly laced with commercialism. Its roots and traditions have intertwined through the centuries, grafting Celtic fire festival and Mediterranean harvest traditions to worldwide practices of veneration of the dead. Throw in the European masquerade and guising traditions along with good old-fashioned ghost stories like "The Legend of Sleepy Hollow" or "Stingy Jack," the tale of a man who, because he tricked the devil, was forever cursed to walk in eternal darkness with only a coal in a turnip to light his way, and you have a holiday with a very diverse family tree.

If you ask some Christians about the roots of Halloween, they will weave for you a frightening tale of a barbarous people who worshiped an evil god whose name was Samhain. The source of this was most likely Charles Vallancey, who in the 1770s wrote a series of historical stories about the Celts and made reference to their worship of a deity known as Samhan, Lord of the Dead, to whom human sacrifices were made at the season of "souls to judgment." And though modern historians have debunked these claims, evangelists the world over still insist that Halloween's origins were evil in nature.

Even the name for this darksome night, when we celebrate the things that frighten us most with parties and parades, has evolved much over time. "Halloween" is a corruption of the term "All Hallows' Even," a Christianization of already established harvest or fire festivals that became a time to commemorate Christian saints. It was later known by many names, including Snap-Apple Night, Mischief Night, and Nut-Crack Night, but by the dawn of the twentieth century, the name Halloween had stuck.

Yes, Halloween has truly become an all-American holiday complete with trick-or-treating, organized haunted houses, and romps through Styrofoam graveyards, and for many of us magickal folk it is the one night we seem to fit in with everyone else. I admit it—I love it! But out there, lost between garlands of bright orange lights and the laughter of pint-sized goblins covered in sticky caramel, are the myths—legends we must pass on so we won't forget its mystical Celtic beginnings.

The truth is, much of what we do know about the rituals of the Celts comes from myth. But like with all stories, somewhere tightly woven within the fiber is truth.

The year for the ancient Celts is divided in two by the beginning and ending of the summer. The light half of the year was marked by the celebration of Beltane. When herds were moved to their hilly pastures to graze on the new green grass, festivities with balefires and fertility rites were held in honor of the sabbat.

Samhain (pronounced SOW-en) marked the dark half of the year when the sun was ritually devoured by the dark cloak of winter. This was the beginning of the Celtic New Year and marked the time when the slaughtering and harvesting were to be completed; according to ancient myth, one must not partake of any fruit left on the branches after Samhain, for the *sidhe* had surely blighted it. Household fires were put out on the eve of Samhain and the hearth was cleansed, to be rekindled from the centralized need-fire.

The silky veil that separated our world from the world of the spirits was at its thinnest on Samhain, and the souls of the dearly departed could return. It was appropriate at this time to honor returning ancestors by leaving a bit of food and drink out for them by the door and maybe lighting a candle so they could find their way on their magickal journey. But because the veil was thin, the Celts believed that not only the souls of loved ones could cross over. Otherworldly spirits (not all friendly) slipped through the mist and shadows and roamed freely throughout the countryside. Their mischievous rustlings could be heard in the scuttling of branches and in the rain that beat upon the thatch.

According to Celtic mythology, you didn't want to trek too far on the night of Samhain. And if you had to go out, it was best to disguise yourself to blend in with the wandering spirits. Be mindful not to look back because you might be taken by prankish *sidhe* traveling in your midst. This was also the one night you could win back a loved one who had become a faerie prize, as portrayed in the ballad of Tam Lin. In this Scottish legend Jennie (or Janet) finds herself at the crossroads on Samhain in a battle with the faerie queen for the soul of her lover, Tam Lin.

On this night when the Celts believed the door between time and space lay open, creating a time out of time, sacrifices were made and the future was revealed through the reading of the burnt sacrificial entrails. Would the crops be successful next year? Who was to wed? Who was to die?

To ancient people this was a time of profound mysteries and of letting go. Just as the earth must give in to winter's shadow, the Celts accepted that death was a part of the ever-turning cycle of life. Through the long, cold months, they held tight to the knowledge that within the hard-packed earth was the hope that transformation was soon to come and their world would once again be fruitful and light.

Embrace the Dark Side

During this season when the earth sheds her green and the Goddess, in her Crone aspect, wraps us with her dark mantle, we are given the opportunity to take our families on a mystical journey to introduce them to their shadowy counterparts. I am talking about shadow work.

Shadow work can be explained as looking at our own hidden darkness—those little demons that lurk just at the edge of our subconscious. What do you see reflecting back? Maybe it's the sooty stain of greed or jealousy's slimy tint. What bad habits need to be dealt with? Or illusions halted?

Here's what I see when I look at my shadow self: the dark residue of procrastination (okay, and maybe a slight sugar addiction). Yeah, you know what I mean.

Some people have asked me, is shadow work really appropriate for kids? You bet it is. Life isn't all unicorns and faerie clouds, and it's important for our children to be able to deal with fear and take responsibility for their own bad behavior or habits at an early age. I'm not saying to force your kids into any situation that might traumatize them for the rest of their lives but to gently guide them to stop bad habits or harmful behavior and to encourage them on new endeavors. Just as the mighty oak must shed her dying leaves, those tiny buds that remain are a reminder that within us all lies the promise of new beginnings.

Enjoy these dark symbols of the season designed to lead your family through the shadowland.

The Hag with Her Cauldron

If you stop by any big-box store between September and October, you will find large plastic cauldrons stacked by the dozens on shelves everywhere. We love them; my daughter used one for years as her trick-or-treat bucket. They are inexpensive and were handy for holding popcorn balls, apples, and other Halloween treats when my kids still wanted large Halloween parties held at our home.

Cauldrons are also attached to that quintessential Halloween character, the hag. She has been used as a tool to scare children and reaffirm our affinity for youth since medieval times. If you ask the mundane what the hag and her cauldron symbolize, they will twist their face and cackle out something like the infamous Shakespearean line, "Double, double toil and trouble..." (you know the rest). Ask a magickal person the same question and they will smile and say, "Transformation."

The Dark Goddess stirs her cauldron of life and smiles knowingly and we shiver. She is known by many names—Cailleach, Hekate, Cerridwen, and Kali to name a few. Her cauldron represents the womb, where all life rests before rebirth. She guards the inner gate and is the keeper of the keys to our deepest mysteries. The most powerful aspect of the Triple Goddess, she is justice, she is wisdom. But most importantly, she is the bridge from the end of one cycle to the next. She is transition. Not to be feared but celebrated, for to face the Dark Mother is to accept change and to accept change is to *transform*.

Call on the Crone to connect with ancestors, perform shadow work, end negativity, deal with the death of a loved one or beloved pet, seek wisdom, and connect with all aspects of aging and menopause.

Cauldron of Wisdom Ritual

This little ritual is designed for a grandmother (or grandmotherly figure) to perform with the kids. Not a lot of setup is involved, so it can be done in the kitchen before trick-or-treating or anytime Grandma's visiting during the Crone's reign. During this ritual, our children will learn to take responsibility for bad or hurtful behavior and to seek wisdom (the Crone) as their guide. It's also a great way for our little ones to get to spend some quality time with their elders.

You will need:

Black central pillar candle (representing the wisdom of the Crone)
1 tea light per child
Candlesnuffer
Apple juice (for wisdom)

1 cauldron suitable for holding liquid (A plastic party-store version will do.)

Cookies

Grandma will light the black pillar candle representing the wisdom of the Crone. One by one, each child will light a tea light (Grandma may need to help the little ones) and name their fear or a bad behavior they would like to conquer (e.g., "I am afraid of my closet" or "I am crabby with my brother"). Grandma will then take the candlesnuffer and snuff each candle, in effect snuffing out the child's fear or bad behavior, and relight it from the black pillar candle. As she does this, she will say, "Let the wisdom of the Crone light your way."

When all candles are relit, Grandma will serve each child a glass of apple juice from the cauldron. When everyone has a glass, Grandma will say, "With wisdom comes transformation." Now it's time for the kids to enjoy cookies and juice with Grandma. Having Grandma tell the story of Cerridwen and her cauldron of regeneration or just stories of her own youth and the lessons she has learned would both be appropriate. Snuff out the black pillar candle but let the tea lights burn out in a safe place. Blessed be the Crone!

Things That Go Bump in the Night

Fear of the things that go bump in the night goes hand in hand with this season, when the fabric between our world and the spirit world grows thin. This may be an especially difficult time for kids who are sensitive to the spirit world and are having a difficult time understanding what they are experiencing. The early darkness that envelops us enhances the spookiness of the scuttles and screeches that on a summer's evening may have seemed benign. And the sometimes macabre decor and creepy lighting, popular this time of year, can be especially frightening for the little ones in our lives.

Fear is not a bad thing; it is natural and has helped us identify threats and survive predators and natural disasters for millions of years. Most fear is learned and developed at a young age. Our fear, for the most part, is influenced by our environment and culture and cued from family and friends. As we grow to adulthood, our reasoning response overrides our senses and we are better able to manage our fears.

But what can we do right now for the five-year-old who is insistent that there is a shark in the swimming pool? (Okay, that was Chloe. She is seventeen now and admits she still takes a second look before diving into a pool.) Or the four-year-old who is convinced there's something under the bed?

Here are a few dos and don'ts that may be helpful with dealing with fear, especially during the Halloween season:

- *Do* share with your child how you have dealt with fear in your own life.

- *Do* encourage and prepare them for a safe interaction with their fear. Maybe Dad could hold the snake while his child touches it.

- *Do* talk with them about their fear and be aware of "unhealthy" fear that might require additional help from a physician.

- *Don't* laugh or belittle their fear. No matter how silly you might think it is (like my daughter's fear of sharks in the swimming pool), it is very serious to them.

- *Don't* force them to face their fears in an unhealthy manner. Forcing a child who is afraid of snakes to hold one is just going to make it worse.

- *Don't* cater to their fears. Encouraging them to unreasonably avoid their fears can be just as bad. Allowing them to stay indoors all the time because they are afraid of snakes is excessive.

Labyrinth of Empowerment Ritual

A labyrinth represents the sacred journey to the center of one's own soul. These circular wanderings have designated a sacred space since prehistoric times and have been found in every culture. The first thing that comes to most people's mind when they hear the word "labyrinth" (besides the movie starring David Bowie) is the Greek myth of Theseus and the Minotaur, the tragic tale of an Athenian prince who takes on the man-eating Minotaur in the heart of his labyrinth home. But the labyrinth has been used as a tool for meditation, prayer, and transition by people of all faiths for thousands of years. There is no wrong way to walk the labyrinth, reminding us that in life it's not the destination that is important but the journey.

This labyrinth empowerment ritual is for releasing fear and is designed to be done as a family.

You will need:

Smooth stones
Washable marking pens
1 bag of flour for drawing your labyrinth
1 cup
Responsibly gathered twigs, leaves, rocks, shells, etc. (optional)
Fireproof tray or stone
1 black candle (for the wisdom of the Crone)
Crone symbols: decorative owl, black cat, black stones, cauldron, or
    raven, etc.

Before the ritual, each family member will gather a few stones and use the washable markers to decorate them with words and symbols that express the fears they would like to release.

In a yard or field use your cup to sprinkle flour to trace out a large spiral. Remember to make it wide enough to walk with your family in a single file. Also remember to make the center large enough to place your tray and still have enough room for the family to gather around it. Gathered leaves, twigs, cones, shells, and other natural objects can be used to go over the flour lines but are not necessary. Set up the tray or stone in the center of the labyrinth with your black candle and symbols of the Crone.

Ground and center before entering the labyrinth. As you file through, symbolically release your fears and burdens by tossing the stones you had previously decorated on the path. Once everyone has reached the center, have an adult light the black candle and say,

Dark Mother, it is of your wisdom we do inquire.
As we journey this labyrinth, help us to inspire.
Release our fears and all that binds
As we circle through, our true, strong selves to find.
Blessed be.

Leave the candle to burn out safely and begin your journey out of the labyrinth empowered with the knowledge that you are not only strong, fearless individuals—but invincible as a family!

Chapter 8

Yule

In the bleak midwinter the trees sparkle with frost,
reminding us that there is beauty to be perceived.
The candles in the window warm my heart,
and I hear my children's soft, excited laughter late into the night.
Hush now, here comes the light …

Growing up, we knew the holidays were upon us when my mother would turn to us girls and belt out the classic Christmas tune by Yogi Yorgesson called "I Yust Go Nuts at Christmas." As a little girl it made my heart flutter, for I knew soon school would be out and old Saint Nick would be visiting our house.

As a teen, the song made me cringe. I would roll my eyes and say, "Can't you please stop singing that?!" In reply, she would sing the next verse … louder. I deserved it. I'm all grown up now and my mom still sings it to us.

As I write this, we are a week from our annual trip to Wight's, a large nursery and gift store near Seattle, two hours south of our beautiful Skagit Valley. My three sisters, my daughter, my nieces, a couple of cousins, sometimes a few friends, my mom, and I rattle down the road in my youngest sister's sixteen-passenger van on a quest to view the store's transformation from ordinary garden center to an indoor fantasy forest of intricately decorated trees. We always pull up to a coffee stand, to the chagrin of the weary barista whose job it is to prepare the orders, and as we finally hit the freeway, that's my mom's cue. She turns back to look at us all uncomfortably banging around (it's tradition for me to get really carsick too) in that old van and she sings "I Yust Go Nuts at Christmas."

After a couple of hours spent in the Christmas tree–lover's paradise, we have a late lunch together and then crawl back into the van to head back to our quiet valley. The light has already diminished, making it hard to compare our store-bought treasures, but we still try. We talk about our favorite holiday memories, and someone always brings up the time our mom passed gas while loading the car outside of a big-box store, proclaiming, "Smell the glorious odor!" She didn't see the woman loading her car beside us, but we did and roared with laughter as Mom tried to apologize.

It's dark and usually the rain that pelts us is so close to turning to snow that you can smell it. We exchange long hugs and Mom always slips each of us an ornament. "I love you," she says.

And I always reply, "Mom, you shouldn't have." I try to hold back the tears, but I'm weak that way. "I love you too, Mom."

It's those kinds of memories that are truly the light of the Yuletide season, that time of year we hold our breath as the sun seems to stand still for a few days before finally conquering the darkness that has overpowered it since Samhain. We rejoice as, little by little, the light increases, rekindling our hope that spring will surely come.

New Beginnings

The winter solstice marks the shortest day and the longest night of the year. Rituals and celebrations for welcoming back the sun have been practiced and celebrated for thousands of years.

But leave it to the Romans to really kick it up a notch with their Saturnalia celebrations. Their festival, in honor of Saturn, the god of agriculture, was a carnival with social norms turned upside down. This event, turned weeklong festival, was a time when roles were reversed, courts were out of session, schools closed, and war could not be decreed. Held December 17 through 23, celebrations included masked balls, candlelit processions, gambling, and drunken revelry—and all this was overseen by the *Saturnalicius princeps*, king for a day and precursor to the better-known Lord of Misrule.

Some of the holiday trappings you can thank the ancient Romans for include the bedecking of the household with greens including garlands and wreaths, ornamenting trees (decorated outdoors where they grew), gift exchanges, and maybe even the first holiday cards, for it was common to write a little poem to accompany your gift.

The anticipation for a rejuvenated earth was most felt by our ancestors to the north. For the Norse, Germanic, and Celtic peoples, the dark half of the year would have felt particularly dreary. In these northerly realms the December sun was a dying ember that glowed just above the horizon for only a few fleeting hours, a very frightening thing for people who depended so on the land.

To help rekindle the sun's dying flame, a log was chosen and set ablaze. The Yule fire would last for days, and it was said that each spark that rose represented livestock to be born in the spring. Evergreen branches were brought in as a symbol of hope and the perseverance of life, and great feasts were held in celebration, for the butchering had just been done and meat was plentiful.

These are the lands of dark elves and haunted forests, where families held tight around the central hearth and told tales in which spirits, imps, and witches abounded. If we listen carefully to their ancient voices that still echo through their myths and legends, we will find a cast of interesting Yuletide characters. Some will be new, but others you might find surprisingly familiar.

Yule's Ominous Cast of Characters

During the dark days leading up the Teutonic midwinter festival known as Yule, northern people were uneasy because it was during this time of year, when the sun stood still, that one had to be weary of chaotic spirits that tromped through the woodlands and crept near the homes. Here are just a few of the midwinter visitors that might happen upon your door:

- *Odin and the Wild Hunt:* When the wind picked up, tossing the tops of trees and lashing around chimney tops, one was sure to hide, for the Wild Hunt was aloft. Led by Odin (or Wodin), the shape-shifting god of wisdom and magick, with his long white beard whipping the back of his cloak and wide-brimmed hat covering his dark, empty eye socket, he leads the spirits of fallen heroes through the sky on his eight-legged horse named Sleipnir. If you hear the howl of dogs or lightning flashes in the sky, do not answer the huntsman's call, or you may be taken up to forever ride the winds.

- *Jólasveinar (Yule Lads):* If you spy an elvish face peering at you through the window near solstice, be weary, for the Jólasveinar are hanging about. These mischief-makers start arriving during the dark days before Yule. The sons of undead trolls Grýla and Leppalúði who stole and ate naughty children, the Yule Lads arrive one after the another. With names like Pot Scraper, Door Slammer, and Curd Gobbler, you might want to latch your windows and lock your doors.

- *Julbock (Yule Goat):* If you were a child living in Scandinavia long ago, you could expect a nighttime visitor around Yule. But unlike Santa Claus, this visitor wasn't there to fill the stockings with care. Instead, the Yule Goat arrived to accept an offering from the last sheaths of grain in return for a bountiful harvest. How would you know if he was pleased with your offering? He would leave a few grains behind. Eventually, he left gifts in exchange. His effigy can now be seen in Scandinavian holiday markets as an ornament made from sheaves of wheat and tied with a red ribbon.

• *Jólaköttur (Yule Cat):* Prowling about during the harvest season, when all good little boys and girls should be helping with the heavy work, is the Jólaköttur, or Yule Cat. As autumn's leaves faded and the snow began to fall, the Yule Cat was waiting to snatch up any child who had not been rewarded for their hard work with a new set of clothes. Unfortunately, poverty was at one time connected to laziness. If your family was too poor to buy new clothes, let's hope the Jólaköttur was making a list and checking it twice during harvest time, so you wouldn't become his Yuletide dinner!

The cast of Yuletide characters we know and love today are just remnants of their richly tapestried Teutonic past, scraps that have been refashioned to suit a more genteel sensibility. But the legends remain and help piece together a holiday history that is truly magickal. So during this celebration of light and hope, gather the family around the fire, enjoy some eggnog, and rediscover the tales of our Yuletide's pagan past.

A Light in the Darkness

As do a lot of modern Pagan families, our family celebrates both Christmas and Yule. I have never thought of Christmas as a particularly Christian holiday, and the modern cultural focus of the celebration is family and togetherness. Midwinter celebrations were always about the light, and it didn't become a Christian holiday until much later when Christians decided to mark the birthday of their own light-bearing son. For us the reason for the season still remains "the rebirth of the sun." The following is a family ritual to rekindle your family's enduring light.

Family Yule Log Blessing

Yule at its heart is a time of renewal and hope, a time to set aside our differences and spread goodwill. It is a time for reflection and of the promise of possibility, and these ideals are reflected in our holiday traditions. We see them in the evergreen boughs and trees that we use to decorate our homes, a reminder of life's persistence; the candles lit in the windows to guide strangers on their way; and the wreath, symbolizing life's continuing cycle of life, death, and rebirth. We strike up the magick of old when we kiss under the mistletoe, which ensured fertility, or shake harness bells, which scared away evil spirits.

But I believe it's the most evident in the Yule log that people, both magickal and mundane, have represented in their homes in one form or another during the holiday season. Be it an actual log that is decorated and displayed or burned in a fireplace, fire pit, or woodstove; a wooden or log-shaped resin candleholder; or the edible version, the *bûche de Noël*, the traditional French dessert shaped like a Yule log, your family is participating in a ritual as old as time.

The lighting of fires at the winter solstice helped encourage the sun's birth, and the ashes were sprinkled over the fields to encourage abundance. It was customary to keep a bit of the charcoal to kindle the next Yule fire. Our family uses a bit of the trunk from our previous year's Yule tree as our Yule log. This is a fun family tradition if you harvest live trees. We harvest a tree from the same local tree farm every year. We are supporting a small, local farm and are *not* in the forest cutting down native trees.

For this ritual, keep your Yule log small, about six to nine inches long and three to four inches in diameter. This can be responsibly gathered outside, or you can buy a log bundle from the store and use one of the small logs. If you do not have a woodstove, fireplace, or outdoor fire pit in which to burn the log, instead supply enough tea lights for every family member.

You will need:

Yule log
Paper
Pen
Place to burn the log

You will be burning this log, so if you want to decorate it with ribbons or pretty ornaments before the ceremony, remember to take them off before putting the log in the fire. Light a fire in your woodstove, fire pit, or fireplace. Have everyone write on a piece of paper a nonmaterial wish or goal for the coming year (by nonmaterial I mean you don't get to wish for a new Xbox). Attach the paper to the Yule log. The following can be said in unison or by the family member of your choosing:

As the new sun is born, lend us your light,
So we too might shine on this blessed night.
Maiden, Mother, and Crone, blessed power of three,
Grant us these wishes—so mote it be!

Place the Yule log in the flames. If you absolutely do not have a place to burn a log, have everyone light a tea light around the log and let them burn out in a safe place. Afterward, enjoy your family's company with some mulled cider and maybe a little *bûche de Noël*. Have a blessed Yule!

Cinnamon Salt Dough Ornaments

Ringing bells clears the air of negative energy. Add the protective power of cinnamon and you have a pretty powerful addition to your Yuletide celebrations.

You will need:

1 cup flour
½ cup salt
½ cup cinnamon
⅔ cup water
Wax paper
Holiday cookie cutters (moon, star, holly leaf, bell, etc.)
Craft bells
Hot glue gun
Heavy thread

Mix flour, salt, cinnamon, and water. Roll dough to ½ inch thick between 2 sheets of wax paper. Use fun cookie cutters to cut out shapes, and don't forget to make a hole at the top of your ornament. Let the shapes dry for 24 hours. Use hot glue to attach 1 or 2 craft bells. Thread heavy thread through the hole in the top of the ornament and tie off. Hang on your Yule tree. You can paint them or leave them plain for a rustic look. The smell is amazing! Makes about a dozen ornaments.

Chapter 9

Imbolc

A breeze scented with new earth touches my face.
The snowdrops bob their pretty faces,
and I hear the sound of new life coming from our barn.
Welcome, Maiden. You have been missed.

January in my part of the Pacific Northwest can be especially dreary. The rain that falls in icy pellets can last for weeks at a time, saturating the soil until every step is a sloppy mess. You are left mud-coated, drenched, and absolutely chilled to the bone. The darkness that shrouds us doesn't fade until almost seven thirty in the morning, and by four thirty in the evening we are once again cloaked in winter's dispiriting mantle.

But something magickal happens around the first part of February. There is a shift of light and weather that lightens our hearts, freeing us to shake the moss out of our hair and take a much-needed breath. As my family and I venture back outdoors, the rain has lifted and there is a breeze that blows in softly from the south tinged with the scent of new earth. The gardens, upon first glance, may seem mortally defeated by winter's reign, but as we pull back the mulch, we spy the green shoots that tell us that the spark of life remains.

"Oh, Mama!" Elijah, who has always loved to be in the garden and was always the most excited, would say when he was little. "Do you see it?"

"Yes, my sweet." I would take a look at his treasure. "Do you remember the name?"

He would cock his head sideways and bite his lip. "I think it's a columbine."

Always proud of my earthy babes, I give him a big kiss. "You are so smart!"

Chloe is the keeper of our "livestock." I use the term loosely; our livestock consists of a dozen chickens, a Pekin duck, between three and seven dairy goats (depending on sales), and a grouchy miniature donkey who thinks she's in charge. At this time of year Chloe's does give birth, and she spends a lot of time watching so that she can be out there to help with the deliveries. I have seen her drag a lawn chair and sleeping bag to our tiny barn.

"It's February, honey. Don't you think you'll get cold?" I ask.

"No, Mama," she says, busily putting together all she thinks she'll need for the night. "I wanna make sure I'm there for them."

I always let her go but leave the porch light on and the door unlocked. I typically find her on the couch the next morning wrapped with the blanket I left out for her.

February can be a tricky month. There have been times I have been out weeding beds and tying raspberries under a sun that, if I hadn't known better, I would have thought belonged to April. But there have also been Februaries when I've found myself shoveling snow and cussing the cruel sky that dropped that white stuff on me.

But no matter what the month has in store for us, the signs are there, and we can thank the Goddess for its reawakening. Spring is coming!

The Power of Three

Between February 1 and 2, we celebrate Imbolc or *Oimelc* (meaning "ewe's milk"), a cross-quarter festival that heralds the return of new life. This was the time when the Celtic people's livestock, heavy with pregnancy, began lactating. This milk was used sometimes as a late winter food source when food supplies were diminishing. It also marked the halfway point between winter and spring.

For the Celts, the bearer of light and life was the triple goddess Brighid or Brid (meaning "fiery arrow"). She was an extraordinary presence who was part faerie and part god. Her mother was one of the Tuatha Dé Danann and her father was the Dagda. She had two sisters, also called Brighid. It is generally thought the three sisters are three aspects of the same goddess.

A triple goddess, she is the goddess of poetry and was revered by artists and diviners for her spark of clarity and creativity. As the goddess of smithcraft, she held the fire of transformation, and as the goddess of healing, she was adored by midwives and was connected to the hearth and home.

For the early Irish, she was Brigantia, an ancestral goddess who represented the fertility of the land and was a patron in warfare. An important goddess to her people, her shrine was located in Kildare, Ireland, where nineteen priestesses kept her fire continuously burning.

With the onset of Christianity, she was quickly canonized. She became Saint Brighid, the fiery queen of heaven and midwife to the Christ Child. Her legend changed. She became the daughter of a druid who was unable to eat regular food as a child, so she only drank the milk of a white cow with red ears. She was said to have predicted the coming of Christianity and was baptized by Saint Patrick himself. Her festival was Christianized and became Candlemas, a time for clergy to bless candles and distribute them to the people.

Her sacred flame was tended by nuns until 1220 CE when it was finally extinguished. In 1993 her sacred fire was relit by the order of Brigidine Sisters and burns to this day.

The light of Brighid burns on, a constant reminder to be still, even in the darkest of times, for that tiny ember of hope will spark and light will come again.

It's Groundhog Day!

February for early Europeans was a time to check for signs that spring was on its way. One way was to watch the behavior of animals as they came out of hibernation. Bears, snakes, hedgehogs, and badgers were all animals our early ancestors noted as the sign of winter's end.

When German settlers arrived in Pennsylvania in the 1700s, they brought with them their customs and traditions. Along with midwinter holidays and festivals, such as Candlemas, they passed on their practice of weather prediction and the superstitions attached to it.

The first mention of Groundhog Day was in a diary entry dated February 4, 1841, by Morgantown, Pennsylvania, storekeeper James Morris. The entry noted, "Candlemas day, the day on which, according to the Germans, the Groundhog peeps out of his winter quarters and if he sees his shadow he pops back for another six weeks nap, but if the day be cloudy he remains out, as the weather is to be moderate." The first official celebration wasn't until February 2, 1887, in Punxsutawney, Pennsylvania, where Punxsutawney Phil has been forecasting the weather ever since.

I have listed a few folksy weather omens from Imbolc/Candlemas past:

The serpent will come from the hole
On the brown day of Bride,
Though there may be three feet of snow
On the surface of the ground.

If Candlemas be fair and bright,
Winter has another flight.
If Candlemas brings clouds and rain,
Winter will not come again.

If Candlemas Day is bright and clear,
There'll be two winters in the year.

For as the sun shines on Candlemas Day,
So far will the snow swirl until May.
For as the snow blows on Candlemas Day,
So far will the sun shine before May.

This is a great time to take the kids out and take a look at the changes that are unfolding during Brighid's reign. The reddening branches that tell you the sap is moving and the swelling buds are just waiting to unfurl. There may be snowdrops and crocus popping up here and there, and if you're lucky, you might just see some of our furrier friends.

Bird watching is another great family activity in February. In my part of the country, from November through March the largest concentration of eagles in the continental United States spends its time on the Skagit and Sauk rivers feasting on spawning salmon. People come from all over the world to watch these magnificent creatures and attend educational events held throughout the season. Closer to Puget Sound, birders come see the largest concentration of arctic birds that call the flats and fields in the area home for the winter. Check out the National Audubon Society's website for great birding areas in your part of the country.

Remember to have the kids take a journal on your outing. Jotting down notes and drawing pictures is great a way to connect with your environment. Find a quiet place in nature to sit. Have everyone close their eyes and just listen … What did you hear? The quiet shushing of a stream? The breeze rattling the branches? How about the chatter of a tree squirrel or the croak of a raven?

When you get home, curl up on the couch with some hot chocolate and compare notes. Another fun addition is to come up with some weather predictions based on your field notes. Don't forget to make them rhyme! Here's a really bad example: "When the branches turn red, time for bears to get out of bed." The kids could jot down their new weather rhymes in their Book of Shadows. And when spring finally does unfurl her pretty head, check to see how close their predictions were. Finally, before bed, don't forget to light a candle in the window in honor of Brighid.

Transformations

February in most parts of the country can be pretty cold, so it's the perfect time of year to get creative! And Brighid, as the goddess of poetry, is the perfect muse. One fun and very magickal project to work on as a family is your Book of Shadows (or BOS). A Book of Shadows is your very own personal collection of spells, charms, recipes, and rituals—basically, an all-around magickal working journal. A Book of Shadows is very personal and should reflect your individuality. For small children, their BOS might be a series of pages they have drawn to reflect the sabbats, seasons, mythological beasts, or gods and goddesses. As children grow, have them make a new BOS reflecting their maturing understanding of the Craft.

Book of Shadows Blessing

Before the blessing, supply everyone with a blank journal or one of those lined composition notebooks you can pick up for under a dollar. Have plenty of craft supplies, including colorful craft paper, glue or rubber cement, stickers, colored pencils, crayons, and pens. You may want to use rubber stamps, pressed flowers, or scraps from old dictionaries or vintage magazines. Really, the sky's the limit. You may also want to try a theme. Some fun ideas include:

- Faeries
- Mythological beasts
- Celtic (something like the *Book of Kells*)
- *Practical Magic* (Okay, I'm a total sucker for that movie! My daughter and I *attempted* that style—notice emphasis on "attempted.")
- Mermaids

- Steampunk

- Gothic

- Medieval

- Greek or Roman

- Harry Potter

- Gods or goddesses of the world

Before you get started crafting, have everyone lay their hands over the craft supplies and ask Brighid to be your muse by saying the following:

Brighid of poetry, our most sacred muse,
Kindle our imaginations, our stumbling blocks to lose.
For the seed of creativity we must surely see
Has been planted within by the gracious goddess of three.

When everyone is done with their masterpieces, clean up the mess, lay those beautiful new Books of Shadows across the table, and remember to thank Brighid for the inspiration!

One small tip: if using a composition notebook, you can cover the unattractive covers by cutting out two pieces of scrapbooking paper (use the notebook as a template) and rubber cement it to the front and back covers. It's also nice to hot glue a ribbon at the top of the inside front cover. It makes an attractive bookmark.

Candle Magick

Here's a simple Imbolc candle spell for transformation. First, collect a few fallen, bare twigs from outdoors, dried out cones, or dried stalks of grass. If you made a corn dolly during Lughnasadh, add that.

Arrange these items around a yellow or orange pillar candle. Not too closely; safety first.

As the candle is lit, say these words:

Winter has held tight the land
In its icy fingers all around.
As we light this sun flame,

The hope for transformation abounds.
As the Goddess warms the frozen earth
And we see the signs we do seek,
May we in turn transform
Through these words that we do speak.
Blessed be!

Brighid's Cross

Brighid's Crosses were traditionally made and hung above doorways as a sign of protection. Made with rushes as a symbol of new life, these crosses were made in several different styles, including the structure representing facets of the Celtic universe. We will be making the most recognizable four-arm solar cross, representing the rays of the sun.

You will need:

3 dozen wheat, straw, grass, or reed stalks roughly the same size
Twine for tying off the ends

Soak the stalks in hot water for 20 minutes or until they are flexible.

Start with a nice straight stalk, holding it vertical.

Fold a stalk around the center, pointing toward your right hand (figure A).

Fold another stalk over the second, pointing downward (figure B).

Fold another stalk over the third and first, pointing toward your left hand (figure C).

You will now have what is the beginning of a four-armed cross. Continue folding stalks in the same pattern until you have used up the stalks. Tie off the arms with twine and trim if necessary (figure D).

Hang your Brighid's cross above each child's bed and say,

Blessed Brighid, bright arrow of light,
Enfold us with protection all through the night.
The solar cross we invoke with the power of three.
Let the magick hold, so mote it be!

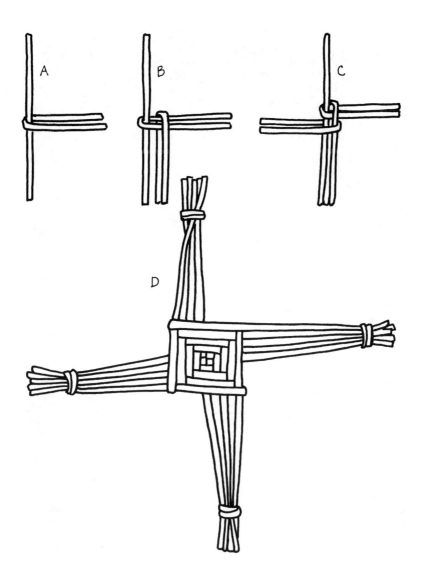

notes

Chapter 10

Ostara

My children sing out for the Maiden to awaken,
and she rewards them with a green fire
that spreads throughout the valley,
kindling the birdsong and our hearts with cheer.

With the approach of spring, we watch the growing sun as he gathers strength, his brilliant fingers stretching higher and higher above the eastern hills, until finally, the golden rays slip through my windows and illuminate a house ... in heavy need of a spring cleaning.

"Are we breathing that?" my daughter asks of the dust particles no longer masked by winter's cloak.

I sheepishly make up something to save my pride. "It's just the play of the light. You know, an optical illusion," I say.

She looks skeptical for a moment and then replies, "Interesting how the optical illusion resembles our cat's hair floating around."

It is about this time we throw open the windows, allowing the breeze to blow out winter's residue. We can't help but take in all that is fresh and new, and it stirs within us a renewed strength. We suddenly feel as if we can take on the world! And if we can take on the world, we can clean this house!

Ostara, or the vernal equinox, has arrived. The Goddess, who stirred the earth's renewal at Imbolc, is fully awake, and the earth revels in her young presence. Light and dark are in balance as the sun lines up with the earth's equator, and all around us the Maiden demonstrates her regenerative power.

Ostara takes its name from Eostre, an obscure Germanic goddess of the dawn, fertility, and new beginnings. Her symbols include the hare and eggs, both potent fertility symbols. And though she is only mentioned briefly by the Venerable Bede in *The Reckoning of Time*, the Goddess in her guise of Maiden, along with the symbols of renewal and fertility, has been venerated in the rites of spring for thousands of years.

And what better way to begin this season of growth and new beginnings than getting the whole family together for a spring cleaning? At our house the doors are thrown open and each family member is designated an area. Curtains are pulled down and furniture moved, windows washed and walls scrubbed—not a dust bunny nor cobweb is safe. After the house is physically clean, Chloe and I use our ritual besoms to sweep away any negativity that might be lurking about. As we come to the end of our clockwise sweep, ending at the double front doors, both opened wide, we say,

> *Farewell to the muck and snow,*
> *And with the light negativity must go.*
> *Welcome, Maiden of greening trees.*
> *Thank you for renewed energy!*

Blessed be the Maiden!

Show Us the Way

Living in the foothills of the North Cascades, we are very close to the land. Our property borders areas of forest that reach hundreds of miles, far into the Canadian border, and our roadways follow rivers that still carry upon their rippling backs the voices of the Sauk-Suiattle Indians that once used them as their byways. We are neighbors to the deer and black bear and to the eagle and salmon, and we do our best to respect the four acres we are borrowing from them for a short time.

We find solace in the forests, meandering along quiet paths created by our animal brothers, and it is under the forest's ancient canopy that we feel the wild energy that pulsates deep within our souls, calling us deeper into the wildwood to follow the Maiden, in the guise of Elen of the Ways. She is an antlered goddess and Green Lady, guardian of the land, guide to ancient pathways, and activator of the fertile energy of the earth.

To find this goddess one must go to where her voice is best heard—the wildwood. Your local park will do. She will be there peeking between the branches and gently brushing past the trees. Spring is a great time to pack a picnic lunch and take the family to the woods, a way for everyone to shake off the winter doldrums and let Elen's forest energy rekindle your spirit. She is not a goddess to be rushed. Take your time as you explore her domain. Walk the trails and listen for the rustlings of animal life. Check out the early spring growth. In the Pacific Northwest, the salmonberries and Indian plum are blooming. The resinous cottonwood buds have opened, releasing a scent that one cannot take in enough of. The delicate, lilylike trilliums litter the forest floor, and the cotton-candy pinks of the flowering currant are my favorite form of eye candy.

Many parks have guided walks with informational boards set up along the route. If you are with the little ones, take the time to read these and get to know your wild areas. Or better yet, do a little advanced research so that when you take the kids out, you will know what you're showing them. Children who are engaged at an early age to understand and respect their wild lands are better stewards of the environment as adults.

When you have finished your picnic, make sure everyone does their part to clean up, and then take a minute to say thank you to Elen of the

Ways for showing you a little bit of her realm. Have the kids trace (lightly) the outline of a heart with their finger on the forest floor and then say,

Thank you, Elen, horned goddess of the wild.
You are the heartbeat of the forest, and I am your child.
I promise to protect forestlands wild and free.
I will be your steward—you can count on me!

Magickally, parents with children can call on Elen of the Ways to fire up new environmental undertakings, be they trail, beach, or road cleanup (anything to do with protecting the earth), gardening projects, or protection on camping and hiking trips. For parents with college-aged or adult children (empty nesters), she is the goddess to invoke concerning your next leg of your personal journey. Be it spiritual, creative, or emotional pathways, whatever mysteries you need to unfold, Elen can help guide you on your trek.

Here are magickal correspondences for working with Elen of the Ways:

Colors: Red, green, and brown

Direction: East

Time: Dawn and dusk

Symbols: Deer, antlers, apples, leaves, flowers

Egg Traditions

When Josh was thirteen and Elijah was nine, they started a very *boyish* egg decorating tradition: the Phallic Egg. Yes, it is exactly what you are thinking—a large erect penis done in crayon relief on a beautifully dyed egg. I caught them snickering as they placed their masterpiece in an egg carton.

"What's so funny?" I asked.

"Oh, nothing, Mama," Eli said, in a voice way too sweet. Then they both burst out with laughter.

I grabbed the egg. But instead of reacting with complete shock, probably to their dismay, I laughed. I laughed hard. "I cannot believe you guys!" I said. "I've taught you well. It's all about fertility!"

I lifted the egg so their father could see it. He rolled his eyes before opening the fridge to graze. It wasn't until the next year, when I found they had created another, that I made it our Ostara "golden egg," worth ten dollars to the child who could locate it. That was enough to secure its placement in Crosson family Ostara traditions forever.

The egg has been used to symbolize renewal and fertility since ancient times. In Germany, egg was smeared on the plows to ensure the fertility of the land. Early Europeans hung eggs from trees and buried them beneath burgeoning roots to symbolize life's regenerative forces. In ancient China and parts of India, women proposed marriage by handing a man an egg. And if a woman wanted to become pregnant, North European folk magick dictated tossing her an egg. Even early Christians believed that if eggs laid on Good Friday were cooked on Easter, it promoted fertility of the crops.

The practice of coloring eggs goes all the way back to Paleolithic Africa, where painted ostrich egg shells 60,000 years old have been found. Ancient Persians colored eggs for their New Year festival known as Nowruz as far back as 500 BCE, the tradition continuing to this day. The ancient Egyptians placed ostrich eggs covered with gold and silver in their tombs. Central European folk customs made egg coloring an art with the Ukrainian pysanka and Polish pisanka. They are lovingly created with intricate symbolism and color by a method known as *batik* (wax resist).

It was German immigrants who brought the practices to America along with their tales of an egg-laying hare (the *Osterhase*). Children would make a nest the night before Easter, and the next morning it would be filled with dyed eggs. Dying eggs, as a rite of spring, has had a long history. The egg itself has taken new forms—plastic, marshmallow, and chocolate, to name a few. But the passage of time has not changed the meaning. With spring comes renewal, and with renewal there is hope.

Eggstra Nice Garden Blessing
Here is an "eggstra" nice garden blessing for your whole family. This is a fun ritual that will bring out your inner artist. We will be burying

an egg (or eggs) in the garden for fertility of the land. If you live in an apartment or have a small yard, you could bury your egg in a flowerpot or window box.

You will need:

Enough eggs for everyone involved
Permanent fine-tipped markers
Egg dye (commercial is fine)
Garden spade (or spoon)

The evening before Ostara, prepare enough eggs for every member to decorate. You can boil them, blow them out by pricking a hole at both ends, or just leave them uncooked. We boil the eggs for our egg hunt and leave the ones for burying uncooked. They decompose pretty quickly.

For your ritual egg take a fine-point permanent pen and write blessings, draw spirals, runes, sigils, or whatever symbols suit you. I like to start at the top and spiral the entire egg with an appropriate poem. Sometimes I write it myself, sometimes I go to Yeats (his stuff is great!). Little kids might draw a picture of a blooming flower with a bright sun. As you do this, remember to focus on growth!

Now dye your egg in whatever manner you typically do, whether it is with commercial egg dye or natural dyes you make from spices and or vegetables—that's up to you.

On the morning of Ostara (as the sun is rising is nice, but it isn't always convenient) go to the garden. Use your garden spade to dig a hole approximately 6 inches deep for each egg. Before burying your egg, say together or elect someone to say,

> *With this egg I place in the earth*
> *We ask the Maiden for rebirth.*
> *Sprouts of green please return for us to see.*
> *As I speak this, so mote it be!*

As you cover your eggs with dirt, focus for a moment on the growth of your garden. Picture full, mature plants with beautiful blossoms. When you're finished, thank the Maiden for her regenerative powers.

Felt Blessing Egg

Another way to promote fertility to the land was to hang eggs in trees. This simple felt egg is fun to make and can be used for Ostara celebrations for years to come.

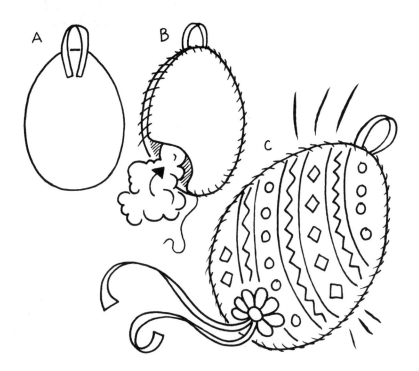

You will need:

1 colorful piece of felt

Scissors

Decorative ribbon cut in 6- to 8-inch lengths

Hot glue gun

Glue stick

Needle

Matching thread
Craft stuffing
Fabric paint

Cut out 2 egg shapes about 3 inches long. Take your ribbon, fold in half, and glue the open ends to the top of 1 of the egg halves (figure A). Put the other egg shape on top of the piece with attached ribbon. Sew the pieces together, leaving a gap to insert the stuffing. Stuff the egg and sew the gap closed (figure B). Now use the fabric paint to decorate your felt egg with magickal symbols (figure C). Once dry, hang and enjoy the blessings of spring!

Chapter 11

Beltane

May's raucous joy calls us to the greenwood.
I watch my children dancing amongst the trees
and grow intoxicated by the scent of wild rose.
I am home in the wildwood!

I have always believed that winter's dreams are fulfilled in May. For it is in the dreary din of winter that I close my eyes and dream of the God's green embrace and hear the distant echo of faerie song. The promise of May keeps me going as I spend long, dark hours poring through seed catalogs and drawing new gardening plans. It comforts me as I watch, through fogged glass, the rain that seems to fall nonstop.

The reminder of warmer days sifts through my kid's reminiscences too.

"Do you remember when we set that mortar off upside down on the Fourth of July?" Josh asks as he throws another log in the woodstove.

"Yes, I remember." I wear a smirk.

"Good times. We almost killed Dad, though."

"Yes, we did." I try not to laugh too much.

In May, my daughter and I run with our headlamps tightly secured at five o'clock in the afternoon. "Mom," she says.

"Yes." I try not to sound out of breath.

"Last summer at this time we would've said it was too hot to run. Remember how we'd wait and run at eight thirty or nine and it was still light?"

"Yes, I remember."

Though we consider ourselves children of the greenwood in the Pacific Northwest, where every season is accented with the color green, it is May that keeps its promises best. I see it in the flowers that add color to our world. I hear it in the birdsong and the never-ending chirping of tree frogs, who elaborately perform for potential mates. It rises with the new shoots that appear in my vegetable gardens.

May is a month of growth and fertility, when the God takes on the aspect of the Horned One and becomes consort to the Goddess, and with their union comes the promise of life.

Kindling Summer

Beltane (meaning "bright fire" in Old Irish) is a cross-quarter Celtic festival that marks the beginning of the light half of the year. It was a time when agricultural people took their herds back to the grassy hillsides. It is thought that Beltane may be derived from the worship of Belenus, a Celtic god of the rising sun who symbolized the vigor of life and the land. Fires were lit high in the hills, and the cattle were driven between them to ritually purify the herd and ensure their protection. It was also common practice for villagers to dance deosil (sunwise) around the fires, a way to ensure their luck for the year. Social behavior was relaxed at Beltane, and after a night of dancing and jumping through the fertile flames, young people were free to wander into the forests or fields to engage in a little fertility magick of their own.

Lighting the Beltane fire was a ritual unto itself. All fires in the community were extinguished, and material for the need-fire was gathered from the wood of the nine sacred trees. Oak (the sun's tree) was hand-drilled to create spark. An easily combustible fungus that grows on birch trees, known as *chaga*, was then added, and it crackled and popped and finally inflamed the most sacred of fires. Coals from the ritual fire were used to rekindle the villagers' own fires, and the ash was used in charm bags and was sprinkled over the fields to increase fertility.

Here is a list of the nine sacred woods and their correspondences to kindle your own Beltane fire:

Birch: The Goddess

Oak: The God

Hazel: Wisdom

Rowan: Life

Hawthorn: Faerie magick

Willow: Death

Fir: Rebirth

Apple: Love

Vine: Joy

As the veil was thin, it was also a good time for our Celtic ancestors to commune with the nature spirits that enlivened the land. The sídhe (or "the good people") were believed to be responsible for milk production and the maturing of crops, so offerings of milk were set out at Beltane. And because it was known that there were faeries that mingled in the mortal world, especially during Samhain and Beltane, one had to be careful. These otherworldly beings that could at times be helpful could also be mischievous—an invitation to dance by one of the handsome sídhe may seem tempting, but the price for such a delight could be to stay in the land of Fae forever.

A Festival for Flora

Many of the Beltane practices we are familiar with started with the Roman celebration of Floralia. A "moveable" festival to gain protection for the flowering blossoms and the propagation of crops, the Romans honored Flora, the goddess-nymph of blossoming plants and fertility, by bedecking the streets with garlands of flowers. The citizens wore floral wreaths and brightly colored clothing and threw handfuls of lupine, vetch, and bean flowers about as they perused the city for the never-ending splendors the festival offered.

There was dancing, banqueting, gladiatorial games, and competitions of all sorts. Theatrical plays and mock combats were performed in the nude by female prostitutes for cheering crowds, and the drink flowed endlessly. Chickpeas were freely thrown at passersby as a sign of fertility, and sexual freedom was celebrated. The symbols of fertility were also *hunted* during this time, for goats and hares were free to roam. It was a flower-strewn, alcohol-enhanced, bawdy party that ensued for five full days.

Here We Go 'Round the Maypole

There is something about the Maypole that, for me, conjures sweet, innocent images of my children dressed in filmy faerie attire and clumsily weaving ribbons under a yellow sun. Our Beltane parties were never complete without one. What I found interesting was the number of my mundane friends who were not aware of what this iconic symbol of spring symbolized. When I would explain that the Maypole was a classic phallic symbol, representing the male organ literally being thrust into the Mother's fertile soil, the response sometimes bordered on horror. "Why are we letting our kids do this?" I usually didn't make it to the part where I told them that the red and white ribbons that were plaited intricately down the pole's shaft symbolized the mixing of female blood and male sperm. Why ruin a good party?

The Maypole has a long history that goes all the way back to the ancient Roman celebration of the resurrection of Attis in a weeklong festival known as *Hilaria* ("the cheerful"). A pine was festooned with wool wrappings and violets. It was then ceremoniously paraded to the temple of Attis's mother/consort, Cybele, where priests danced in frenzied, bloodletting circles around it.

As Roman legions moved and their culture spread, so did some of their customs. Most prevalent in Germany and Britain, Hilaria's frenzied dances evolved into circular dances around a garland-topped pole that we might find more familiar today.

In 1644, the Puritans had the custom of the Maypole outlawed for its blatant display of sexuality. By 1660, the law was repealed and many English villages set up permanent poles in their town centers. Some of these poles measured up to ninety feet tall! It was during the eighteenth century that the interweaving of ribbons became a popular part of the Maypole dance in both France and Italy. Soon troupes of dancers were performing the Maypole dance all over Europe. It was even incorporated into some physical education programs in both England and the United States until the 1950s.

The Maypole almost died out in the twentieth century, but thanks to a resurgence, the tradition has made a comeback. I loved the Beltane celebrations we held when my children were small. Now that they're older we go to Camlann Medieval Village for their Renaissance Beltane celebrations. We dress up, pack a lunch, and spend the day lost in time, for in Camlann it is always 1376. We enjoy listening to minstrels, dancing, candle making, and archery. And after the May Queen is chosen, she leads us in a Maypole dance to the playful sound of pipes, drums, and the hurdy-gurdy. Believe me, the energy raised would make our ancestors proud!

Maypole Dance for Growth

Setting up a Maypole as part of your family or coven Beltane ritual is easier than you might think. No need to go into the forest and cut down a tree. This one is made from PVC pipe, which makes it portable, so you can celebrate the sabbat in a park, backyard, or field and then safely store your Maypole for the next celebration. Note that pipe is sold in ten-foot lengths. You can keep it that long or have the store trim it to the size you want.

You will need:

10-foot-long 1-inch PVC pipe
1¼-inch PVC cap
Lightweight sand paper
Brightly colored spray paint
Colorful ribbons (10 feet by 1 inch)
Hot glue gun
Hammer or mallet
Old weighted umbrella stand or an old holiday tree stand

To make the Maypole, first gently sand the PVC pipe and cap to remove the shiny surface and allow the paint to stick. Spray paint both the pole and the cap in whatever bright color suits your family (figure A). Let dry. As part of the ritual for growth, have everyone involved in the Maypole ritual pick a color of ribbon that suits their intention. I have included some examples.

Green: work, luck, balance

Red: love, strength, courage

Pink: good will, friendship, peace, healing

Light Blue: opportunity, quests, tranquility

Dark Blue: protection, change

Yellow: harmony, creativity

Orange: success, encouragement, vitality

White: truth, purity, justice

Violet: self-improvement

Purple: psychic growth, wisdom, self-assurance

You will then take the ribbons and hot glue them into the top of the pole (figure B). If you have to layer them on top of each other, that's fine. When you are finished, tap the cap over the ribbons with a rubber mallet or cover the cap with a dish towel and gently hammer it onto the top of the pole (figure C). Place it in the umbrella stand. Now you are ready to perform your ritual.

Have everyone hold their ribbons. Focus on the color and its meaning. Imagine your intention growing and gaining strength. Finally, imagine it fully formed. Then say together,

> 'Round the Maypole we shall go a-dancing
> During this time when all things grow.
> We ask for the Lord and Lady's blessing
> And to share with us all they know.
> For as we weave these pretty ribbons,
> The magick intensifies three times three.
> As we circle, we shall will it.
> Let the magick hold—so mote it be!

As you weave around, focus on your intent. Imagine your goal in full bloom. As you end tightly around the pole, everyone raises their hands and yells, "Blessed be!"

When finished, the cap can be easily removed and the ribbons replaced with other colors.

A-Maying We Will Go

A favorite Beltane custom I enjoyed as a child was to leave bouquets for nearby friends and relatives secretly on their front porches. We would put the bouquets in tin cans or mason jars with pretty ribbons and a card with a funny poem that contained clues to the giver's identity.

"Going Maying" is a custom that has deep European roots. Villagers would go into the countryside and bring back leaves, branches, and flowers to decorate themselves, their loved ones, and their abodes with garlands that relayed a statement. Floriography, also known as the language of flowers, hit its peak in the Victorian Age. In a very genteel society, flowers could be used to convey messages that a "proper Victorian" would not dare to speak.

We will be using discarded cans to make pretty little containers for Beltane bouquets to send messages to friends and family.

You will need:

Discarded aluminum vegetable or coffee cans
Hammer and nail
Colorful ribbons
Paper tag material (scrap paper or premade tags to write a poem or wish on)
Flowers!

For each bouquet you will need a clean aluminum can with the label removed. Use a hammer and nail to pound a hole on opposite sides near the rim. Run a ribbon through each side and knot it inside the can. Now fill with flowers and hang! For added fun, you can create your own fun tags to write a poem or riddle and tuck into the bouquet.

If you are doing this for coven-mates or other magickal friends, bewitch your gift by using magickal correspondence for the ribbons and flowers.

I created a very short list of some common garden flowers, weeds, trees, and nuts easily found in many yards to get you started. Some of the meanings are sweet, some funny, and some downright mean! If you are interested in learning more about floriography, there are many books on the topic as well as websites that offer some great information. Enjoy the research!

Acorn: Immortality

Apple Blossom: Beauty and goodness

Bachelor Button: Single blessedness

Bluebell: Humility

Bouquet of Withered Flowers: Rejected love

Bramble: Loneliness, envy, remorse

Buttercup: Ingratitude

Chamomile: Energy in hard times

Columbine: Folly

Daffodil: You're the only one, thinking of you

Daisy (Garden): I share your sentiment

Daisy (Oxeye): A token

Dandelion: Faithfulness, happiness

Dead Leaves: Sadness

Fern: Magick, fascination

Fern (Maidenhair): Secret bond of love

Fir: Time

Forget-Me-Not: True love, memories

Garlic: Courage, strength

Geranium: Stupidity, folly

Grass: Utility, submission

Hydrangea: Thank you for understanding

Iris: Your friendship means so much to me

Ivy: Fidelity, friendship, affection

Lemon Balm: Health

Lily-of-the-Valley: Sweetness

Moss: Maternal love, charity

Nasturtium: Conquest, victory

Nuts: Stupidity

Petunia: Your presence soothes me

Pine: Hope, pity

Queen Anne's Lace: Come home

Red Clover: Industrious

Rose (Lavender): Enchantment

Rose (Pale Pink): I like you, joy

Rose (Red): Romantic love

Rose (Single Full Bloom): I love you

Rose Leaf: You may hope

Rosemary: Remembrance

Sage: Wisdom

Sweet Pea: Thank you for a lovely time, goodbye

Violet: Modesty

Violet (White): Let's take a chance on happiness

White Clover: Think of me

Zinnia: Thinking of an absent friend

notes

Chapter 12

Midsummer

There is faerie magick in the air.
I see it in the tangled flowers clinging to arbors and stone walls.
It rises with the heat and swirls about, making the very air quiver.

In June, when the sun stands still in its fiery glory during the summer solstice, the hand of the Oak King is most evident in the garden. The plants that were just sprouts a month before are lush and beautiful, and the air is alive with the buzz of bees and the sweet song of the evening grosbeak.

As the sun hits its northernmost point, it crosses the sign of Cancer, a watery sign connected to emotions and the home. And it is at home you will find us this time of year—in the garden working the soil, relaxing under shady trees with iced tea and a good book, roasting marshmallows under a twilight sky on the banks of the Sauk, and communing in our own private ways with the spirit of nature who now dons his leafy green cloak.

My oldest son does this by taking a vintage typewriter into the woods. "Nature is my muse," he says. "Inspiration wrapped in green."

Elijah takes his mountain bike out early in the morning and rides to a small hidden lake about five miles from our house. He finds solace there. "It is my church," he says, his expression turning wistful.

Chloe hikes the bluff behind our house to an old maple tree with a large moss-covered branch. "That's where the faeries talk to me," she says. "I made them an altar there and they leave me presents sometimes." She shows me her faerie treasures, which include feathers, hazel nuts, and shriveled forget-me-not and buttercup blooms.

My husband, Steve, takes long evening walks along the river. He is quiet about his revelations, but his eyes reflect a soul at peace. As for me, I enjoy a mile and a half walk to a section of forest that I serendipitously stumbled upon almost fifteen years ago. It is there, where the moss and sword fern are carpet for giant hemlock and Douglas fir, that I feel nature's green presence best. And within this bower as my heart beats to a primordial rhythm, I dance. I feel free.

Midsummer is a celebration of growth, abundance, and, most of all, life! Go to those places where you feel most alive as the sun reaches his peak of strength and celebrate.

Keep the Fire Strong!

Midsummer, or *Litha* (an Old English word roughly translating to June and July), is a fire festival that occurs between June 20 and 22 at the time of the summer solstice. For the ancients, this time between planting and harvest, when the Goddess was pregnant with the ripening fruits of the fields, was celebrated with bonfires, fire wheels, and torchlit processions that were lit to ritually strengthen the sun.

The fires were kindled from oak, which is the sun's tree, and fir to symbolize the continuing cycle of rebirth. Villagers danced around the fires as they tossed mugwort and vervain into the flames, ritually burning their bad luck and guaranteeing good fortune to come. Another custom was to hold branches of larkspur in front of their eyes as they circled. This was thought to protect the health of their eyes for the remainder of the year. Branches of gorse were also dipped into the flames and then carried around herds; the cleansing smoke was thought to aid in the prevention of disease.

Fire wheels were another part of the festivities. Villagers collected straw and attached it to cart wheels, which were brought to the tops of hills by the male participants. The wheel was flung and sent rolling toward whatever body of water lay below. There was much revelry as the fiery circle blazed toward its inevitable end. If the wheel continued to burn as it hit the banks and extinguished in the stream, river, lake, or well, it was a sign of an abundant harvest in the fall. And all of these activities were led by torchlit processions from village centers to sacred ritual areas.

As the firm grip of Christianity took hold, Midsummer rites continued in the guise of Saint John's Day. The balefires that set the hilltops alight no longer aided the sun's dying strength as it took its southerly turn but were set to drive away heathenly dragons. These dragons, it was told, became aroused by the midsummer heat, mated in the sky, and poisoned wells, streams, and rivers by releasing their seed into them. Yikes! In Christian iconography the dragon represented Satan and his cunning temper that destroys mankind. Much like John the Baptist spiritually cleansed Jesus through baptism in the river, the villages were cleansed through the baptism of fire.

Midsummer traditions are still celebrated to this day, especially in Europe, where balefires and fire wheels can still be seen lighting up the hillsides on the eve of the summer solstice. In several Northern European countries Midsummer is a national holiday, with trappings including the Maypole, singing, dancing, flower gathering, special meals, and, of course, fire!

Midsummer (or the weekend closest to it) is a great time to hit the beach or a favorite park with your family and enjoy a little of the sun's strength-gaining benefits, such as the increase in white blood cell production, which boosts the immune system; vitamin D production, to keep depression at bay; increase in oxygen content, which boosts stamina; and the sun's healthy effects on skin disorders like acne and eczema. Of course, too much of a good thing can also be harmful: remember to stay hydrated, stay close to a shaded area, and for Goddess's sake, don't allow yourself to get sunburned. Get out there and enjoy the sun!

Mixing Kids and the Fae

Ancient people knew that faerie magick stirred in the midsummer heat that settled throughout the land. This being so, Midsummer was known as one of the three great faerie festivals (including Samhain and Beltane). It was believed that at midnight on Midsummer you could see throngs of faerie folk dancing around great balefires, and it was rumored, as the magick sparked within the heat of the flame, that animals could speak, songs could burst forth from the surrounding hillsides, and the fern would bloom at midnight, bestowing the gifts of wealth and invisibility.

Faeries have been guardians to the elements and enlivening the earth since the beginning of time. And faeries have been thought responsible for everything from winning wartime battles and successful marriages to disfigured babies and bloody milk ever since. In truth, faeries are spirit beings and are tightly connected to the land. And when called upon to empower our personal sacred spaces, the results are nothing but extraordinary. That being said, they have a moral code that is very different from our own, and when offended, they can become very, shall we say … mischievous. This can be difficult for children to understand, so I don't recommend parents giving their children creative license on this one.

Here are a few dos and don'ts for mixing kids with the Fae:

- *Do* become a steward of the land. You don't have to drag the family to the top of an old growth tree or chain yourself to a logging truck, but you can do your part with small changes; recycling, composting, creating a butterfly garden, and feeding the birds are all small ways to make a difference and are much appreciated by the Fae.

- *Do* plant flowers and herbs to entice them. (Refer to page 115 for faerie garden ideas.)

- *Do* make faerie houses! Having the kids involved in creating a faerie house, altars, or a complete faerie garden is a great way for them to work with the Fae.

- *Do* invite faeries into your garden. Yes! And the blessings will be evident. Your garden will take on an otherworldly feel. The flowers will seem more vibrant and scents more intoxicating. Once the Fae have blessed your garden space, you'll never want to go back indoors!

- *Do* show the faeries respect. Once you have dedicated your garden to the Fae, create an altar for them. My daughter made hers on a wooded hill behind our house where the property is still wild. If you don't have a wild space, tuck faerie statuary near a fern with some tumbled stones and maybe a few shiny objects. Leave them a few sweets from time to time too!

- *Don't* let small children work with faeries alone. If you have a small child who is interested in working with faeries, either do a little research on your own and work with your little one, or go to a circle or coven-mate who has experience working with nature spirits and would be willing to work with your child.

- *Don't* invite them into your home. This is a recipe for disaster. You may find that things like car keys, jewelry, and coins have been misplaced or are missing altogether (they like shiny objects). Items may be knocked off counters and shelves. And because they're spirit beings, they may give your home a spooky feel. And that scratchy noise you hear … it's not mice.

- *Don't* call on the Fae if you're not living a green lifestyle. What do I mean by this? If you are not doing your part (however small) to be an environmental steward, why would you dare call on a nature spirit? Have you ever read the popular garden sign "Don't Piss Off the Faeries"? Yeah, this might do it.

Working with the Fae, if done correctly, can be rewarding for both you and your children. And remember, if you're lucky enough to wake up late one night to the tinkling sound of bells and ethereal voices softly singing, you have pleased the faeries and you are truly blessed.

Here's a fun way to invite faeries into your garden:

Set up a flat stone in a pretty section of your garden. Set out a little honey and maybe a few shiny coins or a pretty crystal. String some bells and give each of your children a set to shake.

As the kids dance about, shaking their bells, say,

Nature spirits far and near,
We call for you, our song is clear,
To enchant our flowers each and every day
And enliven our garden with your faerie play.

Thank the faeries in your own way!

Sunny Stepping-Stones

Add a little of the sun's enchantment to your Midsummer faerie garden with these sunny stepping-stones. This craft will make approximately ten stepping-stones. If you are only making one or two, you can purchase five-pound boxes of concrete in any craft store. For the molds, anything that will hold concrete will do: old cake pans, pie tins, cardboard cereal boxes, or old food-storage containers. You can also pick up stepping-stone molds at any craft store.

You will need:

Newspaper
Molds
Nonstick cooking spray
Rubber gloves
Large spoon or paint mixer
1 50-pound bag of concrete
Water
Old bucket
Pretty glass beads, stones, or mosaic tiles in bright, sunny colors

Lay newspaper down on the lawn to protect grass from concrete clumps. Prepare clean, dry molds by giving them a nice coating of the nonstick cooking spray to prevent the concrete from sticking. Wear gloves to mix desired amount of concrete with water in your bucket until it is the consistency of brownie batter. Pour into molds, gently tapping them so the mixture will spread evenly and release any bubbles.

Now it's time for the fun! Use your glass beads, tiles, or stones to create large sun shapes on your new stepping-stones. When complete, let them dry for 24 to 48 hours. Pop them out and let them cure for another 5 to 7 days before putting them in the garden.

Blessed be and enjoy the sun!

The Oak King and the Holly King

May and June are my favorite months in Washington State. I wake early to slender streaks of golden sunlight that stroke my face, fueling my soul. I make coffee to take out to the gazebo, where I sit for just a little while taking in the green workmanship of the Oak King's hand. I gaze at eagles catching thermals near peaks to the south. Crows are nesting in trees to the west, and they croak in sweet harmony. The river also softly sings its morning song, a lullaby to calm my nerves from a sometimes-hectic week. The garden is lush and the air is sweet, and it is on these mornings that I tell myself there is no place I would rather live than right here. It would be worth 364 days of rain to experience this one perfect morning.

But on the morning of the summer solstice, as I sit and take in my surroundings, I feel somewhat bittersweet. For the sun has hit his crescendo. The Oak King takes off his leafy crown and the reign is handed over to the Holly King. The light decreases little by little, and my beloved green canopy fades and shrivels as darkness takes an ever-increasing hold. But just as the Holly King's dark cloak threatens to blot the light out completely, the Oak King takes back his crown and I wait patiently for the green.

The Oak King and the Holly King represent an ongoing battle between the light half of the year and the dark. As aspects of the Horned God, the two are solar twins or, basically, two sides of the same coin. The Oak King with his powers of growth and fertility can still be seen in cathedrals all over Europe as the Green Man. The Holly King represents reflection and introspection. Their tale has been compared to other mythological battles, including those of Lugh and Balor, Gawain and the Green Knight, and Balan and Balin.

Their ongoing battle has been acted out for centuries by dance troupes and mummers during the time of the solstices, and many covens and circles continue the practice to this day.

So how about it? Get the kids together and put on your own production of a classic battle. The summer solstice is a perfect time to take the fun outdoors. You don't need to write lines if the kids aren't into it—just play really cool music and add some epic sword play (with fake swords, of course)! Costumes can be as simple, with leafy, silk chaplets and face paint, or as elaborate as you please, complete with robes decorated with seasonal flair and gnarly wood staffs with bells.

If you don't feel comfortable writing a play, use the script below. It can be easily modified for families with more than two children by adding narrators who can tell the story as the kings battle out the seasons!

Battle of the Oak King and the Holly King

It is summer and the Oak King proudly looks over his domain.

OAK KING: Ahh! Look at the flowers in bloom. (*Sniffs the air.*) And there is a scent of honey in the air.

Enter Holly King.

HOLLY KING: Brother, though the sun is high, the time has come.

OAK: Your icy fingers will not touch leaf, bud, nor limb. (*Circles around the Holly King.*)

HOLLY: I am sorry, dear brother. Look. (*Points toward the sky.*) Darkness is winning even now in the heat of the sun.

Both circle around each other, threatening each other with their chosen weapons.

OAK: You say it is time, but I say it is not. For the land still shines with the work I have done!

HOLLY: Your work is truly finished, dear brother, and for everything that has bloomed and every seed that has sprouted, I shall place them in my cold hands until they wither and die. (*Laughs villainously.*)

OAK: Noooo!

The two kings battle it out until, finally, the Holly King is victorious. The Oak King, wounded badly, struggles to stand.

OAK: This is not over, brother. I will be back to fight another battle. (*Limps off stage.*)

The Holly King proudly looks over his domain.

HOLLY: Ahh! Look at the flowers; they are already fading. (*Sniffs the air.*) And there is the scent of frost in the air!

notes

Chapter 13

Lughnasadh

A golden sun illuminates the rewards of our labor
as we play hide-and-seek within the cornrows and sunflowers.
The air is tinged with plum and apple ... The harvest season has begun.

The Goddess takes on her aspect of Grain Mother as the August sun lays golden across the land. And though some of our warmest days are yet to come, there is a shift in light and mood. The chatter of bird-song has silenced and long shadows begin to form. The heaviest work in the garden begins, and the whole family chips in to help with the harvest.

There are beans to snap and corn to pick, cabbage to ferment and berries to process. Long, sultry days are spent filling freezer bags, hanging herbs, and drying legumes. We braid garlic and onions and pickle our beets, beans, and cucumbers. Finally, we spend many hot hours transforming our tomatoes into gallons of tomato sauce.

If we're not in the garden, we're helping my daughter prep for the county fair. There are goats to bathe, clip, and trim to show-ring perfection, songs for Chloe to practice for performing arts, and photographs to mount. We choose the finest canned goods and vegetables for competition and pack enough supplies for a week of camping behind the goat barn at the Skagit County Fairgrounds.

Though the week is nothing less than exhausting, we enjoy taking part in an enduring piece of Americana whose roots reach back to ancient Eastern Mediterranean feast days, when markets, trade, and revelry were the norm.

One of the longest-running fairs is the Irish Puck Fair (meaning "fair of the he-goat" in its original Irish), which occurs every August in Killorglin and has been in written existence since 1603. There are contradicting stories of its inception, but is it thought to be traced back to ancient Lughnasadh celebrations. It was a harvest festival in which the he-goat reigned as a symbol of fertility.

The fair itself is three days long. On the first day, called the Gathering, a wild he-goat is brought into town from the hillsides and crowned by the Puck Queen, a local schoolgirl. There is a carnival atmosphere and horses are brought into town to auction. The second day, Fair Day, is when the cattle fair occurs. The final day, or the Scattering, is when King Puck is escorted back to his mountain home and set free. All three days include markets, dancing, fireworks, parades, music, and fun.

As I sit by a crackling fire at our makeshift fair home, I listen to the carnival-goers' revelry and the bleats and bays of restless animals and think about the agricultural fairs of our ancestors. For those of us lucky enough to be living in a first-world country, the need to grow our own food has been obliterated. We can easily drive to a supermarket and buy not only what is in season but also what is not. And because of this, the old-fashioned county fair is becoming a thing of the past.

While strolling through various tents and pavilions, instead of rows and rows of giant pumpkins, bushels of tomatoes, and hand-stitched quilts, you are more apt to see hundreds of vendors barking the wonders of their products, everything from massaging chairs to robotic vacuum cleaners. But take a sudden turn and there, behind the large commercial area, is the goat barn. My daughter's face shines as she educates fair-goers about the joys and struggles of goat husbandry.

Not far from the goat barn is the very small garden pavilion where you will find my name and names of many of my dear friends paired with our vegetables, shining examples of the garden's delights. I have to smile—I am proud to be among the few families in our valley who grow most of their own food and are passing these skills down to their children. We are helping keep alive an annual rite that still celebrates the first foods of the harvest. Our ancestors would be proud!

Assembly of Lugh

Lughnasadh (meaning the "assembly of Lugh" in Irish) is a Celtic cross-quarter festival in celebration of the harvest of the first fruits of the land. Legend holds that Lugh, a Celtic god who was the inventor of all arts, patron of commerce, and hero of the Tuatha Dé Danann (securing for them the secrets of planting and ploughing), inaugurated this day as an assembly in memory of his foster mother, Tailtiu. She died from exhaustion while clearing forested land for planting near Teltown in County Meath.

Tailtiu is connected to Ireland as an earth goddess, and her death was a way of ensuring a successful harvest as long as the funerary games were held.

Interestingly, Lugh had several wives who upon death were commemorated by Lugh with their own assembly sites in other parts of the country. Carman's site is in County Wexford; her festival ensured that the first corn and choicest fruits would be plentiful and households full of cheer. Nás's site is connected with an assembly in Naas in County Kildare, and Buí's is connected with Knowth.

These hilltop sites were inaugural gatherings where kings had to ritually marry the sovereign goddess of the land to earn their right to rule. Marriages, legal matters, feasting, markets, and fairs were all held at these sites. So in some part, Lugh became responsible for the relationship between king and earth goddess, as well as the people and the land itself.

Proceedings to hilltop assembly sites continue to this day in parts of Ireland during the first part of August, though no longer in the name of Lugh but its Christianized form, Lammas (from Old English *hlāfmæsse,* "loaf mass"). The most famous of these assembly sites takes modern pilgrims to the top of Croagh Patrick, a 2,510-foot mountain in County Mayo. At sunset twice a year in April and August, the sun seems to wrap around the remains of a standing stone at its peak and "roll" down the western side of the mountain. The pilgrimage is typically done barefoot, a penance for bad behavior, and is followed by dancing and drink.

Lughnasadh is a great time to take your family on a hike, explore your surrounding countryside, or visit a local farm that offers U-pick berries. By doing the work yourself, it's cheaper and a lot more fun! Both blueberries and blackberries are at their peak (in most of the country) around Lughnasadh and are easy to pick, even for your littlest helper. Take your beautiful fruit home and use it to make jam or eat it fresh. As you enjoy these first fruits of the season, remember to thank the living spirit within these plants for the sustenance they provide.

Honoring the First Fruits

As we celebrate this sabbat, we must remember the earth goddess in her guise as Demeter. She is the harvest queen and Corn Mother, and her daughter Kore is the grain that is dropped deep into the earth and returns to us as Persephone, the Maiden of spring. For our European ancestors, the word "corn" meant any type of "grain," and grain is the staff of life.

The extreme importance of grain (or corn) is seen in the folk customs and ballads connected to harvest time. The first cuttings were often made into bread, brewed into beer, or saved for seed, to ensure the continuance of life. The last sheaf was typically made into a corn dolly. The corn dolly (roughly meaning "grain idol") represented the spirit of vegetation and was ritually placed above the hearth or the entrance of the home as a symbol of protection and abundance. It was then returned to the land when the first furrows were plowed into the still cool spring soil, a symbol to remind us that what dies is reborn.

This is also illustrated through the ballad of "John Barleycorn," a somewhat violent song (might be too scary to read to very young children) of English origin that tells the regenerative story of barley. I have to say, I've always loved this old ballad and read it freely to my boys at Lughnasadh, who thought the cutting and thrashing of poor old John Barleycorn was pretty cool. Their favorite line: "John Barleycorn must die!" In the end, John Barleycorn does not die, of course. He is harrowed in again spring after spring, where he grows thick and strong continuing his yearly sacrifice for our nourishment.

First Fruits Ritual

Here's a ritual in honor of nature's sacred gift—the first fruits.

You will need:

Green, orange, or red candle (the Grain Mother)

Fresh fruit, veggies, or flowers that you grew yourselves, received from family or friends, or bought from a local farmers' market

Corn dolly (optional)

Fresh-baked bread or scones
Fresh juice or milk

This is a nice ritual to perform outside, maybe at a picnic table, spread out on a blanket, under the shade of a tree, or near your garden. Set your candle up safely on a fireproof dish. Around the candle, place your "first fruits." Before the ritual, have your family ground and center themselves or cast sacred space in their own way.

This is a chance for each of your kids to talk about what "first fruits" means to them. Hopefully some of the produce or flowers that were placed around the candle were fruits they had helped propagate.

First, have someone light the candle and say,

Thank you, Goddess of the earth, for these fruits a-plenty.
Thank you for the grains and berries, of which there are a-many.
Thank you for enchanting these foods with your loving hand
And spreading your blessings lovingly across this beautiful land.

Each family member now can pick up a favorite fruit, vegetable, or flower and express why they are thankful for it. It's okay if all the kids want to be thankful for the blueberries and no one picks the green beans—the Goddess understands. When everyone has had a turn, snuff out the candle for another use, open your circle in your own way and enjoy some fresh-baked bread, scones, or what have you with some juice or milk. After you are done, play a few old-fashioned games like red rover, capture the flag, or Marco Polo; read poetry; or play checkers or chess in honor of Tailtiu and her funerary games.

Corn Dolly

Corn dollies represent the spirit of vegetation and were hung above the hearth or entrance of the home for protection and abundance. Later, they were used as a badge of trade at hiring fairs. If you were a shepherd, you would plait wool into your dolly; a carpenter would add a bit of wood. They were also given to friends and neighbors as gifts around the harvest to ensure luck for the community and as love tokens from potential suitors.

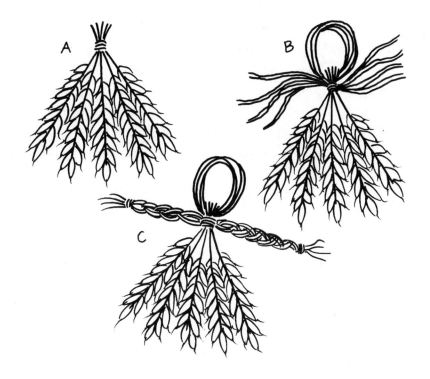

Corn dollies are made from sheaves of wheat, barley, rye, or oat straw plaited into intricate shapes. Many of the examples we have now are British in origin, and that is reflected in the design names. Some of the most beautiful include the Stafford Knot, Essex Terret, and the Yorkshire Spiral. I have included directions for a corn dolly that is a little more kid friendly but, hopefully, keeps the essence of the art alive. Stalks can be obtained from a farmer's field or bought at a craft store or online. If we are unable to acquire wheat stalks from a neighbor, we typically use stalks of field grass that have a nice seed head. Because it's not real cool to plow field grass or grain into your vegetable or flower garden bed in the spring, we bury ours in the compost at Ostara.

You will need:

3–5 stalks of grain (wheat, rye, barely, or oats) per dolly

A package of raffia

The seed heads of grain will compose the bottom of the skirt, so take the stalks and bundle them in a way as the seed heads lay attractively. Trim to desired length and tie off at top with a piece of raffia (figure A).

Use more raffia to create a head and the top layer of skirt. You will do this by looping raffia over your bundle of straw and tying it securely. Leave a nice loop at the top. This creates the head and allows the remaining raffia to hang freely over the stalks of grain (figure B).

Braid pieces of raffia and tie around your dolly for arms. You could also braid raffia for hair (figure C).

There you go! You can hang her up for protection and abundance or put her to bed until spring.

Chapter 14

Mabon

The sun grows weary and autumn's chill breath
clings to the alder and maple.
Children chase tumbling leaves under a Harvest Moon
as the last canned goods are stored.
The hearth calls to me ... Time to rest.

September is a spark that ignites the fires of autumn. This time of equal day and night hints of the fiery beauty to come. In Washington, vine maples begin to turn scarlet and the swallows gather in large groups, organizing their departure. The sun mellows and casts a golden light, dappling the fields and pathways with shadow, and we are drawn to our hearth fires to pursue quieter tasks.

As a child, I would travel in September with my sisters and our mother, aunt, and grandmother to the flat, wide farmland that seemed to stretch for miles near the edge of Puget Sound. Upon first glance, these fields seemed used up, wasted. But once we got out into the loamy, dark soil and began to pull back the yellowed and broken foliage, we found treasure: plump peas, tender bush beans, beautiful squash, and, my favorite treasure of all to dig, Yukon Gold potatoes. My family was part of a group of gleaners. What do gleaners do? Well, they are volunteers who go into agricultural fields after the harvest and gather the fruits and vegetables that may have otherwise gone to waste. The produce is then separated and distributed between gleaning organization members and food banks, and a small percentage of the crop goes back to the farmer.

Mentioned both in the Old Testament and the Koran, gleaning has been a successful community action program since ancient times. The practice provided farmers with a way of cleaning up their fields and making use of fruit, vegetables, and grain that may not have been suitable for market or that may have been missed by laborers, while also providing much-needed nutritious food to families in need.

Today, gleaners are not only in the fields gathering agricultural waste, but they are also involved with local grocery stores, clothing stores, restaurants, and bakeries. They collect items that have an expired shelf life but still pack a nutritious punch or much-needed warmth for families in need.

By definition, a gleaner is someone who gathers gradually. I like that. So during this time, after the hard work of the harvest and just before the darkness sets in, this is a good time to sit down with a cup of tea and mentally glean memories and events of the past year. Did you keep those resolutions you had made on New Year's Day? Yeah, I know … me neither. But what about the great memories made with family, coven- or circle-mates, and friends? What did you accomplish magickally? I'll bet you and your family raised some amazing energy over the year. Be proud of your accomplishments, for you have worked hard to glean those small pieces that make a difference in the lives of your loved ones.

Harvest Home

Most modern Pagans call the autumn equinox Mabon in recognition of the Welsh god Mabon ap Modron (meaning "the great son of the great mother" in Welsh). Mabon's story is one of a son who is abducted from his mother, the goddess of the otherworld, when he is just three days old. And it is only through the wisdom of the stag, crow, owl, eagle, and salmon that Mabon is released from his captivity.

Mabon's story is similar to that of other solar deities, as it follows an outline of our agricultural year. He was born of a divine mother, abducted and taken to an otherworld, and released to perform great deeds, and, finally, he won the devotion of the divine maiden. It is a story of power and rebirth that repeats its telling year after year, but our family has always associated this second harvest festival with family and *home*. And for this I look back to the Harvest Home festivals that originated in Britain and continue in some remote regions to this day.

What is the first thing you think of when you hear the words "Harvest Home"? Is it the Thomas Tryon novel of the same name or the miniseries starring Bette Davis based on the novel (which scared the bejeezus out of me in the 1970s)? Because if it is, I think we could be best friends. It's a seriously fun read about modern-day Eleusinian mystery cult initiates who perform a literal sacrifice every seven years. I have a copy of it on my fireplace mantle and whenever I'm irritated with my husband, I just point to it. Luckily, we both have a sense of humor.

But, seriously, true Harvest Home celebrations embodied the jubilation felt after a year's hard labor finished. For our ancestors, a successful harvest brought relief and gratitude to the God and Goddess that bellies would be full during the dark, long months to come and there would be seed in the spring to begin the cycle all over again. It's hard for modern people to imagine a world without supermarkets, where our food is packaged neatly and ready for us on a whim, and crazier still to imagine that this has only changed within the last hundred years. In fact, you probably could talk with any of your older living relatives who could tell you stories of their own family's joys and tribulations of working closely with the land for their sustenance.

Harvest Home marked the end of the backbreaking labor that came from weeks of mowing stalks and processing grain, not to mention the harvesting and processing and storing of vegetables, fruits, and berries.

There was much celebration as the last sheaf was cut, and many rituals and customs arose to keep the grain safe throughout the winter, enabling planting to begin anew in the spring.

Celebrations typically began with the bringing in of the last of the grain from the field on what was sometimes called the "hock cart." These carts would be decorated with garlands of seasonal flowers and corn. The children riding on top of it would ring bells and sing songs or just shout out for joy. The harvest feast followed and was typically held in the barn. Hosted by the farm owner for friends, family, and laborers who had helped with the harvest, meals included beef, mutton, potatoes, seed cakes, and plenty of beer and ale. This was followed by more beer and ale, toasts, dancing, and merriment. And all of this was overseen by the Harvest Lord. Who was the Harvest Lord? Well, he was typically the foreman of the laborers. As overseer, he was in charge of wage negotiations, enforced punishment for unruly workers, and implemented fines (known as a largesse) to strangers who happened to stumble upon the working field. He was sometimes ceremoniously crowned at the harvest feast and led the toasts to the farm owner and his family.

Beheading the Sheaf

Cutting the last sheaf of grain was an event marked with much ceremony and superstition. In some parts of England, the last sheaf was known as the "head" or the "neck." Because the spirit of the grain was known to dwell in this last sheaf, superstitious laborers did not take cutting the last sheaf lightly. They would typically tie off the sheaf and stand back and throw their sickles at it until it dropped to the ground, only then crying out in excitement, "We have it! We have it! We have it! A neck! A neck! A neck!" In parts of Ireland, it was the girls who were invited to try their skill at beheading the sheaf. The lucky one who skillfully took it off in one swipe would be married by the year's end.

But as lucky as it was to cut the last sheaf of wheat in some regions, in others it was quite the opposite. In South Ayrshire, Scotland, where the last sheaf was known as the "hare," it was not desirable to be the one whose sickle struck it because of the hare's connotation with witches. In some regions of Ireland, the last sheaf was called the *Cailleach* (hag) and, as an insult, thrown into the field of a neighbor who had not yet completed his harvest. The last farmer to finish the harvest had to take care of the Cailleach throughout the winter.

After the sheaf was cut, it was gathered and taken back to the farmer's house, where it was exchanged for a meal by the farmer's wife. It was intricately plaited into a corn dolly and was sometimes paraded on the hock cart and used as a centerpiece during the harvest feast. The dolly was then ritually hung for abundance above an entrance or "put to bed" until the first plowing in the spring.

A custom in Scotland dictated that if the harvest was good and completed before All Hallow's Eve, the corn dolly was woven into the form of a young girl. But if it was a poor harvest or finished after All Hallow's Eve, she was woven into the form of the hag.

The vast amount of customs and rituals that surround the harvest reflect a reliance on nature that modern-day people find hard to comprehend. So the next time you're in the grocery store, as you reach for the box of oats or the presliced whole grain bread and place it in your shopping cart, keep in mind the farmers who work with our Mother Gaia to provide us with nutritious food.

Witch's Thanksgiving Prayer

The second of three harvest festivals, Mabon, is known as the Witch's Thanksgiving. And what better way to celebrate than at your home with your family? We prepare a traditional thanksgiving meal and carry it down to the riverfront, where I decorate with true Martha Stewart flair, including burlap table runners, buckets of sunflowers, and festive garlands. I hang tea lights in mason jars from the low branches of the maples and have a campfire blazing to ward off an evening chill and maybe to roast a few marshmallows on, as well. Sometimes it's just our family, but we have also included friends and neighbors (magickal and mundane) who want to join in on our fun.

There is one rule we abide by at our Mabon feast, and that is everything prepared must contain local or homegrown ingredients (flour and sugar are my exceptions). Chloe and I prepare the vegetable dishes, salads, and a pie. Elijah makes beet pancakes from his own beets and our apples, and Josh helps Steve with the smoking of ham and cheese we buy from local farmers. It all smells heavenly. I took a cheese-making class this past summer and am excited to have Steve smoke our own cheese next fall.

Something we always do before we eat our Mabon dinner is say a prayer of thanksgiving to the God and Goddess for the gift of nature and the bounty it provides. I have to say, it's very satisfying to sit under the giant sweeping branches of our maple trees and gaze at a table laden with fruits of the earth that we help cultivate. We stand around our table and raise joined hands toward the sky.

I usually start out with something weepy and sappy, and then each family member adds to the prayer. The energy raised from our words is palatable and still hangs prickly and electric as our guests arrive.

Your Mabon feast certainly doesn't have to be as elaborate as the one I just described. But including locally or homegrown ingredients in a dish or two at Mabon is a nice way to acknowledge Harvest Home celebrations of the past and to thank the God and Goddess for the fruits of the earth. Our family does not typically pray before meals, but at Mabon thankfulness is a key element of the sabbat, and acknowledging those blessings we have received through the practice of prayer feels suitable.

As modern Pagans we have so much to be thankful for—the fruits of the earth that nourish our bodies, the fruits of the soul that provide balance in a sometimes hectic world, and, not to mention, the freedom to walk with our loved ones under a starry sky and worship our gods in the manner we feel appropriate. So on this day, before your meal of thanksgiving, join your loved ones in raising your hands to the sky and give thanks. Families linked hand in hand are a powerful kind of magick.

Here is a simple Mabon blessing to get you started:

Balance in light, heart, soul, and mind,
Balance between the Lord and Lady Divine.
We give thanks for the bounty the harvest brings.
We give thanks for the reassurance of new life in the spring.
Blessed be.

Apple-Faced Soul Dolly

Our ancestors didn't have big-box stores with aisles and aisles of movies, video games, and action figures to buy for their children, nor did they have Amazon Prime to order from at a whim. Most families had to create their own entertainment or make toys and games from what they had on hand.

One popular primitive toy was the apple-faced doll. And with the apple's connection to the soul, Mabon is a great time to create apple-faced dolls that can later be used in Samhain ritual.

You will need:

1 large apple per person
Vegetable peeler
Paring knife for carving (butter knife or spoons can work for the little ones)
Lemon juice
Salt
1 ½-inch wood dowel per apple
Mason jar
Scraps of natural fiber, corn husks, or grain or grass stalks for decorating

Peel your apples. Use the paring knife (or butter knife or spoon) to carve out facial features. If this will be used in ritual, concentrate on your magickal intent as you carve. You may even want to carve symbols or your intention into the back of your apple head. When finished, coat your apple head in lemon juice and salt to help preserve your dolly. Poke a dowel into the apple and stand it in a mason jar. Place the jar in a sunny window and let the apple dry approximately 3 to 4 weeks. Decorate the dowel with natural fiber, husks, or stalks of grass or wheat.

During your Samhain ritual you can ceremoniously bury your soul dolly—your intentions to be reborn and become fruitful.

Conclusion
Reap What You Sow

It's been a wonderful journey, and I have enjoyed our time together. But the twilight hues are seeping into a tired sky, and I hear the sounds of family calling me back. There is a fork in the road just up ahead, and that is where I'll leave you to scatter the seeds we have gathered together along the way.

As you continue along your path that winds between the worlds, don't forget to take off your shoes, play freely, and look for the magick in the mundane.

Remember well that within each of us lie the seeds of hope for a better way—cultivate them so that others may know the importance of sustainability and keep true to the stewardship of this beautiful planet we inhabit.

Slow down. Take time to delight in the Goddess as the Wheel of the Year turns slowly but surely, never ceasing. Celebrate the little things in life—the scent of rain on new spring foliage, the newborn sun at Yule, or the first tinted leaf that falls on a brisk autumn morning. Relish the sound of silence.

Teach your children to appreciate their own beautiful souls as they, in turn, learn to appreciate the differences of others. Remember, the rose doesn't try to out-blossom the tulip. They just bloom, and we are better for it.

Keep your hands close to the soil. Share the secrets of our agricultural past with the gift of a seed. Create your own tea blends and sip slowly from china cups as the wind tickles the wind chimes and whispers ancient teachings.

Never forget that you are never too old to make faerie houses, blow dandelion wishes, or climb a favorite old tree. And most definitely, remember to dance under a warm Thunder Moon with your family.

Blessed be your journey!

Bibliography

Amref Health Africa. "Female Genital Mutilation Has No Place in Africa." Accessed December 2016. http://amref.org/news/news/female-genital-mutilation-has-no-place-in-africa.

Arnold, Catherine. *The Sexual History of London: From Roman Londinium to the Swinging City—Lust, Vice, and Desire Across the Ages.* New York: St. Martin's Press, 2011.

Arroyo, Stephen. *Astrology, Psychology and the Four Elements: An Energy Approach to Astrology & Its Use in the Counseling Arts.* Sebastopol, CA: CRCS Publications, 1975.

Carmichael, Alexander. *Carmina Gadelica: Hymns and Incantations.* Vol 1. Edinburgh: T. and A. Constable, 1900. Electronic reproduction by John Bruno Hare for Internet Sacred Texts Archive, 2005. http://www.sacred-texts.com/neu/celt/cg1/.

Carretani, Jessica. "The Contagion of Happiness." Harvard Medical School. Accessed February 2016. https://hms.harvard.edu/news/harvard-medicine/contagion-happiness.

Chevallier, Andre. *The Encyclopedia of Medicinal Plants: A Practical Guide to Over 550 Key Herbs & Their Medicinal Uses.* New York: DK Publications, 1996.

Cole, Adeline P. "The 17th Century Still-Room." *The Herbalist.* Boston, MA: Herb Society of America, 1935. http://www.neuhsa.org/The17thc.StillRoom.pdf.

Congreve, Celia. "The Firewood Poem." *The Times,* March 2, 1930. http://www.skyline-sooty.co.uk/history-poems.

Conway, D.J. *Maiden, Mother, Crone: The Myth & Reality of the Triple Goddess.* St. Paul, MN: Llewellyn Publications, 1999.

Coon, Nelson, Louise Hyde, Bonnie Fisher, Marion Wilbur, Barbara Foust, Heinze Grotzke, and William Hylton. *The Rodale Herb Book.* Emmaus, PA: Rodale Press, 1974.

Cooper Marcus, Clare. *House as a Mirror of the Self: Exploring the Deeper Meaning of Home,* Boston, MA: Conari Press, 1995.

Crosson, Monica. "Conjuring Up a Good Night's Sleep." In *Llewellyn's 2015 Magical Almanac,* 317–27. Woodbury, MN: Llewellyn Publications, 2014.

———. "Seed Saving … Pass It On." In *Llewellyn's 2015 Herbal Almanac,* 9–19. Woodbury, MN: Llewellyn Publications, 2014.

———. "Under a Blood Moon: A Family Ritual." In *Llewellyn's 2017 Witches' Companion,* 166–177. Woodbury, MN: Llewellyn Publications, 2016.

Cunningham, Scott. *Encyclopedia of Magical Herbs.* St. Paul, MN: Llewellyn Publications, 1985.

Dugan, Ellen. *Garden Witchery: Magick from the Ground Up.* St. Paul, MN: Llewellyn Publications, 2003.

———. *Herb Magic for Beginners: Down to Earth Enchantments.* Woodbury, MN: Llewellyn Publications, 2006.

Dunwich, Gerina. *A Witch's Halloween: A Complete Guide to the Magick, Incantations, Recipes, Spells, and Lore.* Avon, MA: Provenance Press, 2007.

El Issa, Erin. "2016 American Household Credit Card Debt Study." NerdWallet. December 14, 2016. www.nerdwallet.com/blog/credit-card-data/average-credit-card-debt-household.

Fleming, Fergis, Shahrukh Husain, C. Scott Littleton, and Linda Malcor. *Heroes of the Dawn: Celtic Myth.* London: Duncan Baird Publishers, 1996.

Franklin, Anna. *Hearth Witch.* Lear Books, 2006.

Franklin, Anna, and Paul Mason. *Lammas: Celebrating the Fruits of the First Harvest.* St. Paul, MN: Llewellyn Publications, 2001.

Frazier, James. *The Golden Bough: A Study in Magic and Religion*. Oxford: Oxford University Press, 2009.

Freeman, Mara. *Kindling the Celtic Spirit: Ancient Traditions to Illumine Your Life Through the Seasons*. New York: HarperCollins, 2001.

Fustel De Coulanges, Numa Denis. *The Ancient City: A Study on the Religion, Laws, and Institutions of Greece and Rome*. Baltimore, MD: Johns Hopkins University Press, 1980.

Grieve, Margaret. *A Modern Herbal*. Vol. 1, A–H. Mineola, NY: Dover Publications, 1971.

———. *A Modern Herbal*. Vol. 2, I–Z. Mineola, NY: Dover Publications, 1971.

Grimassi, Raven. *Beltane: Springtime Rituals, Lore & Celebration*. St. Paul, MN: Llewellyn Publications, 2001.

Head, James G., and Linda MacLea. *Myth and Meaning*. Evanston, IL: McDougal, Little & Company, 1976.

Hupping, Carol. *Stocking Up*. Emmaus, PA: Rodale Press, 1986.

Johnston, Hannah E. *Children of the Green: Raising our Kids in Pagan Traditions*. Alresford, UK: Moon Books, 2014.

Jung, C. G. *Memories, Dreams, Reflections*. New York: Pantheon, 1963.

Knight, Sirona. *Celtic Traditions: Druids, Faeries, and Wiccan Rituals*. New York: Citadel Press, 2000.

Knowles, Elizabeth. *How to Read a Word*. Oxford: Oxford University Press, 2010.

Kondratiev, Alexi. *The Apple Branch: A Path to Celtic Ritual*. New York: Citadel Press, 2003.

Kosmin, Barry A., and Ariela Keysar. "American Religious Identification Survey (ARIS 2008)." Trinity College. March 2009. http://commons.trincoll.edu/aris/surveys/aris-2008/.

Kraft, Nina. "Rotter fetere av genmat." Forskning.no. July 11, 2012. http://forskning.no/genmodifisert-mat/2012/07/rotter-fetere-av-genmat.

Louv, Richard. *Last Child in the Woods: Saving Our Children From Nature-Deficit Disorder.* Chapel Hill, NC: Algonquin Books, 2006.

Lowry, C. A., J. H. Hollis, A. de Vries, B. Pan, L. R. Brunet, J. R. F. Hunt, and J. F. R. Paton. "Identification of an Immune-Responsive Mesolimbocortical Serotonergic System: Potential Role in Regulation of Emotional Behavior." *Neuroscience* 146, no. 2 (May 2007): 756–72. doi:10.1016/j.neuroscience.2007.01.067.

MacEowen, Frank. *The Mist-Filled Path: Celtic Wisdom for Exiles, Wanderers, and Seekers.* Novato, CA: New World Library, 2002.

Mathews, John. *The Green Man: Spirit of Nature.* Boston, MA: Weiser, 2002.

Mayo Clinic Staff. "Antidepressants for Children and Teens." Mayo Clinic. May 27, 2016. http://www.mayoclinic.org/diseases-conditions/teen-depression/in-depth/antidepressants/art-20047502.

McCoy, Edain. *Ostara: Customs, Spells & Rituals for the Rights of Spring.* St. Paul, MN: Llewellyn Publications, 2003.

Morrison, Dorothy. *Yule: A Celebration of Light and Warmth.* St. Paul, MN: Llewellyn Publications, 2000.

Mountain Rose Herbs. "DIY Guide to Tea Blending." September 3, 2013. mountainroseblog.com/guide-tea-blending/.

Muller-Ebeling, Claudia, Christian Ratsch, and Wolf-Dieter Storl. *Witchcraft Medicine: Healing Arts, Shamanic Practices, and Forbidden Plants.* Rochester, VT: Inner Traditions, 1998.

National Academy of Sciences. "Educating the Student Body: Taking Physical Activity and Physical Education to School." Health and Medicine Division. May 23, 2013. http://www.nationalacademies.org/hmd/Reports/2013/Educating-the-Student-Body-Taking-Physical-Activity-and-Physical-Education-to-School/Report-Brief052313.aspx.

Patterson, Rachel. *A Kitchen Witch's World of Magical Herbs & Plants.* Alresford, UK: Moon Books, 2014.

Pickering, David. *Dictionary of Superstitions.* London, UK: Cassell Books, 1995.

Punxsutawney Groundhog Club. "Groundhog Day History." Last modified 2017. http://www.groundhog.org/about/history/.

Raedisch, Linda. The *Old Magic of Christmas: Yuletide Traditions for the Darkest Days of the Year.* Woodbury, MN: Llewellyn Publications, 2013.

Restall Orr, Emma. *Living Druidry: Magical Spirituality for the Wild Soul.* London: Piatkus, 2004.

Rickey, Lisa. "Groundhog Day Notes." *Out of the Box* (blog), February 4, 2015. Wright State University Libraries' Special Collections & Archives. https://www.libraries.wright.edu/community/outofthebox/2015/02/04/groundhog-day-notes/.

Skagit Audubon Society. "Birding Skagit." Last modified June 29, 2014. http://www.skagitaudubon.org/birding/birding-skagit.

United States Environmental Protection Agency. "Reduce, Reuse, Recycle." Last modified January 4, 2017. www.epa.gov/recycle.

Vallancey, Charles. *Collectanea de Rebus Hibernicis.* Vol. 3. Dublin: 1786.

Walker, Barbara. *The Woman's Encyclopedia of Myths and Secrets.* New York: HarperCollins, 1983.

Wilde, Francesca Speranza. *Ancient Legends, Mystic Charms and Superstitions of Ireland.* London: Ward and Downey, 1887. Kindle edition by CreateSpace, 2016.

Zenner, Charlotte, Solveig Herrnleben-Kurz, and Harald Walach. "Mindfulness-Based Interventions in Schools—A Systematic Review and Meta-Analysis." *Frontiers in Psychology* 5, no. 603 (June 2014): 1–20. www.ncbi.nlm.nih.gov/pmc/articles/PMC4075476.

Acknowledgments

This wouldn't have been possible without the support and encouragement of my own magickal family—Steve, Joshua, Elijah, and Chloe—who gave me the gift of time to fully immerse myself in the writing of this book.

To my family, friends, and coworkers, who listened to me talk nonstop about the struggles and joys of writing nonfiction. To Mardi McLaskey and the talented wordsmiths of Writers of the North Cascades, who were there with kind words and sage advice and continue to support me in my writing career.

To Neil Brigham for the amazing cover art.

To the talented staff at Llewellyn Publications, who helped to make this dream a reality. To Elysia Gallo for providing me this opportunity and to Lauryn Heineman (you rock!) for all your hard work and dedication to this project. Thank you all!

Index

To Write to the Author

If you wish to contact the author or would like more information about this book, please write to the author in care of Llewellyn Worldwide Ltd. and we will forward your request. Both the author and publisher appreciate hearing from you and learning of your enjoyment of this book and how it has helped you. Llewellyn Worldwide Ltd. cannot guarantee that every letter written to the author can be answered, but all will be forwarded. Please write to:

Monica Crosson
% Llewellyn Worldwide
2143 Wooddale Drive
Woodbury, MN 55125-2989

Please enclose a self-addressed stamped envelope for reply,
or $1.00 to cover costs. If outside the U.S.A., enclose
an international postal reply coupon.

Many of Llewellyn's authors have websites with additional information and resources. For more information, please visit our website at http://www.llewellyn.com.

GET MORE AT LLEWELLYN.COM

Visit us online to browse hundreds of our books and decks, plus sign up to receive our e-newsletters and exclusive online offers.

- **Free tarot readings • Spell-a-Day • Moon phases**
- **Recipes, spells, and tips • Blogs • Encyclopedia**
- **Author interviews, articles, and upcoming events**

GET SOCIAL WITH LLEWELLYN

Find us on Facebook

www.Facebook.com/LlewellynBooks

Follow us on

www.Twitter.com/Llewellynbooks

GET BOOKS AT LLEWELLYN

LLEWELLYN ORDERING INFORMATION

Order online: Visit our website at www.llewellyn.com to select your books and place an order on our secure server.

Order by phone:
- Call toll free within the U.S. at 1-877-NEW-WRLD (1-877-639-9753)
- Call toll free within Canada at 1-866-NEW-WRLD (1-866-639-9753)
- We accept VISA, MasterCard, American Express and Discover

 Order by mail:
Send the full price of your order (MN residents add 6.875% sales tax) in U.S. funds, plus postage and handling to: Llewellyn Worldwide, 2143 Wooddale Drive Woodbury, MN 55125-2989

POSTAGE AND HANDLING

STANDARD (U.S. & Canada):
(Please allow 12 business days)
$30.00 and under, add $4.00.
$30.01 and over, FREE SHIPPING.

INTERNATIONAL ORDERS:
$16.00 for one book, plus $3.00 for each additional book.

Visit us online for more shipping options. Prices subject to change.

FREE CATALOG!

To order, call
1-877-
NEW-WRLD
ext. 8236
or visit our
website

Supermarket Magic
Creating Spells, Brews, Potions & Powders
from Everyday Ingredients
Michael Furie

The tools of magic don't have to be expensive or difficult to find—they're right in your supermarket aisles! This easy-to-use book provides clear instructions for working simple and powerful spells—with only common ingredients.

Perfect for Witches and all practitioners of natural and herbal magic, this essential guide explains all the basics of magic including ethics, meditation, timing, and basic charging techniques. There are clear instructions for working a wide variety of simple and powerful spells: clearing and cleaning, increasing harmony, healing, love, lust, beauty, luck money, protection, and honing psychic abilities. Discover how to whip up magical brews, powders, and oils using inexpensive items that can be conveniently purchased at your local grocery store.

978-0-7387-3655-6, 288 pp., 5³⁄₁₆ x 8   **$16.99**

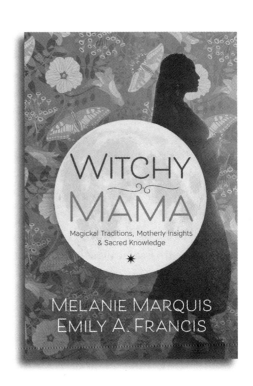

Witchy Mama
Magickal Traditions, Motherly Insights
& Sacred Knowledge
Melanie Marquis and Emily A. Francis

Written for mothers, by mothers, *Witchy Mama* offers practical and magickal ideas, inspiration, and information to help you overcome stress and exhaustion, banish bad dreams, soothe boo-boos, create a magickal home, achieve personal goals, and more.

Discover stones, scents, and colors to increase energy and attract good fortune to yourself and your family. Use simple charms and rituals to ease conflicts, remove fears, protect children, and boost happiness. Connect with your body during pregnancy through magick and meditation, which will infuse your growing baby with positive energy. Guided by dozens of photos, you'll master stretching exercises, breathing techniques, and easy yoga moves that will help you feel healthy, beautiful, and comfortable throughout pregnancy and beyond. *Witchy Mama* contains a wealth of insight gathered from centuries of mother's wisdom as well as from the authors' own personal experiences. This book won't tell you how to parent, but it will help you be happier and more successful as a parent, while still being your own person, too.

978-0-7387-4830-6, 312 pp., 6 x 9   **$17.99**

To order, call 1-877-NEW-WRLD or visit llewellyn.com
Prices subject to change without notice

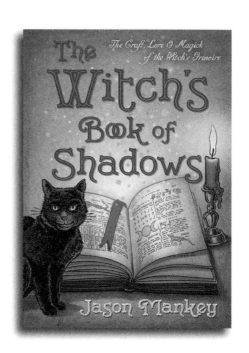

The Craft, Lore & Magick
of the Witch's Grimoire

The Witch's Book of Shadows

Jason Mankey

The Witch's Book of Shadows
The Craft, Lore & Magick of the Witch's Grimoire
JASON MANKEY

Discover the fascinating history, tradition, and modern uses of the Book of Shadows. This fun and easy-to-use guide provides essential information on creating and consecrating a Book of Shadows, as well as how to make it a part of your practice.

Learn about the various types of Books of Shadows, their roles throughout history, and how they differ from regular spellbooks. Enjoy advice and excerpts from the grimoires of well-known modern and historical Witches. Explore a wide variety of ideas for what to include in your own Book of Shadows. Like a magical chart showing where you've been and where you're going, this wonderful tool is your personal guide to Witchcraft.

978-0-7387-5014-9, 312 pp., 5 x 7   **$15.99**

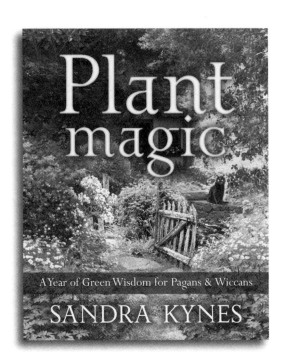

Plant magic

A Year of Green Wisdom for Pagans & Wiccans

SANDRA KYNES

Plant Magic
A Year of Green Wisdom for Pagans & Wiccans
SANDRA KYNES

Connect to the natural world in ways you never expected with the many magical uses of ordinary and classically witchy plants. *Plant Magic* presents a unique approach to working with plants in concert with the cycles of nature. Learn which ones best align with the sabbats on the Wheel of the Year and which are most useful for the time between them.

Sandra Kynes guides you through a year of plant magic, providing significant dates and detailed information on garden, wild, and household plants associated with each month. Discover activities to grow your connection with nature, such as plant-based rituals to celebrate the seasons and incense burning to attract love and prosperity. Explore ways to develop your self-expression in the craft, from placing flowers on your altar to using herbs in your divinatory practices. Featuring lore, recipes, spells, and more, *Plant Magic* helps you better understand and be inspired by the green world.

978-0-7387-5017-0, 264 pp., 7½ x 9¼   **$19.99**

CLIFF SERUNTINE

SEASONS
OF THE
SACRED EARTH

FOLLOWING THE OLD WAYS ON AN ENCHANTED HOMESTEAD

Seasons of the Sacred Earth
Following the Old Ways on an Enchanted Homestead
CLIFF SERUNTINE

Join the Seruntine family on a magical journey of green living at their homestead hollow in the Nova Scotia highlands. Share their magical experiences as the family lives in harmony with the land and respects nature's spirits. Growing and hunting most of their food, Cliff and his family share hands-on practical home skills you can use, too.

With a warm, personal style, *Seasons of the Sacred Earth* chronicles the Seruntine family's adventures following the old ways. They celebrate the Wheel of the Year by leaving apples for the Apple Man, offering faerie plates during Samhain, and spilling goat's milk for the barn *brua-nighe*. In return, the land blesses them with overflowing gardens, delicious ales, and the safety of their farm animals. Through their journey, you'll discover the magical and the mystical are never farther than Earth and Sky.

978-0-7387-3553-5, 336 pp., 6 x 9   **$16.99**

Witchy Crafts

60 Enchanted
Projects for the
Creative Witch

LEXA OLICK

Witchy Crafts
60 Enchanted Projects for the Creative Witch
LEXA OLICK

The most powerful magical objects a Witch owns are those she makes with her own hands. When it comes to crafting, however, it is difficult to find projects that reflect the magical arts. Jam-packed with fun and imaginative ideas, this unique book is designed specifically for Wiccans, offering step-by-step instructions for 60 delightfully witchy craft projects.

Weave magic into essential ritual items such as your Book of Shadows and wands. Create magical home décor and concoct recipes for health and beauty. Learn to make a goddess cornucopia, crochet pentacle coasters or a ritual capelet, recycle old tarot decks, make runes out of bottle-caps, create accessories like bags and jewelry, and build a charm box.

Witchy Crafts also gives tips on the basics of Wicca, forming a craft group, crafting by the seasons, and preventing common mistakes. Includes color photos, line drawings, and correspondence charts.

978-0-7387-2618-2, 312 pp., 7 x 10   **$19.99**

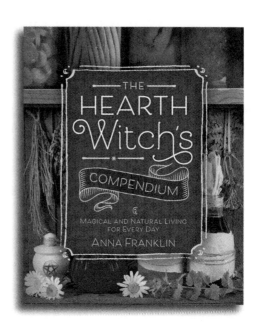

The Hearth Witch's Compendium
Magical and Natural Living for Every Day
ANNA FRANKLIN

Live greener and find magic in the world around you with this comprehensive sourcebook to living the hearth witch way. Featuring homemade recipes, instructions for making everything from wine to soaps, and a variety of potions and spells, *The Hearth Witch's Compendium* helps you incorporate spiritual practice into everyday life.

The contemporary hearth witch inherits the mantle of the village wise woman; she is part shaman, part seer, part herbalist, part spiritual healer, and entirely witch. Anna Franklin guides you through each project, from growing your own herbs and making remedies for simple ailments to creating natural household products and mixing oils. By following the hearth witch life, you'll save money, reduce waste and exposure to potentially toxic chemicals, and have a lot of fun along the way.

978-0-7387-5046-0, 528 pp., 7½ x 9¼   **$27.99**

Garden Witch's Herbal
Green Magick, Herbalism & Spirituality
ELLEN DUGAN

Enrich your Craft—and your spirit—by working with the awesome energies of nature. In this follow-up to *Garden Witchery*, Ellen Dugan takes us further down the path of green magick, revealing the secret splendors of the plant kingdom.

From common herbs and flowers to enchanted shrubs and trees, Dugan digs up the magickal dirt on a wide variety of plant life. Encouraging Witches to think outside the window box, she shares ideas for incorporating your garden's bounty into spellwork, sabbat celebrations, and more. Tips for container gardening ensure that city Witches can get in on the green action, too.

This stimulating guide to green Witchery—featuring botanical illustrations of nearly fifty fascinating specimens—will inspire you to personalize your Craft and fortify your connection to the earth.

978-0-7387-1429-5, 336 pp., 7½ x 7½   **$19.95**